Hugo Chávez and the Bolivarian revolution

MANCHESTER
1824

Manchester University Press

Hugo Chávez and the Bolivarian revolution

Populism and democracy in a globalised age

Barry Cannon

Manchester University Press
Manchester and New York
distributed exclusively in the USA by Palgrave Macmillan

Published by Manchester University Press
Oxford Road, Manchester M13 9NR, UK
and Room 400, 175 Fifth Avenue, New York, NY 10010, USA
www.manchesteruniversitypress.co.uk

Distributed exclusively in the USA by
Palgrave Macmillan, 175 Fifth Avenue, New York,
NY 10010, USA

Distributed exclusively in Canada by
UBC Press, University of British Columbia, 2029 West Mall,
Vancouver, BC, Canada V6T 1Z2

British Library Cataloguing-in-Publication Data
A catalogue record for this book is available from the British Library

Library of Congress Cataloging-in-Publication Data applied for

ISBN 978 0 7190 7771 5 hardback

ISBN 978 0 7190 7772 2 paperback

First published 2009

18 17 16 15 14 13 12 11 10 09   10 9 8 7 6 5 4 3 2 1

The publisher has no responsibility for the persistence or accuracy of URLs for external or any third-party internet websites referred to in this book, and does not gurantee that any content on such websites is, or will remain, accurate or appropriate.

Typeset
by Helen Skelton, Brighton, UK
Printed in Great Britain
by CPI Antony Rowe Ltd, Chippenham, Wiltshire

Contents

List of abbreviations and terms

Abbreviations

AD	Acción Democrática (Democratic Action), one of the two main *puntofijista* political parties
ALBA	Alternativa Bolivariana para las Américas (Bolivarian Alternative for the Americas)
ANC	Assamblea Nacional Constituyente (National Constituent Assembly)
APRA	Allianza Popular Revolucionaria Americana (Popular Revolutionary American Alliance), Peruvian political party
CAN	Community of Andean Nations
CCD	Congreso Constituyuente Democrático (Democratic Constitutional Congress). Constituent Assembly, Peru
CEPR	Center for Economic and Policy Research
CICPC	Cuerpo de Investigaciones Científicas, Penales y Criminalísticas (Scientific, Penal and Criminal Investigation Force), the Venzuelan forensic police
CITGO	US-based subsidiary of PdVSA
CNE	Consejo Nacional Electoral (National Election Council)
COPEI	Comité de Organización Política Electoral Independiente (Independent Electoral Committee for Political Organisation), the second most important *puntofijista* party
COPRE	Comisión Presidencial para la Reforma del Estado (Presidential Commission for the Reform of the State)
CTV	Confederación de Trabajadores de Venezuela (Venezuela Workers Council)
DAI	Development Alternatives Inc.
DC	Democratic Coordinator
DEA	US Drug Enforcement Agency

DISIP	Dirección de los Servicios de Inteligencia y Prevención (Directorate of Intelligence and Prevention Services), the Venezuelan political police
EAP	economically active population
ECLAC	Economic Commission for Latin America and the Caribbean
FAN	Fuerzas Armadas Nacionales (National Armed Forces), the Venezuelan armed forces
FARC	Fuerzas Armadas Revolucionarias de Colombia (Revolutionary Armed Forces of Colombia), Colombian guerrilla group
FEDECAMARAS	Federación de Camaras de Comercio y Produción (Federation of Chambers of Commerce and Production), the peak Venezuelan business association
FTA	free trade agreement
FTAA	Free Trade Area of the Americas
GDP	gross domestic product
GN	National Guard
HDI	human development index
IDB	*Impuesto Débito Bancario* (Banking Debit Tax)
IFI	international financial institutions, e.g. World Bank, IMF
IMF	International Monetary Fund
IOs	international organisations
ISI	import substitution industrialisation
MAS	Movimiento al Socialismo (Movement Towards Socialism)
MBR-200	Movimiento Bolivariano Revolucionario (Bolivarian Republican Movement)
MERCOSUR	Mercado Común del Sur (Southern Common Market)
MVR	Movimiento Quinta Republica (Fifth Republic Movement), Venezuelan ruling party under Chávez
NED	National Endowment for Democracy
NGO	non-governmental organisation
NICs	newly industrialised countries
OAS	Organisation of American States
OIT	USAID Office of Transition Initiatives
OPEC	Organisation of the Petroleum Exporting Countries
PCV	Partido Comunista Venezolano (Venzuelan Communist Party)
PdVSA	Petróleos de Venezuela (Venezuelan Petroleum), the Venezuelan state oil company
PP	Polo Patriotico (Patriotic Pole)
PPT	Patria Para Todos (Motherland For All)
PSUV	Partido Socialista Unido de Venzuela (United Socialist Party of Venezuela); replaced the MVR in 2007
SAP	structural adjustment policy

SENIAT	Servicio Nacional Integrado de Administración Aduanera y Tributaria (National Integrated Service for Customs and Taxation Administration), the Venezuelan tax agency
SIN	Servicio de Inteligencia Nacional (National Intelligence Service), Peru's intelligence agency
SUNAT	Superintendencia Nacional de Administración Tributaria (National Superintendent for Taxation Administration), the Peruvian tax agency
TNCs	transnational corporations
TSJ	Tribunal Supremo de Justicia (Supreme Tribunal of Justice)
UNASUR	Unión de Naciones Suramericanas (Union of South American Nations)
UNDP	United Nations Development Programme
UNT	Unión Nacional de Trabajadores (National Worker's Union, Venezuela)
USAID	United States international development cooperation agency
WTO	World Trade Organisation

Terms

autogolpe	self-coup
caracazo	massacre carried out by the security forces during the second Pérez presidency in February 1989
caudillo	leader, usually military
chavismo	refers to the ideology of the movement led by President Chávez and to the movement itself
Constituyente	the process of forming a new Constitution for Venezuela
democradura	substantive dictatorship within formal democracy
fujimorismo	refers to the ideology of the movement led by President Fujimori of Peru and to the movement itself.
mestizaje	miscegenation
misiones	the various social programmes installed by the Chávez government
pardo	mixed race
paro cívico	lockout/strike of 2002–03
partidocracia	political system entirely dominated by political parties and their associates
pueblo	the people
Punto Fijo	the pre-Chávez period in Venezuela (1958–93)
puntofijismo	bipartisan democratic regime which ruled Venezuela between 1958 and 1999. So named after the agreement or pact signed between the main political parties in the home of Rafael Caldera, leader of COPEI, named Punto Fijo

rondas campesinas military-controlled vigilante groups, Peru

venezolanidad   the concept of being Venezuelan; Venezuelan identity

List of tables

Acknowledgements

I would like to extend my thanks to the following individuals and institutions for the help, encouragement and/or companionship they provided me during the time spent preparing this document:

Professor Peadar Kirby, University of Limerick who while in the DCU School of Law and Government had faith in me and gave me the opportunity to realise this project, as well as providing constant and rigorous guidance. The rest of the staff of Law and Government, especially Dr John Doyle, Dr Gary Murphy and Mr David Doyle.

Particular thanks goes to Julia Buxton, Senior Research Fellow, Department of Peace Studies, University of Bradford, for a comprehensive review of the manuscript of this book and key recommendations without which it would not have achieved its present form. Thanks also to Diane Raby, Honorary Research Fellow, Institute of Latin American Studies of the University of Liverpool for reviewing the manuscript of this book and advising on its contents.

A number of people provided information for this book or reviewed sections of this book, either in its thesis form or in its present book form. These were: Maxwell Cameron, University of British Columbia, Canada; Ronaldo Munck, DCU; Margarita López Maya, FACES, University of Caracas, Venezuela; Steve Ellner, Universidad del Oriente, Barcelona, Venezuela. Special thanks goes to, Dr Mo Hume, University of Glasgow – sorry about the lack of a gender perspective Mo! Thanks to all those who agreed to be interviewed in Spain, Venezuela and Peru. Also to the library staff of CICOB Barcelona, Spain, special thanks to staff of the Interlibrary Loans Section of DCU Library, and to all staff in the libraries and institutions which I visited in Ireland, Spain, Peru and Venezuela.

This work is dedicated to my mother, Madeleine Cannon Walsh, my father, Michael Cannon, and my brother, Aiden Cannon, may they all rest in peace. The book is also dedicated to the people of Venezuela, *un abrazo*!

Fieldwork for this study was partly financed by what was the National Committee for Development Education (NCDE), now subsumed into Irish Aid, the Irish government's division of the Department of Foreign Affairs responsible for international cooperation. The writing of this book would not have been possible without support from Irish Aid for my position as Post-doctoral Fellow in the School of Law and Government, Dublin City University as part of our *Active Citizenship in Central America* programme. All opinions expressed within this work, however, are my own.

Parts of this book were previously published as articles in the *Bulletin of Latin American Studies* and *Third World Quarterly*. Thanks to the publishers of these journals for copyright permission. All translations are the work of the author, unless otherwise stated.

Introduction

The revolutionary potential of *chavismo*

This book aims to explore for the first time in depth the presidency of Hugo Chávez Frías of Venezuela (1999–present) in the context of theory on populism. In this it hopes to fill a gap in the literature on Chávez and to put one of the principal charges against Chávez, that he is a free-spending, authoritarian populist, with the fully negative weight of such a charge, into a more nuanced perspective. To do so the study will look at issues such as the continued relevance of populism itself in Latin American politics, populism's origins in the profound race/class cleavages found in the region, its ideological diversity, with, however, a programmatic emphasis on popular participation, and finally populist claims to legitimacy within a region with weak democratic institutions. Nonetheless, one of the main contentions of the study is that theory on populism in itself is not sufficient to fully explore Chávez as a populist leader.

This introduction will outline how the book will deal with these issues in its second section. In this section, however, more fundamental questions are dealt with such as: Is the Chávez government a populist government at all? If so, does it have within it the wherewithal to go beyond mere populism to something truly revolutionary? Can *chavismo* offer the world the seeds of a new democratic model?

From the outset, this book will contend that in order to answer these questions the meaning of democracy in a globalised world must be explored in greater detail. In it an excessive concentration on form, in other word institutions, over process in the analysis of democracy is warned against – but this does not imply that institutions are unnecessary. Rather the book contends that it is sometimes necessary to step outside and infringe existing institutionality when that institutionality lacks legitimacy and is acting against democracy's progressive tendencies. From such 'transgressive' actions new forms of institutionality more suited to advancing democracy in its full, inclusive and substantive sense can emerge. As David Held states, in his *Models of Democracy*, 'a political system implicated deeply in the creation and reproduction of systematic inequalities of power and opportunities will rarely … enjoy sustained support by groups other than those whom it directly privileges. Or, more contentiously, only a political order that places the transformation of those inequalities at its centre will enjoy legitimacy in the long run.'[1] In order to transform such anti-democratic institutionality the study contends that this may result in a concerted challenge which involves negating those institutions in order to transform them.

D. L. Raby, in her incisive study on *Democracy and Revolution*, affirms that within populism there is the possibility of far-reaching revolutionary change, 'but only when its social base is an autonomous movement of the dominated classes and where its leader is a true representative of that movement, not necessarily in terms of his/her class origins but in terms of cultural and ideological identification and political practice'.[2] What form would this 'truly revolutionary change' take? This book's central contention is that it should aim to a form of democracy similar to the 'deliberative democracy' model as put forward by Held, in the same book mentioned above. This model sets out a blueprint for a more advanced, progressive form of democracy which ensures participation by the citizen in a deliberative manner, in which the citizen can, if he or she chooses, fully exercise citizenship and influence and construct policy. In the deliberative democracy model Held acknowledges that participative democracy represents an advance on other forms of democracy, including liberal democracy, but that it is in itself fraught with difficulties. Most notably the threats to minorities and individuals and to the quality of public reasoning, that is the need to ensure the *quality* of participation itself, avoiding that such participation lapse into 'the reduction of public argument to the lowest possible denominator'.[3]

Hence, Held maintains 'for democracy to flourish today it has to be reconceived as a double sided phenomenon: concerned on the one hand, with the reform of state power and, on the other hand, with the restructuring of civil society', what he calls the 'process of *double democratization*: the interdependent transformation of both state and civil society'.[4] Democratic rights must go beyond simple protections of the individual or groups against the overweening power of the state, or indeed rights as entitlements to specific public goods, such as health and education. Democracy 'would be fully worth its name if citizens had the actual power to be active as citizens; that is to say, if citizens were able to enjoy a bundle of rights which allowed them to demand democratic participation and to treat it as an entitlement'.[5]

Such a system would include, according to Held, a constitution setting out not only the right to cast a vote, 'but also equal rights to enjoy the conditions for effective participation, enlightened understanding and the specifications of the political agenda'.[6] Within this conception, representative institutions, such as parliaments or congresses, would continue to exist, if in a somewhat modified state. These remodelled representative institutions would not only 'ensure formal equality before the law, but also that citizens would have the actual capacity (the health, education, skills and resources) to take advantage of opportunities before them', which 'would radically enhance the ability of citizens to take action against the state'.[7] These rights would include an array of social rights in health and education and economic rights 'to ensure adequate economic and financial resources for democratic autonomy'. It would therefore involve a central concern with distributional questions and matters of social justice 'as anything else would hinder the realisation of the principle of autonomy and the rule of democracy'.[8]

Such changes at the state level, however, must be complemented by changes at the civil society level. Strategies 'must be adopted to break up old patterns of power in civil society' and new structures through which social relations can be conducted should be set up – such as socially regulated enterprises, independent communications media and health centres – 'which allow their members control of the resources at their disposal without direct interference from the state, political agencies or other parties' and these would have participatory mechanisms within them.[9] Furthermore, Held makes clear that those in control of 'vast amounts of productive or financial power' will have to be treated 'unequally'. Indeed the process of 'alleviating the conditions of the least powerful while restricting the scope and circumstances of the most powerful – would apply to a variety of areas marked by systematic inequality (from wealth and gender to race and ethnicity)'.[10] All of this would be on an experimental basis – 'the "music of the future" can only be composed in practice'.[11] It would also, necessitate at times the stepping outside of existing institutionality, as contended above, as existing institutions often work to sustain and support such inequalities, and can be used by the powerful to stymie and overthrow reform processes.

Held also points to some difficulties and further questions to be considered within this process towards what he calls 'deliberative democracy'. For example, within this conception is the citizen obliged to participate, or can he or she choose not to do so? Where does the private realm end and the public realm, that realm subject to citizen deliberation, begin? How would the balance on decision-making between representatives and citizens be determined? In other words, who deliberates and who governs? How will the market be reframed, or rather, how will the balance between market, state and citizen be established? To what extent must equality be established without sacrificing diversity? What are the limits on citizen autonomy? Held provides a number of replies to such questions, which need not be elaborated on here, but which also would be subject to the same form of trial by error referred to above.

Hence in reply to the question if *chavismo* has many of the traits associated with a populist type government the answer must be affirmative. Furthermore *chavismo* has the potential to install a truly revolutionary and foundational project in Venezuela. Raby enumerates the characteristics of a populist movement which can have truly revolutionary potential. Apart from charismatic leadership it must be firmly rooted in popular culture, it must be democratic in political practice and internal structure, ideologically pluralist, encouraging free discussion but always within the context of the advancement of the popular interest, and firmly committed to fundamental, and ultimately revolutionary change.[12] In chavismo we can find many of these characteristics. *Chavismo* is populist with respect to the deeply intertwined relationship between leader and people. The elevation of the people to almost mythical status through the leader's discourse in combination with the emphasis on distributive elements can also be seen as being essentially populist. Nonetheless, in the emerging Bolivarian model of democracy, documented in these pages, some of the elements of Held's deliberative democracy model can also be seen. They can be seen, for example, in the participatory mechanisms used to construct the 1999 constitution. They can also be seen in the popular revolts of April 2002 defending Venezuelan democracy and its legitimately elected leader and government. They can be seen too in the *misiones* (social programmes set up by the Chávez government) and the participatory mechanisms which govern them. They are also apparent in the attempts to democratise the media, and with the explosion of cooperatives, worker co-management of enterprises and the like. More recently, they can be seen in the formation of the new political party – the PSUV – with its grassroots elections of party candidates in mid-2008, the first in Venezuelan history, for the local government, assembly and regional elections in November 2008. None of these processes are perfectly participative, but all of them have sought to be so, which is surely the crucial point. Most certainly *chavismo* can transform itself from populism to a radical participative and deliberative democracy if it strengthens these tendencies and policies and lessens those of the preponderance of the leader, tendencies seen for example in many of the Constitutional Amendments defeated in the December 2007 referendum.

Much work needs to be done within *chavismo* and within Bolivarian Venezuela to ensure that Venezuela strengthens the radical democratic elements referred to. Gregory Wilpert, a US sociologist living and working in Venezuela, for example recommends further emphasis being placed on citizen autonomy, on citizen controls on the means of production, state autonomy, and resource distribution and allocation.[13] He recommends for example further steps to the democratisation of the workplace, as much in the nationalised and renationalised services and industries, including telecommunications, electricity and the all-important state oil company,

PdVSA, in the public administration, as well as in the private sector. He also recommends that issues of patronage and clientelism within emerging participatory structures be eradicated. Structures and mechanisms need to be crafted to ensure the autonomy of the movement from its leadership, including within the nascent PSUV. A profound reform of the state is necessary to ensure the construction of an autonomous bureaucratic structure which will implement policy according to the law and not to party or leader pressures.

Finally and central to these difficulties, Wilpert contends, is the person of Hugo Chávez and it is this last point that this study wishes to emphasise before preceding to substantiate these opening claims in more detail in the following chapters. While on the one hand Chávez is central to the success of the movement he has founded, it is also urgent that the movement find ways to move beyond his leadership. In other words, Venezuela must move on to the stage where it can have *chavismo* without Chávez.

What is crucial, therefore, is the guarding against the preponderance of the leader as the guarantor of popular participation – in other words the over-identification of the people with the leader. In *chavismo* we can detect the curious dichotomy of a powerful, dynamic, intelligent and visionary leader, whose person and leadership skills are absolutely crucial to the process underway in Venezuela but who must lead his people to the point within this process where his leadership is no longer necessary. In this sense Chávez must lead his people to a freedom that does not simply mean a freedom from the shackles of the past, crucial as that is – that is a freedom from the class- and race-based fissures which have divided Venezuelan society since the conquest and from the semi-colonial dependence of the Venezuelan economy on the more powerful nations of the globe. Chávez must also work to become mere *symbol*, to free the Venezuelan people from a leadership that is *his* to a leadership that is *theirs*. The leader is crucial in the current context as the harbinger of change – but the leader must work towards his or her own oblivion as a centre of power, and ensure that this process takes place guided by principled democratic values. It is within this possible process that we find the truly revolutionary potential of *chavismo*.

Populist theory and *chavismo*

The following chapters will substantiate these claims by looking at the issues enumerated at the beginning of this introduction. In Chapter 1, a central dispute in the theoretical literature on populism will be examined which is that between what one analyst, Kenneth Roberts termed the 'historical/sociological perspective' of Germani and others, and the 'ideological perspective' of Laclau.[14] Central to Germani's theories was the belief that modernisation processes formed the context in which populism emerged in Latin America.

Furthermore, Germani argued that populism was essentially social democratising, in that it gives the popular classes an 'experience of participation' which is of more value to them than liberal democratic freedoms of, for example, association and expression.

Laclau, however, emphasises that populism's difference lies not in any relation to modernisation processes, but rather its particular *logic of articulation*. Laclau shows us that there are not any actual *contents* identifiable as populist, but rather that populism arises out of a series of unsatisfied demands which translate themselves into antagonism and then into a populist rupture. He identifies a number of stages in the constitution of a populist moment. First, different social demands aggregate themselves into what he calls an equivalential chain, forming a 'popular subjectivity'. An 'empty signifier', in other words a 'leader', emerges to give coherence, to provide a 'totality', to these demands. Through various politico-discursive practices, the leader constructs a popular subject (the 'people') and divides the social space, forming an 'internal frontier', between the 'people' and the existing power bloc. Laclau therefore provides a more logical thesis as to why populism presents such programmatic variety.

In Chapter 2, the study will show that modernisation processes can have a bearing on the emergence of populism, in that they can create the conditions in which crises emerge, leading to gaps between democratic governments and the population which can provide a space for populist leaders to gain power. Nonetheless, this explains more about democracy's weaknesses and the reasons for populism's emergence, rather than the nature of populism itself. Such theory does not delve deeply enough into the underlying causes for Latin American democracies' recurrent weaknesses.

By examining Habermas's theory on legitimation in democratic regimes we can find answers to this question. If a democracy seeks legitimacy it must provide its people with a participative experience in every sphere of national life. Most people must have jobs, the state must be able to provide education, health and housing to the broad mass of the people; the majority must identify culturally with the prevailing ideology of competition and privatism – education, careers, leisure must be shared and realisable goals for the majority. And of course, there must be political participation, through elections at the very least. On most of these levels, however, except perhaps on the political level, Latin American democracies have failed the majority of their peoples, thus they have been unable to gain legitimacy: most people do not have jobs, or are seriously underemployed; large sections of the population do not identify culturally with capitalist values, large groups do not have access to education and to health care, and for those that do, its quality is often poor. By looking further into the historical, economic and social context we find that these exclusions are based on the inherited, and often interchangeable, cleavages of race/ethnicity and class. Moreover, change is very difficult to achieve due to the entrenched ties the elite have with the dependent economies found in Latin America, and thence onto the most powerful nations of the world, a situation further exacerbated and entrenched by globalisation. In sum, investigation into why populism emerges in Latin America must go well beyond the literature on populism to other theoretical frameworks such as Habermas and dependency theory – or rather analysis of populism must refer to these wider contexts and analytical theories.

The characteristics of populist regimes are neatly summed up in Laclau's 'people/power bloc' equation, above. Further to that, however, Venezuela shows us that the manner in which populists gain power are aptly explained by Gramsci's theory of hegemony. Broadly speaking, Chávez gained power through hegemonic strategies which gave centrality to the concept of the people, which provided a direct relationship between the people and the leader, a relationship established through a discourse antagonistic to the status quo.

What is argued here, however, is that ideology has a profound impact on the characteristics of populist movements, governments and its policies. Populism has been used to further a variety of ideological models. Alberto Fujimori of Peru (1990–2001), for example, used it to implant a radical neoliberal model into Peru, which has survived its maker even while he languishes in jail on corruption and genocide charges – fujimorismo without Fujimori. This model emphasised the market, individualism and the minimal state, but also entailed a demobilisation of the popular classes and the poor in favour of a hyper-presidentialism, where the president becomes the sole actor on the national stage. The Chávez government, on the other hand, has used populism to further the preservation and reconstruction of a state-interventionist economy, but with a radical social democratising content, emphasising equality and participation. Rather than hyper-presidentialism, we have a duoply of power between the popular classes and the president, with a recomposition of institutions to reflect this emerging new model.

In this way, Laclau's theories have proven to have greater analytical power than Germani's to explain the nature of the Chávez government. Laclau's theories nonetheless are indebted to Gramsci's theory of hegemony. In Chapter 3 we find that in Gramscian theory, hegemonic strategies are independent of ideology. While populism can be articulated to any ideology or mix of ideologies, what this study contends is that the nature of the populist movement will be strongly influenced by the ideology to which it is articulated. This central finding is borne out in the following chapters. In Chapter 4, the book shows how there are heightened levels of social and economic participation in a number of areas of national life, with greater involvement of the popular classes in the economic life of the country through cooperatives, micro-credits, increased educational opportunities, worker co- or self-management of enterprises etc. Similarly participative mechanisms have been put in place in the popular committees informing policy on health, water, land and in the new communal councils. In Chapter 5 the study also finds high levels of political participation in Venezuela with a vibrant participatory culture in the areas of electoral contests, institutional and associational autonomy, human rights and the media. It is argued that these participatory policies are grounded on Bolivarian ideology which places a premium on popular participation and engagement.

Chapter 6 brings the tension between anti-democratic and democratic elements in Venezuela into focus. Here we find that it is the historical context, further bolstered by the current international context of neoliberal hegemony, which wrests legitimacy from democracy, preventing it from fulfilling its potential. Populism, rather than being a cause of the deinstitutionalisaton of States, as much of the literature asserts, is instead a reflection of democratic regimes' and their institutions' inability to gain legitimacy. Fundamentally, this failure is due to their unwillingness or inability to act decisively and consistently towards the reduction of inequality, based on race and class. The existence of democratic institutions is not in itself evidence of the existence of democracy. Rather, it is the perceptible lessening of inequality on the economic, social and political levels, which is a true sign of increasing democratisation and which will then be reflected in new types of institutions which will act to preserve the gains made. Democracy in this sense is, or should be, as Nef calls it, 'a genuine participatory system of governance based on justice and equality'.[15]

Rueschemeyer et al. assert that 'it is the contradictions of capitalism that advanced the cause of democracy' providing the impetus to those affected most by that inequality, the working or popular classes, to insist on greater participation, putting democratic curbs on capitalism.[16] Often, as Nabulsi points out, that insistence must sometimes step outside the realm of institutionality in order to further the agenda of increased equality and populism, it is argued, is one of the major vehicles used by Latin Americans to attempt to achieve that.[17]

Indeed rather than populism being an opposite of democracy, as much of the literature seems to suggest, this study underlines populism's intimate relationship with democracy. As Canovan explains the hope that democracy gives in its promise of equality, its redemptive side, can be compromised by its equally powerful pragmatic side that is 'democracy [as] a way of coping peacefully with conflicting interests and views'.[18] Yet 'the power and legitimacy of democracy as a pragmatic system depend ... on its redemptive elements. That always leaves room for the populism that accompanies democracy like a shadow.'[19] Indeed, populism is, as Arditi clarifies, commenting on Canovan, 'a possibility embedded in the very practice of democracy'.[20]

Therefore, we must also, in accepting the 'embeddedness' of populism in democracy, accept the populist claim to democratic legitimacy.[21] Analysts, in counterposing populism to democracy, and criticising the former for 'deinstitutionalising' the latter, forget the context and reasons why populists such as Chávez achieve power in the first place; the existence of inequality and the failure of democracy's redemptive power in overcoming it. Even those analysts such as Roberts who do recognise this, suggest institutional reform as a means to prevent populism emerging, again reinforcing the assertion that democracy and populism are somehow separate. In Chapter 6, we argue, however, that only by being seen to tackle the root causes of inequality can democracy gain legitimacy, a task much greater than mere institutional reform and, to an extent, dependent on global conditions.

In Chapter 6, the book underlines and expands on the role of neoliberal globalisation in increasing inequality in the region, and consistently undermining many democratic governments' effectiveness in tackling that inequality. Increasingly in Latin America, democratic regimes are seen not as the protectors of the liberties of their peoples, all their peoples, but as agents of neoliberalism. They have become, as Nef terms them, 'receiver states', 'highly transnationalised and weak ... [acting] in partnership with foreign creditors and international financial institutions as manager, executor, and liquidator of [their] own bankruptcy'.[22] This role limits democratic governments' ability to tackle inequality, which should be the central role of democratic institutions, making their task to gain legitimacy even more difficult still.

Yet it is not just in Latin America that inequality is increasing, the book argues, but rather it is a worldwide phenomenon. Democracy is in peril as neoliberalism advances in the region, as the United Nations Development Programme's (UNDP) 2004 report on democracy in Latin America attests, and, as Jacques maintains, throughout the globe.[23] We have then the curious dichotomy whereby in Latin America there have never before been so many democratically elected governments in power, which nonetheless are powerfully constrained in meeting their electors' wishes and furthering an agenda of equality. These constraints are primarily as a result of the one-size-fits-all straitjacket of neoliberal globalisation, which in the form of the Washington Consensus has drastically reduced states' room for manoeuvre in formulating policy which can create a truly participatory political, social and economic environment.

In this way, the present study underlines the importance of placing populism firmly within the global context. Populism in Latin America, we contend, is usually a local response to global structural conditions, which can act to accommodate those conditions or to attempt to change them and their effects. In either case, the main justification for the adoption of a particular ideology, be it neoliberalism or Bolivarianism, is to further development. Hence, as found in Chapter 7, populist governments pursue their development strategies within an unequal international context, or as Payne terms it, within the 'global politics of unequal development'. In the current context of neoliberal globalisation, characterised by deepening asymmetries between nations, the Venezuelan government has pursued a foreign policy seeking to lessen those asymmetries by promoting a multi-polar world, countering the dominant power of the United States, and thus seeking to create a space within the global order for it to pursue its alternative development model without interference. Populism therefore, does not happen in a geopolitical vacuum, but rather is a reaction to the prevalent international order and orthodoxy, either seeking to insert the specific country deeper into those processes, or to distance itself from those processes, seeking new positions from which to negotiate them. But as populism is born in crisis, so it is often the harbinger of profound change, usually embarked upon from within existing democratic structures, to alleviate that crisis and ostensibly tackle its root causes.

These issues will be explored in much more detail in the following seven chapters. In the next, first, chapter, however, the book will begin by exploring in more detail the issues raised in this introduction in the literature on populism, constructing through that exploration the book's theoretical framework which will form the basis of its structure and content.

Notes

1 Held, D., 2006, *Models of Democracy*. Cambridge: Polity, p. 289.
2 Raby, D., 2006, *Democracy and Revolution: Latin America and Socialism Today*. London, Ann Arbor, MI: Pluto Press and Toronto: Between the Lines, p. 256.
3 Held, *Models of Democracy*, p. 277.
4 Ibid., p. 276. Italics in original.
5 Ibid., p. 277.
6 Ibid.
7 Ibid., p. 278.
8 Ibid., p. 278.
9 Ibid., p. 280.
10 Ibid., p. 286.
11 Ibid.
12 Raby, *Democracy and Revolution*, pp. 256–257.
13 Wilpert, G., 2007, *Changing Venezuela by Taking Power: The History and Policies of the Chávez Government*. London: New York: Verso, pp. 231–235.
14 Roberts, K. M., 1995, 'Neoliberalism and the transformation of populism in Latin America: the Peruvian case', in *World Politics* 48(1): 82–116; Germani, G., 1965, *Politica y Sociedad en una Epoca de Transicion: de la Sociedad Tradicional a la Sociedad de Masas*. Buenos Aires: Editorial Paidos; Laclau, E., 1977, *Politics and Ideology in Marxist Theory: Capitalism-Fascism-Populism*. London: New Left Books; Laclau, E., 2005, *On Populist Reason*, London: Verso.

15 Nef, J., 1995, 'Demilitarization and democratic transition in Latin America', in S. Halebsky and R. L. Harris (eds), *Capital, Power and Inequality in Latin America*. Boulder, CO: Westview Press, pp. 81–107; p. 104.

16 Rueschemeyer, D., Stephens, E. and Stephens, J. D., 1992, *Capitalist Development and Democracy*. Cambridge: Polity Press, p. 7.

17 Nabulsi, K., 2004, 'The struggle for sovereignty', in *The Guardian*, 23 June.

18 Canovan, M., 1999, 'Trust the people! Populism and the two faces of democracy', in *Political Studies* XLVII: 2–16; p. 10.

19 Ibid., p. 16.

20 Arditi, B., 2004. 'Populism as a spectre of democracy: a response to Canovan', *Political Studies* 52(1), March: 135–143; p. 141.

21 Canovan, 'Trust the people!', pp. 6–7.

22 Nef, 'Demilitarization', p. 93.

23 UNDP/United Nations Development Programme, 2004, Ideas and Contributions: Democracy in Latin America. Available from: www.undp.org. Accessed 10 June 2008; Jacques, M., 2004, 'Democracy isn't working', in *The Guardian*, 22 June.

1 Populism and Latin America: context, causes, characteristics and consequences

Introduction

Populism is viewed by many as a negative concept. Donald Rumsfeld, one time United States Secretary for Defence under President George W. Bush, in a speech given in March 2006, expressed his concern about Latin Americans turning to 'populist leadership ... that clearly are worrisome'. Alejandro Toledo ex-president of Peru (2001–06) believes that 'cheap empty populism is the danger to democracy'.[1] *The Economist* warns that 'populists are leading Latin America down a blind alley'[2] while British newspaper, *The Independent* concurs.[3] Nor is such sentiment unusual in the academic world, albeit in a more nuanced manner. Argentine analyst Celia Szusterman in an article published in 2006, for example, warns that what is currently happening in Latin America is a 'populist resurgence which is currently eroding already damaged political institutions'.[4]

This, however, is not always the case. Others see populism as a much more nuanced concept and this is the position adopted in this book. Many academics, including Margaret Canovan and Ernesto Laclau amongst many others, argue against dismissing populism out of hand. Indeed, Joseph Stiglitz, the Nobel prize-winning economist and ex-chief economist and vice-president of the World Bank, for example, exclaims in one article that 'Populists are sometimes right!'[5] The book accepts that populism is a highly contested concept, not only in terms of its being seen as negative or positive for countries which experience it, but also, at a more fundamental level, about what defines populism. This chapter, however, will attempt to unravel these discussions and produce a working concept of populism which will serve as a theoretical framework for our ensuing examination of *chavismo*.

The discussion in this chapter will be based on four apparently simple but important questions: What is populism? Why does populism emerge? What are its characteristics? What impact does it have, or rather what are its consequences? In other words the book will look at what has been termed the four Cs; the *context, causes, characteristics* and *consequences* of populism. It will be argued here, however, that while the answers to these questions provide us with our required working concept of populism, they also lead us to broader and more profound questions which the literature on populism sometimes does not fully answer, such as: What is democracy? Why is democracy so fragile in Latin America? What is political legitimacy? How is political legitimacy gained and secured? For answers to questions such as these it is necessary to enter into broader, more universal, literatures, on the nature of democracy, on politics, on international political economy, on history and on ideology. To begin, however, the first of these questions will be examined: What is populism?

What is populism?

As stated above, populism is a highly contested concept with approaches to its study, which are often a reflection of the analyst's own academic prejudices.[6] Broadly speaking, following Roberts, there are four approaches or perspectives to the study of populism.[7] First, there is what he terms the *historical/sociological* perspective, emphasising populism as a consequence of and necessary stage towards economic and social development. Second there is the *economic* perspective, which identifies populism with expansionist and redistributive economic policies. A third perspective is what Roberts terms an *ideological* perspective, emphasising an ideological discourse based on the 'people' against those in power, the 'underdog' against the 'elite'. Finally there is the *political* perspective, which equates populism with vertical or leader-led popular mobilisation and the sidelining of existing democratic institutions to foster direct leader/people communication. Roberts concludes that each of these perspectives on their own is valid, as populism is a multidimensional phenomenon and indeed he recommends that any definition of populism should be a synthesis of all four.[8] It is worthwhile therefore to have a more detailed look at each of them.

The Italian/Argentinean sociologist Gino Germani, along with other contemporaries of his such as Di Tella and Ianni, argue that economic and social modernisation in developing societies creates a situation of permanent change.[9] Change is experienced in a conflictive manner in peripheral societies, in other word 'crises', which become a normal part of transition. This change, primarily rooted in urbanisation and industrialisation, produces what he calls a 'disposable mass' of people, usually from the newly urbanised popular classes, which, it is argued, is prone to support authoritarian leaders and/or movements. These political leaders then facilitate and encourage the mobilisation and participation of the popular classes in the exercise of power. Populism then is a result of modernisation and is part of a developing nation's route to modernity.

Linked to this perspective is the *economic* perspective. Here populism is associated with a policy of import substitution industrialisation (ISI), supporting national industries through high tariff regimes and subsidies, thus protecting internal markets from external competition. It has a nationalist industrial and economic strategy, protecting jobs in local industry and through nationalisation, the control of local raw materials and key industries. By prioritising local industrial growth and social welfare it builds cross-class alliances between different classes, such as the domestic industrial classes, the industrial working classes or the bureaucratic and mercantile middle classes. It is interventionist, state-led, and distributivist.[10]

According to some, such as Dornbusch and Edwards, and Sachs, these policies historically ignored risks to inflation, balance of payments and debt. As such they were 'fiscally irresponsible', leading to the economic crises of the 1980s, the so-called 'lost decade' of Latin America which produced zero growth, runaway inflation and huge international debt repayments causing steep declines in employment and rises in poverty. It has also been argued, however, that these policies were a form of 'Third Way' to national development, between capitalism and communism, which sought to satisfy demands for social equity and so head off threats of socialist revolution.[12]

The main exponent of our third perspective, the *ideological* perspective, strongly questions many of the assumptions behind our first *developmentalist* perspective. Laclau argues that this perspective is based on a teleological assumption of modernisation theory, which presupposes Latin America will develop a similar form of modernity as Europe and the United States.[13] Laclau argues that this, however, is not certain. For him populism has little to do with a determinate stage of development but rather is linked to a 'crisis of the dominant discourse which is in turn part of a more general social crisis'.[14] In other words populism emerges as a result of an ideological crisis of the dominant sectors within, and indeed caused by, a generalised economic and social crisis. Central to such a crisis is the extreme weakness and ineffectiveness of Latin American democratic institutions, such as courts, the legislature, ministries and political parties – the *political* perspective. This perspective posits the idea that the weaker democratic institutions are, the more likely that populism will emerge. The main function of institutions is to mediate between government and people and in the context of Latin America they very often fail in this role. Indeed, Latin Americans often view their democratic institutions as hopelessly corrupt and ineffective. In times of social and economic crisis this can lead, according to Philip, to people seeking strong executive leadership, a leader/people, top-down form of political organisation.[15] Furthermore, each instance of populism reinforces the original context of institutional weakness thus paving the way for more populism. Populism then can become 'a defining characteristic of a political culture'.[16] Celia Szusterman, cited above, would also subscribe to this perspective.

Looking critically at these different perspectives, three things stand out for the purposes of this study. First, while they are different in their emphasis, as Roberts points out they are not necessarily mutually exclusive. Each has something to offer in helping to explain populism. Second, there is the acceptance of the centrality of *crises* in the emergence of populism, and the inability of democratic institutions to withstand such crises. Finally, on the negative side, they fail satisfactorily to explain the context in which populism emerges. For example they do not always explain to a satisfactory degree why these crises occur. In order to do this, a central argument of this book is that analysis of populist experiences should be placed within a broader context on both the national and international level. The next section will examine these issues in more detail beginning with the first question: *Why does populism emerge?*

Populism: context and causes

As established above populism emerges due to *crises*: economic, social and political crises – in other words an entire crisis of all the established systems in a country which give that country stability. But this observation leads us to another deeper question: *Why do these crises take place?* The literature on populism, as we found above, points to issues such as institutional weaknesses, economic failures, and the pressures of modernisation processes. These crises, however, are linked to global issues, to global economic crises rooted in structural change, the resulting populist regimes being often responses to these global events but rooted in their national historical trajectories. The *developmentalist* perspective in particular shows how, in the context of Latin America, the historical exclusion of the dominated sectors, based on class and race, the dependent capitalist situations of states in the region, and the fractures and instabilities which result from these conditions contribute to a situation conducive to crises. It is important therefore to pay attention to this historical context.

When we examine Latin American history we see that democracy has had great difficulty in establishing itself, despite Latin America being considered by elites in the region as firmly within western political and cultural traditions. This fact points to a failure on the part of these elites to acknowledge the peculiar historical trajectory of the region, which has created a unique environment that may not be conducive to a traditional western-style liberal democracy. Liberal democracy in Latin America as it has been practised over the twentieth century could be said indeed to lack legitimacy, despite it finding qualified favour with most Latin Americans.[17]

Why then does democracy 'work' in developed societies, such as Western Europe, and not in developing societies such as in Latin America? Or to put it another way; how is it that democracy in Western Europe and other developed countries does not face these periodic crises which analysts claim lead to populism in Latin America? It is worthwhile here to look at Jürgen Habermas's work on legitimacy and crises in Western Europe to seek answers to this problem.[18]

Habermas argues that in advanced capitalist democracies liberal democracy maintains legitimacy, despite being based on class exploitation, as there is sufficient spreading of material and motivational rewards to achieve mass loyalty. Crises in this way are avoided by spreading costs throughout a plethora of weaker groups. This balancing act, and access to sufficient resources, ensures the survival of democracy despite its deficiencies in terms of participation. It is further bolstered by a widely diffused ideological outlook based on privatism – that is the private pursuit of public goods, such as careers, leisure etc. – and competition.

Habermas's model used comparatively can help show us why Latin American democracies fail. Essentially, while mass political participation is, nowadays at least, the norm in Latin America, these democracies fail to provide the sufficient material resources for an adequate number of people to ensure the mass loyalty which liberal democracy needs to survive. For this reason, while Latin Americans may favour democracy in theory they are nonetheless prepared to abandon it in order to have their material needs satisfied. Participation therefore must go beyond the political sphere and include also the economic, social and cultural levels in any democratic society.

Here Latin America faces a number of further barriers, principal among these being historically rooted social fractures based on the intertwined fissures of class and race, as we will see in the case of Venezuela in the following chapter. These fundamental cleavages are important deciding factors on access to housing, education and employment, for example. The lack of employment, and huge underemployment, leaves large groups – mostly indigenous, *pardo* (mixed race) or black – outside the formal economy. Inequitable and inefficient tax systems prevent the formulation and execution of policies to benefit the majority. Cultural differences, coupled with the lack of material rewards, discourage the spreading of capitalist social norms of competition and private endeavour, causing a 'motivation crisis'. The absence of these factors leaves these democracies prone to a greater degree of systemic crises, as was seen in the 1980s, and hence, in some cases, to the emergence of strong personalist leaders.

Habermas's theory of legitimation crises therefore provides a pertinent comparative model by which Venezuela can be compared with advanced capitalist democracies. It also provides the study with a structure by which we can examine the level of participation in each sphere of society – social, economic, cultural – to seek reasons as to why Chávez achieved the legitimacy denied his more immediate 'democratic' predecessors.

Dependency theory can also facilitate examination of this lack of legitimacy. Cardoso and Faletto characterised the economy of the Latin American region as being basically dependent on the export of raw materials to the advanced, or core capitalist economies in exchange for capital and manufactured goods.[19] Dependency theory holds that developing countries cannot follow the development route of advanced industrial countries, as developing countries need core country investment for development. Developing countries are therefore dependent on the core countries, which, however, insist on terms of trade which are unfavourable for Third World development. 'The effect of these conditions is that capital is drained out of the periphery into the core', preventing the former's development.[20]

This economic dependence coupled with the social cleavages identified above on class and race provide the basic context in which decision-making on access to economic, social, political and cultural participation is made. Modernisation processes brought improvements in these areas for many but also sharpened inequalities, particularly economic inequality in many societies. This prompted demands for a deepening of this move to greater participation to eradicate these inequalities. Yet structural change on a global level led to debt crises and retraction rather than the expansion of such participation. The result was crises – systemic crises leading to legitimation crises preparing the way for the possible emergence of a populist leader.

This points to a further concept which is helpful to explain crises and the emergence of populism in the current context – globalisation. In general it can be said that at the time of writing the pressures of globalisation are causing great strains on Latin American democracies. Liberal democracy is the principal form of government in Latin America, with only Cuba an exception. Furthermore, Latin American governments, through the Organisation of American States (OAS) have taken measures to safeguard liberal democracies' survival, such as the InterAmerican Democratic Charter.[21]

Globalisation has manifested itself in the region primarily through neoliberalism, and in 'boundary blurring', that is a reduction of state sovereignty in favour of international organisations and transnational corporations.[22] Both these phenomena have had a negative impact on the quality and effectiveness of Latin American democracy.

The neoliberal model implemented in Latin America, outlined by the so-called 'Washington Consensus' formulated by Williamson,[23] recommended the following measures:

- Fiscal discipline.
- A redirection of public expenditure priorities toward fields offering both high economic returns and the potential to improve income distribution, such as primary health care, primary education, and infrastructure.

- Tax reform (to lower marginal rates and broaden the tax base).
- Interest rate liberalisation.
- A competitive exchange rate.
- Trade liberalisation.
- Liberalisation of FDI inflows.
- Privatisation.
- Deregulation (in the sense of abolishing barriers to entry and exit).
- Secure property rights.

These measures, applied to greater or lesser degrees throughout most of Latin America, led to a reduction in the role of the state in favour of the market, which was to become 'the principal mechanism for regulating society, resolving conflicts, and determining directions of change'.[24]

Yet the achievements of the reforms, now going into their third decade, have been sparse. Growth has benefited mostly multinational companies and large economic groups.[25] Overall growth has not been as high as under the import substitution industrialisation policy of the previous few decades, primarily associated with populism as previously seen. Furthermore a large proportion of the income from this growth ends up being sent to developed countries in the form of interest payments on the debt, or as repatriated profits.[26]

Reforms have had a negative effect on job quality, with the informal sector increasing substantially.[27] Social provision has also been reduced, in favour of debt repayment, and much of it transferred into the private/non-governmental organisation (NGO) sector, increasing inequality of access.[28] The percentage of those living in poverty in Latin America rose from 40.5% in 1980 to 44.0% in 2002. Not once did the poverty level go below the 1980 figure during those twenty-two years and income inequality increased.[29]

This poor socio-economic showing has had a knock-on effect on democracy's credibility, liberal democracy being seen as the natural corollary of neoliberal reform. As Tedesco puts it, Latin Americans have to live with 'the paradox of a democratic system seeking the political inclusion of all and an economic system characterised by the economic exclusion of the majority'.[30] As Kirby maintains, an elitist political system is being consolidated in Latin America that, if anything, limits popular influence on decision-making.[31] The system has more to do with social control by wealthy elites than different projects of social transformation, leading to high levels of disenchantment and apathy with politics.

This situation has led to a decline in support for democracy. A report on democracy published by the UNDP shows that Latin Americans have little faith in democracy's ability to improve living standards or in the institutions of democracy.[32] Political parties and the judicial system score particularly low levels of trust with Latin Americans according to the report. Most Latin

Americans (57% in 2002) express support for democracy, but of those that do so, almost half (48.1%) value economic development more highly, and would support an authoritarian government if it solved the country's problems (44.9%).[33] Furthermore, those who show the least faith in democracy are those who live in countries with higher levels of inequality, illustrating graphically the link between a lack of confidence in democracy as it currently exists and inequality.[34] These dichotomies and dualities in Latin America are strengthened rather than lessened by globalisation. As Laclau succinctly puts it, the greatest danger to Latin American democracy 'comes from neoliberalism and not from populism'.[35]

Hence, while crises are, as shown in the literature, the principal *cause* for populism's emergence, it is important to place these crises into a wider regional and global political economy *context* and how a particular country interacts with that context. This is one of the principal aims of this book in its quest to explain *chavismo*. Moreover, in general these factors have to be taken into account in explaining the characteristics of populism, in particular with respect to 'populist' ideology, as will be shown in the next section.

The characteristics of populism

Populism and ideology

As seen with the *economic* perspective outlined above, populism was generally accepted as linked to growth and redistribution, ISI, and cross-class alliances between those who benefited most from these policies; the working class, local bourgeoisie and the bureaucratic and mercantile middle classes. These policies were deemed irresponsible by some analysts, leading to inflation, indebtedness and poverty.

Castañeda, however, argues that this point of view is guided by a prejudice against such policies.[36] Wide variations existed between distinct national populist regimes and populism changed and adapted to local and international demands and trends. Varying policy emphases were to be found depending on the nature of the coalition, the national political culture, and the socio-economic situation of the country with regard to levels of urbanisation and industrialisation. Different currents could be found within the same movement, be they corporatist, redistributive, democratic, authoritarian, technocratic etc., and this could vary from country to country.[37]

In effect many of these measures were not unusual in the international context of the time. In Western Europe, for example, in the same period, there was a general post-war consensus on the benefits of state intervention and the corporatist, dirigiste state.[38] Furthermore, the re-emergence of populist, or neopopulist, regimes in the late 1980s and in the 1990s, often in tandem with neoliberal restructuring policies, forced analysts to reconsider this orthodox view of populism. Neoliberal restructuring policies were, it was said, incompatible with traditional or classical populist economic policy, yet it was clear that the new breed of leader in Latin America, such as Fujimori in Peru, Fernando Collor in Brazil, and Carlos Menem in Argentina, amongst others, were using populist strategies to achieve and maintain power. Weyland argued that populism, or 'neopopulism' as he termed this new phase, had certain underlying affinities with neoliberalism.[39]

It can be argued then that as 'classical' populism was as much a product of a state-led international political economy context, so contemporary populism is a product of a globalised, neoliberal age. Populism as a political system, therefore, cannot be solely identified with a specific set of economic policies but must be seen in the context of international economic norms, and must be set within a wider sociopolitical and geopolitical context. As Roberts points out, populism's 'multiple expressions allow it to survive, and even thrive, in a variety of economic and political situations'.[40] Additionally, however, populism must also be seen within the context of the consistent demands from the population, and those who vote for populist leaders, for increased economic, social and political participation. Both these constants are the parameters within which populist leaders must design and execute their policies.

It is these central facts which can determine the characteristics of specific populist regimes. Differing ideological outlooks can give distinctly different flavours to different populist regimes, which in turn can affect the response to popular demands for participation. For this reason it is necessary to go beyond the literature on populism to analyse the influence and effect of ideology on specific regimes. In the present age this is particularly relevant within the overarching context of globalisation. The characteristics of a specific populist movement can vary, in its organisational structure for example, depending on that movement's position with regard to neoliberalism.

The people and the leader

Another major characteristic of populism found in the literature is the authoritarian, charismatic leader who uses the concept of the 'people' as central to his or her strategy to gain and maintain power. The identity of the 'people' in populism is unclear, as the term can be specific and vague, inclusive and exclusive, 'empty of precise meaning and full of rhetorical resonance'.[41] Laclau argues that the 'people' are defined through the discourse of the leader.[42] By discourse Laclau does not simply refer to language, that is to speech and writings, but also to the relations built up between the different elements of a populist movement.[43] A first step in building up this relationship is an 'appeal to the people' by the populist leader. The main objective of the 'appeal to the people' is to isolate mediating institutions (such as political parties and even parliament) and establish a direct unmediated relationship between the populist leader and the people. It is through these appeals to the people that the entity of the 'people' is defined in each individual populist episode.

This definition is developed through a process of 'antagonism'. Laclau sees three stages in the formation of the 'people'.[44] First, there must be a plurality of democratic demands being put forward to the government which remain unsatisfied. These demands coalesce to form an equivalential chain of popular demands, which then become of equal weight. Second, the leader, through his discourse, divides society into two camps, what Laclau calls the 'people/power bloc' dichotomy.[45] Third, the relationship between both camps is one of antagonism, as the people reject the status quo and seek out new forms of rule.

But who are 'the people'? The people are not so much a coalition of identities, as portrayed by many analysts, but rather invest their diverse identities into one privileged identity. Laclau illustrates this with the distinction between the people as *populus*, the body of all citizens, and as *plebs*, the underprivileged. The 'people' of populism comes about when the *plebs* come to represent the *populus* – 'that is, a partiality which wants to function as the totality of the community'.[46] He gives the examples of Solidarnosc, a trade union representing shipyard workers in the port of Gdansk in 1980s Poland, the *descamisados* or 'shirtless ones' in Perón's Argentina, and more recently the rise of the *informales* or informal workers in many Latin American states, such as Peru. All of these identities became representative of the entire *populus*, the people, within their respective countries at these times.

Central to this process of construction of the 'people' is the role of the leader. Populist leaders are often drawn by analysts as strong, charismatic, and paternalistic *macho* men, with an autocratic, authoritarian bent, who present themselves as honest and wilful, determined to guarantee the fulfilment of the people's wishes.[47] They are seen as 'outsiders', part of but estranged from elites, but unhappy with elite policies and customs, and are portrayed as manipulative of the 'people', autocratic, power hungry and ambitious.[48]

Laclau, however, resists attributing the prominence of the leader in populist movements to these characteristics.[49] As we have seen for him, populism is a chain of demands whose unity is expressed through one element of those demands (the *plebs*; Solidarnosc, *descamisados*, *informales*). In other words the *totality* is expressed through a *singularity* and the extreme form of a singularity is an individuality. The group then, the totality of the *populus*, becomes symbolically unified around an individuality, in this case the leader. The 'leader' therefore 'is inherent in the formation of a "people"'.[50] 'Leader' and 'people' are one, two sides of the same phenomenon in a populist formation.

Populist leaders' main strategic weapon to gain power is to appeal to the people, over the heads of established institutions and intermediary organisations in an antagonistic, direct, personalised manner. These appeals generally occur, as we have seen above, at times of crises, be that a general social/economic crisis and/or a related institutional crisis.[51] Their objective is to isolate the established institutions in order to form a direct unmediated relationship between the populist leader and the people. A central feature of these appeals is their antagonism to the status quo.[52] This antagonism is central in the formation of the identity of the 'people'.

Laclau's theories on populism point to, and are strongly influenced by, Gramscian theories on hegemony. It is through an antagonistic discourse against the status quo that the social space is divided into two clear camps – the *populus* and the powerful. As Laclau points out, discourse is not simply speech, although this is central to any hegemonic strategy, but also encompasses the totality of actions of a leader and movement. These actions can be analysed along Gramscian lines.

In his *Prison Notebooks* Gramsci develops his theory of 'war of manoeuvre' and 'war of position' as two parts of an overall strategy to achieve hegemony.[53] The 'war of manoeuvre' is a strategy to capture the institutions of state by a swift campaign of almost military precision. The 'war of position' is a subtler and longer strategy establishing consent from the people by winning their hearts and minds. Gramsci's theory can provide us with a framework to help understand better populist hegemonic strategies. As we shall see in Chapter 3, populists leaders can gain power through the legal (e.g. elections), the barely legal (ruling by decree) and the illegal (coups). These strategies can be conceptualised effectively by Gramsci's 'war of position' and 'war of manoeuvre' theories

Laclau and Mouffe point to a further and interlinked dimension of populism which is at the core of questioning around it.[54] Many if not most analysts recognise that populism and democracy are deeply intertwined. Laclau and Mouffe point out that the power strategies discussed above can lead to a 'logic of democracy' or a 'logic of totalitarianism'. Other analysts point out that populism can sometimes lead to an uneasy balance between the two.[55] Canovan indeed claims that populism is democracy's shadow.[56]

Most analysis in the literature on populism, however, seems to concur that populism is ultimately harmful for democracy. Conniff, Crabtree, and Roberts amongst others argue that populism damages democratic institutions and inhibits or retards democratic development in Latin America, precisely because of the supposed authoritarian personalism of populist leaders.[57] This discussion points to a need to widen the debate to embrace conceptions of democracy, conceptions which will be discussed more fully in the following section.

Consequences of populism

In general, there is little investigation into the consequences and impact of populism on the societies that have experienced it. Generally speaking analysts identify some positive aspects, namely popular participation and, more commonly, negative impacts on institutions and institutionalisation and a failure to tackle structural inequalities, thus failing to implement real change.

On the positive side a number of analysts note that at the very least populism encourages the participation of the popular sectors in societies' structures and institutions, thus dissipating the meekness of those classes and encouraging their assertiveness.[58] Amongst the gains made by these sectors are increased democratic rights, unionisation, industrialisation and welfare reform. Furthermore, Conniff argues that populism particularly encouraged a new cultural awareness among the masses, and a revival of interest in indigenous cultures.[59]

On the whole, however, analysts see populism as a negative phenomenon. Although some recognise that populism brought the masses into the political life of Latin America, this participation is not seen as genuine or thorough, but rather a pseudo-participation which ultimately perpetuates the inequality and exploitation characteristic of the region. Real structural change is shied away from and deferred, so that the root causes of populism (social inequality, poverty and political exclusion) remain intact. Representative institutions are weakened, thus exerting central control over popular participation, discouraging group autonomy, and reinforcing the political context which can lead to a re-emergence of new populist movements and regimes. Thus a consequence of populism is populism itself.[60] Bresser-Pereira et al. argue that this institutional weakening personalises politics and generates a climate where politics is reduced to fixes;[61] the political culture therefore becomes one of short-termism and politicians of all persuasions are expected to deliver quick-fix solutions to complex problems. This, it is argued, can only damage even further the chances for democratic development and long-term economic improvement.

In assessing these arguments, however, one must return to previous discussions in this chapter about the origins and causes of populism. If for example, weak institutions are a structural feature of Latin American political and social life, to what extent can populism be blamed for weakening institutions? Philip comments for example, that politics in Latin America generally tends towards short-termism.[62] Furthermore with regard to populism's inability to deliver on structural reform, is this due to the inability of populist leaders, or to strong, often illegal, resistance on the part of vested interests against such reform, or rather to structure or agency or both? Structural change in Latin America has been fiercely resisted on a number of occasions by a variety of groups, often receiving outside support. One need look no further than the coup against President Allende in Chile in 1973, or the long war against the Sandinistas of Nicaragua in the 1980s, for proof of resistance to structural change on the part of powerful national and international interests. As Diane Raby points out, however, true radical populism, precisely because it builds deep and binding ties between leader and mass, can actually facilitate implementation of a long-term transformative project; indeed, that in the face of hostile neoliberal pressures, something like this may be the only way to implement a serious transformative project.[63] Finally institutional weakness not only can give rise to populism, but also to authoritarianism in Latin America – why then is populism specifically related to institutional failure? Ultimately in order to shed further light on these questions it is necessary to go beyond the literature on populism and explore more fully the concept and meaning of 'democracy'.

What do writers on populism generally mean when they refer to 'democracy'? There is a generally agreed recognition that genuine democracy must have popular participation and strong institutions. Yet as we have seen popular participation in current liberal democracy is limited to the political level – in other words voting in elections – and excluding the economic and social spheres. Democratic institutions, while recognised as weak, are rarely analysed critically – despite their extremely low credibility amongst Latin Americans.[64] In effect liberal democracy – *really existing democracy* – is a correlate of neoliberal globalisation in Latin America as defined by the Washington Consensus, thus explaining to a great extent its weaknesses. Conversely many of the most lasting institutions in the region with high levels of popular participation, such as trade unions and political parties, were bequeathed by populist regimes.

Clearly then, in any discussion on populism, the nature of democracy and the effectiveness of democratic institutions are fundamental questions. For this reason these two questions are considered in various chapters of this study, particularly in Chapter 5, where the relative democratic and authoritarian characteristics of Chávez will be discussed, and on a more general level in Chapter 6, where the global state of present-day democracy will be reviewed in order to assess Chávez within a broader international and regional context.

Conclusion: populism as an analytic framework

The above discussion can provide us therefore with the following basic framework (shown in Table 1.1) to structure this study's enquiries based on the four guiding questions, the four Cs as discussed in the introduction: *context, causes, characteristics* and *consequences*.

Table 1.1   *Analytic framework*

Context and causes	Context of institutional weakness
	Generalised crises
Characteristics	Authoritarian, charismatic leaders
	The 'people'
	Appeals to the people
Consequences	Increased participation of popular sectors in social, economic and political life of country
	Deinstitutionalisation of state and society

The review, however, has also served to highlight a number of failings in the analysis of populism. One failing in the literature is the emphasis on defining populism to the neglect of researching its origins, causes, and impact. By concentrating on the nature of populism, analysts sometimes lose sight of the bigger picture, blaming populism for many ills afflicting the region, which have their origins in more permanent structural deficiencies affecting the region's economies and societies. A review of the wider geopolitical context, specifically on globalisation, and in the context of this study on the specific historical context of Venezuela, will help us to remedy that failing.

Moreover, there is a failure in the literature to enquire critically into the reasons for democracy's lack of legitimacy in Latin America, especially with regard to the role of institutions. Institutions are, more often than not, taken as intrinsically good, and as the sum of democracy rather than a reflection of its effectiveness, or lack thereof. As Terry Gibbs puts it there is a strain in North American political science approaches to political movements which 'tries to encapsulate social struggle in often ahistorical, institutional and theoretical categories that tend to weed out agency and obfuscate or even ignore the broader ideological context'.[65] Habermas can aid us here through his theory of legitimation crisis which explains the importance of popular participation on all levels of national life – political, social, economic and cultural – for the survival of democracy.[66] We thus can glean clues as to the reason for its failure in Latin America and the consequent emergence of populism. Moreover, Laclau foregrounds the role of ideology redressing the absence identified by Gibbs in the literature, while providing a credible solution to the problem of the lack of sufficient explanation as to populism's ideological variety, through his theory on ideological articulation.[67]

Finally, the literature on populism, by concentrating on specific regimes or on comparative studies within the region, often neglects the wider international context to help explain why some populist regimes adopt specific ideologies or policies. It is for this reason that this study is framed within a wider discussion on globalisation to help explain why it is that the Chávez regime can emerge at the end of the twentieth century, when not only populism, but socialism was pronounced dead. Furthermore, to address this absence in the literature we include a chapter of the Chávez government's foreign policy, showing the interaction of the internal, the national, and the external, the international in the formation of a populist regime framed by Anthony Payne's theory of the 'global politics of unequal development'.

In sum, though Chávez has been widely described as populist, the existing literature on populism is inadequate to provide a convincing analysis of his emergence as a political leader, the ideological differences in *chavismo* from more orthodox Latin American governments and differences in their style and substance of governing. A framework provided by a synthesis of the literature on populism and of these other literatures discussed above should allow a better explanation of the emergence, ideology and mode of governance of the Chávez government. Therefore taking this into account a revised version of the framework in Table 1.1 would look somewhat as shown in Table 1.2 (specific authors are in parentheses).

Table 1.2   Populism in a wider theoretical context

Question	Literature on populism	Other literatures
Context and causes	Context of institutional weakness	Historical context (various)
	Generalised crises	Legitimacy (Habermas, 1976)
Characteristics	Authoritarian, charismatic leaders	Ideology (Laclau and Mouffe, 2001)
	The 'people'	Hegemony (Gramsci, 1977)
	Appeals to the people	Democracy (various)
Consequences	Increased popular participation	Globalisation (various)
	Deinstitutionalisation of state and society	Democracy (various)
		International relations (Payne)

In the following chapter therefore the book will begin this process by looking at the national and regional structural contexts and causes for the emergence of *chavismo* in Venezuela.

Notes

1 For Rumsfeld see Rumsfeld, D., 2007, 'Remarks by Secretary Rumsfeld to the 35th Annual Washington Conference of the Council Of Americas', in US Department of Defense, Defense Link. Available from: www.defenselink.mil/transcripts/2005/ tr20050503-secdef2681.html Accessed 3 May 2005. For Toledo see Sustainability Tank, 2008, 'LATIN AMERICA: growth perspective in a shifting political landscape'. Available from: www.sustainabilititank.info. Accessed 14 June 2008.

2 See for example *The Economist* (2006), 'The return of populism'. Available from: www.economist.com/opinion/displaystory.cfm?story_id=6802448. Accessed 17 May 2006.

3 Usborne, D. (2006), 'The big question: should we be worried by the rise of the populist left in South America?', in *The Independent* 4 May 2006. Available from: http://news.independent.co.uk/world/americas/article361780.ece. Accessed 17 May 2006.

4 Szusterman, C. (2006) 'Latin America's eroding democracy: the view from Argentina'. Available from: www.opendemocracy.net/democracy-protest/argentina_ erosion_3607.jsp. Accessed 7 June 2006.

5 Stiglitz, Joseph, 2003, 'Populists are sometimes right'. Available from: www.project-syndicate.org. Accessed 5 October 2006.

6 Wiles, P., 1969, 'A syndrome not a doctrine', in G. Ionescu and E. Gellner (eds), *Populism: Its Meaning and National Characteristics*. London: Weidenfeld and Nicolson, p. 166.

7 Roberts, K., 1995, 'Neoliberalism and the transformation of populism in Latin America: the Peruvian case', in *World Politics* 48(1): 82–116.

8 Ibid., pp. 84–89.

9 Germani, G., 1965, *Politica y Sociedad en una Epoca de Transicion: de la Sociedad Tradicional a la Sociedad de Masas*. Buenos Aires: Editorial Paidos; Di Tella, T., 1965, 'Populism and reform in Latin America', in C. Veliz (ed.), *Obstacles to Change in Latin America*. London: Oxford University Press, pp. 47–75; Ianni, O., 1976, 'Populismo y relaciones de clase', in G. Germani, T. di Tella and O. Ianni, *Populismo y contradicciones de clase en Lainoamérica*. Mexico DF: Serie Popular Era, pp. 83–150.

10 See Dornbusch, R. and Edwards, S. (eds), 1991, *The Macroeconomics of Populism in Latin America*. Chicago: University of Chicago Press; Cardoso, F. H. and Faletto, E., 1979, *Dependency and Development in Latin America*. Berkeley: University of California Press; and O'Donnell, G., 1979, *Modernization and Bureaucratic Authoritarianism*, 2nd ed. Berkeley: Institute of International Studies, University of California.

11 Dornbusch, R. and Edwards S. (eds), 1991, *The Macroeconomics of Populism in Latin America*. Chicago: University of Chicago Press.; Sachs, J. Y., 1990, *Social Conflict and Populist Politics in Latin America*. San Francisco: ICS Press.

12 Drake, P. W., 1982, 'Conclusion: requiem for populism', in M. L. Conniff (ed.), *Latin American Populism in Comparative Perspective*. Albequerque: University of New Mexico Press, pp. 217–247, p. 233.

13 Laclau, E., 1977, *Politics and Ideology in Marxist Theory: Capitalism-Fascism-Populism*. London: New Left Books.

14 Ibid., p. 175.

15 Philip, G., 1998, 'New populism in Spanish America', in *Government and Opposition* 33(1): 81–87, p. 96; Mouzelis, N. P., 1986, *Politics in the Semi-Periphery: Early Parliamentarism and Late Industrialisation in the Balkans and Latin America*. New York: St. Martin's Press.

16 Crabtree, J., 2000, 'Populisms old and new: the Peruvian case', in *Bulletin of Latin American Research* 19(2): 163–176, p. 165.

17 UNDP/United Nations Development Programme, 2004, *Ideas and Contributions: Democracy in Latin America*. Available from: www.undp.org. Accessed 10 June 2008.

18 Habermas, J., 1976, *Legitimation Crisis*. Cambridge and Oxford: Polity Press.

19 Cardoso and Faletto, *Dependency and Development*.

20 Calvert, P., 2002, *Comparative Politics: An Introduction*. Harlow: Longman, p. 77.

21 The InterAmerican Democratic Charter was approved by the Organisation of American States (OAS) in Lima in 2001. The Charter states that if any member country experiences an unconstitutional interruption of the democratic order or an unconstitutional alteration of the constitutional regime norms they can be suspended from the OAS (See Article 19, OAS/Organisation of American States, 2001, *Inter-American Democratic Charter*. Available from: www.oas.org/OASpage/eng/Documents/Democratic_Charter.htm. Accessed 14 June 2008.

22 Calvert, *Comparative Politics*, pp 76-85. For a fuller discussion on globalisation in its neoliberal form and its effects on developing countries see Chapter 6.

23 Williamson, J., 1990, 'What Washington means by policy reform'. Chapter 2 from *Latin American Adjustment: How Much Has Happened?* Available from: www.iie.com/publications/papers/williamson1102-2.htm. Accessed 8 March 2004.

24 Kirby, P., 2003, *Introduction to Latin America: Twenty-First Century Challenges*. London: Sage, p. 56.

25 Kirby, *Introduction to Latin America*, pp. 65–66.

26 Veltmeyer, H., Petras, J. and Vieux, S., 1997, *Neoliberalism and Class Conflict in Latin America: A Comparative Perspective on the Political Economy of Structural Adjustment*. Basingstoke: Macmillan, p. 24.

27 Ibid. p. 14; Kirby, *Introduction to Latin America*, p. 60; Gwynne, R. N. and Kay, C. (eds), 1999, *Latin America Transformed: Globalisation and Modernity*. London: Arnold, p. 22.

28 Gwynne and Kay, *Latin America Transformed*, p. 24.

29 ECLAC (Economic Commission for Latin America and the Caribbean), 2003. *Anuario Estadistico de America Latina y el Caribe 2002*. Available at: www.eclac.cl. Accessed:14 November 2003, pp. 50–75.

30 Cited in Kirby, *Introduction to Latin America*, p. 76.

31 Ibid., p. 79.

32 UNDP, *Ideas and Contributions*, pp. 24–25.

33 Ibid., p. 52.

34 Ibid., p. 58.

35 Laclau, E., 2006, 'La deriva populista y la centroizquierda latinoamericana', in *Nueva Sociedad* 205, Septiembre/Octubre: 57–61, p. 61.

36 Castañeda, J. G., 1993, *Utopia Unarmed: The Latin American Left After the Cold War*. New York: Alfred A. Knopf, p. 40.

37 Drake, 'Conclusion', p. 234.

38 Cammack, P., 2000, 'The resurgence of populism in Latin America', in *Bulletin of Latin American Research* 19(2): 149–161, p. 156.

39 These were: a reliance on unorganized largely poor informal groups and an adversarial relation to organized groups, such as unions and the political class; a strongly top-down approach and strong state to effect economic reform and boost the position of a strong leader; and distribution of costs through restructuring to organized sectors and benefits, and benefits to informal sectors through the end of hyperinflation and targeted welfare programmes. See Weyland, K, 1996, 'Neopopulism and neoliberalism in Latin America: unexpected affinities', in *Studies in Comparative International Development* 31(3): 3–31.

40 Roberts, 'Neoliberalism', p. 112. Roberts identifies as a core property of populism:

'an economic project that utilizes widespread redistributive or clientelistic methods to create a material foundation for popular sector support' (p. 88).

41 Canovan, M., 1981, *Populism*. New York and London: Harcourt Brace Jovanovich, p. 286.

42 Laclau, E., 2005, *On Populist Reason*. London, New York: Verso.

43 Ibid., p. 68.

44 Ibid.

45 Laclau, *Politics and Ideology*.

46 Laclau, *On Populist Reason*, p. 81.

47 See Stein, S., 1980, *Populism in Peru: The Emergence of the Masses and the Politics of Social Control*. Madison and London: Harcourt Brace Jovanovich. Canovan, in *Populism*, cites a quote from Perón illustrating this point: 'If my government is to have merit it must interpret completely the wishes of my people. I am no more than the servant. My virtue lies in carrying out honestly and correctly the popular will' (p. 145).

48 See for example Roberts, K. M., 2006, 'Populism, political conflict, and grass-roots organization in Latin America', in *Comparative Politics* 38(2) January: 127–147.

49 Laclau, *On Populist Reason*.

50 Ibid., p. 100.

51 See Cammack ('The resurgence of populism', p. 154) where he states that appeals to the people arise when there is a crisis of political institutions and political and institutional mediation. See above for a discussion on crises and its role in populism.

52 Laclau's definition of populism is 'the presentation of popular-democratic interpellations as a synthetic-antagonistic complex with respect to the dominant ideology' (*Politics and Ideology*, pp. 172–173). Mouzelis argues that Laclau does not refer to the organizational implications of his theories on populism (See Mouzelis, N., 1987, 'Ideology and class politics: a critique of Ernesto Laclau', in *New Left Review* 107: 45–61, p. 10).

53 Gramsci, A., 1971 [1947] (edited and translated by Q. Hoare and G. Nowell Smith), *Selections from the Prison Notebooks*. New York: International Publishers.

54 Laclau, E. and Mouffe, C., 2001. *Hegemony and Socialist Strategy: Towards a Radical Democratic Politics*, 2nd ed. London and New York: Verso.

55 Dix, R. H., 1985, 'Populism: authoritarian and democratic', in *Latin American Research Review* 20(2): 29–52.; Germani, *Politica y Sociedad*; Roberts, K. M, 2000, 'Populism and democracy in Latin America', Paper delivered to *Threats to Democracy in Latin America* Conference, University of British Columbia, Vancouver, Canada, 3–4 November 2000. Available from: www.iir.ubc.ca/pwiasconferences/threatstodemocracy/. Accessed 25 August 2004.

56 Canovan, M., 1999, 'Trust the people! Populism and the two faces of democracy', in *Political Studies* XLVII: 2–16.

57 Conniff, M.L., 1982, 'Introduction: toward a comparative definition of populism', in M. L. Conniff (ed.), *Latin American Populism in Comparative Perspective*. Albequerque: University of New Mexico Press, pp. 3–29; Crabtree, 'Populisms old and new'; Roberts, 'Populism and democracy'.

58 See for example Germani, *Politica y Sociedad*; Lynch, N., 2000, 'Neopopulismo: un concepto vacío', in N. Lynch (ed.), *Política y Antipolítica en el Perú*. Lima: DESCO Centro de Estudios y Promoción del Desarrollo, pp. 153–180; Stein, *Populism in Peru*, p. 14; Torres Ballesteros, S., 1987, 'El Populismo: Un concepto escurridizo', in J. Alvarez Junco (ed.), *Populismo, Caudillaje y Discurso Demagogico*. Madrid: Centro de Investigaciones Sociologicas: Siglo XXI, pp. 159–180, p. 177.

59 Conniff, 'Introduction', p. 20.

60 Ibid., pp. 14–15; Crabtree, 'Populisms old and new', p. 176.

61 Philip, 'New populism in Spanish America', p. 94.
62 Ibid., p. 94.
63 Raby, D. L., 2006, *Democracy and Revolution: Latin America and Socialism Today.* London and Ann Arbor, MA: Pluto, Chapter 7.
64 Ellner, S., 2002, 'The tenuous credentials of Latin American democracy in the age of neoliberalism', in *Rethinking Marxism* 14(3): 76-93; UNDP, *Ideas and Contributions.*
65 Personal communication, 20 December 2006.
66 Habermas, *Legitimation Crisis.*
67 Laclau, *Politics and Ideology; On Populist Reason.*

2 Structural fractures, crises, the state and the emergence of Chávez

Introduction

Crises, as we have seen in the previous chapter, are one of the principal paths through which a populist government can come to power. But why is it that developing countries and Latin American countries in particular seem particularly prone to such crises resulting in populist eruptions? In other words, why is it that advanced capitalist countries can successfully withstand crises without losing mass support whereas developing countries can face comprehensive systems crises as a result of external economic shocks, sometimes leading to the emergence of populist regimes?

In Chapter 1 it was argued that crises are a central element in the emergence of populism, citing Jürgen Habermas's 'legitimation crises' model. In this chapter it is argued that in all three areas of Habermas's model – the economic, the administrative (the political) and the sociocultural - Venezuelan society did not manage to achieve sufficient levels of robustness and inclusiveness to avoid a legitimation crisis of the entire system. On the economic level an historical situation of economic dependency, specifically based on petroleum exports, led to a failure to develop a strong independent economy. On the administrative/political level, while great strides were made towards inclusion of the poor this was not sufficient to withstand the economic crises of the 1980s. In particular a failure to build strong institutions led to their rejection by the majority of society during these crisis years. Finally on a sociocultural level the persistence of historical fractures in the structure of society, specifically along race and class lines, failed to achieve sufficient spreading of rewards to ensure legitimation of the existing democratic regime. Ultimately the Venezuelan state could not execute the policies needed to ameliorate these social fractures, illustrating the inability of successive governments in Venezuela to ensure legitimacy and avoid chaos, thus paving the way for the emergence of Chávez.

This chapter will look at these issues in an integrated manner, as each area is interlinked. The main point of the chapter is that social fissures based on class and race have been integrated into Venezuela's development strategy, undermining it, as they perpetuate, and in turn are perpetuated by, Venezuela's economic dependency on the advanced capitalist countries. To prove this the book will first look briefly at data supporting the thesis of Venezuelan economic dependence and then go on to examine the rise and fall of the Punto Fijo system. In following sections class/race fissures in Venezuelan society from an historical perspective will be examined, showing how they eventually contributed to a profound system crisis which opened up a space for the emergence of *chavismo*. It will be further argued that Chávez's emergence signals a polarisation around race and class, with Chávez finding support amongst the poorer darker skinned groups while the opposition support rests in the lighter skinned middle and upper social groups. These divisions are further reflected in discourse emerging from both groups.

Economic dependency and sociocultural fractures

Most Latin American countries are to some extent or other economically dependent on the export of primary products to advanced capitalist countries and a concomitant importing of manufactured and capital goods from those countries. Venezuela is no exception. Of a total of $34,218.7 million dollars of exports in 2005, primary products accounted for 90.6% of those, little changed from the 85.8% recorded in 1995.[1] Oil, of course, is the country's main export and in 2005 crude oil or oil products accounted for 85.3% of Venezuela's exports, a significant rise on the 76.3% of exports it accounted for in 1995.[2] Furthermore much of that oil is dependent on one market, the United States, Venezuela being that country's fourth largest supplier. This dependence on oil leaves the country particularly exposed to the vagaries of market pricing, affecting its ability to plan its growth, as there is a constant downward pressure on prices (and OPEC) by powerful consumer countries.[3] Recasting Cardoso and Faletto's theory of dependency, Fernando Coronil identifies countries subjected to this phenomenon as 'nature-exporting societies': 'Even when these nations seek to break their colonial dependence on primary exports by implementing development plans directed at diversifying their economies, they typically rely on foreign exchange obtained by exporting primary products, intensifying their dependence on those commodities.' As a result they become subject to the infirmiries of so-called Dutch disease, which he renames, 'third-world or neo-colonial disease', whereby export 'booms tend to overvalue the domestic currency, promote imports of manufactured goods, and undermine productive sectors directed toward the domestic market'.[4]

Moreover, dependence on oil revenues obviated the necessity to implement progressive tax regimes, and private industry became dependent on state grants to survive. In effect the state became, as Coronil memorably interprets it, 'magical', acting 'as a single agent endowed with the magical power to remake the nation' into an image of modernity based on Western models.[5] The extreme centralisation of the party system, however, undermined and perverted this aim, ensuring instead that only those businesses closest to party leaderships benefitted, these being the most powerful (such as those of billionaire Gustavo Cisneros), while small and medium-sized businesses lost out. Meanwhile the Dutch disease ensured that imports of goods and services remained high, totalling $30,266.4 million of which consumer, intermediate and capital goods totalled over $20,068 million in 2005, for example, showing a marked dependence on imported consumer and manufactured goods.[6] The US alone, for example, supplies more than one-third of Venezuela's food imports.

In Venezuela structured employment, wealth, taxation and the distribution of social goods are subject to influence by the structural factors of race/class and economic relations with the core capitalist countries rather than national societal needs. An essential difficulty during the latter quarter of the twentieth century for most Latin American countries was that a substantial proportion of the earnings from exports went to pay off crippling international debts, instead of being used for reinvestment in social programmes or in the establishment of new industries. Venezuela was no exception: in 2004, it spent 6.0% of its gross domestic product (GDP) on debt servicing, whereas it only spent 2.0% of GDP on public healthcare in 2003–04. The increased oil revenues during the Chávez years have allowed increased social investment, yet the paying of the international debt remains a priority, as we shall see in further chapters. Consequently, such economic dependence coupled with the pressures of debt servicing preserves underdevelopment, inhibits economic growth and helps perpetuate the existing class/race bifurcation and the inequalities stemming from that basic societal cleavage, which in turn helps further perpetuate such economic dependence.

Both these factors have resulted in stratified societies based on race throughout Latin America with non-white majorities having limited access to the scant formal employment opportunities available. The white or 'near-white' elite on the other hand acts as the mediator between local markets and capitalist centres, with local capitalists playing a reduced role in the local market, providing basic consumer goods (such as beer, wine, flour etc.) to it and few high-value manufactured products. This race/class stratification is reflected in local politics, which has traditionally excluded the demands of the majority either through authoritarianism or through forms of liberal democracy limited by restrictive franchises, such as property and/or literacy requirements. Neoliberal globalisation has further exacerbated this phenomenon as international corporations have become more dominant and local elites more involved in facilitating their dominance, what Gamble and Payne refer to as the 'transnational managerial class'. Gustavo Cisneros is the perfect example of this type of elite, a man whose economic power is deeply embedded in the new global structures emerging as a result of globalisation processes.[9] The result therefore is a society based on the exclusion of large sectors of the population rather than integration as in the advanced capitalist model outlined by Habermas. In following sections this chapter will look at the historical roots of racism and classism in Venezuela. In the next section, however, we will review the rise and fall of Punto Fijo Venezuela to illustrate how this political system faced legitimation crisis due to its failure to reconcile the dichotomy of dependence in its economic and social structures.

The rise and fall of Punto Fijo Venezuela[10]

Foreign investment and dominance of the local economy, especially of the US, became increasingly prominent during the first half of the twentieth century. Foreign oil companies controlled 98% of national production by 1945, the US giant Standard Oil controlling half of that.[11] However, President Medina Angarita (1941–45) imposed tighter regulations on these companies, substantially increasing the government's share of oil revenues. His Oil Law of 1943 became the basis of Venezuelan oil policy right up to nationalisation in 1976, laying the financial foundations for the Punto Fijo populist system.[12] Yet, according to Rómulo Betancourt, founder of Acción Democratic (AD, one of the two main parties during the Punto Fijo era) and twice president of Venezuela (1945–48 and 1959–64), oil multinationals continued to benefit more from Venezuelan oil than did the Venezuelan people.[13] Industrial manufacturing did develop in Venezuela 'controlled from the core (capitalist countries) but managed more and more by members of the expanding local elites'.[14]

Venezuela, however, did develop a reasonable level of cultural homogeneity and, eventually, a strong democratic tradition. Its relatively abundant oil rents facilitated the creation of stable, though relatively restricted, democratic institutions in the latter part of the twentieth century, which ultimately, however, proved ineffective in the face of economic crisis, leading to political polarisation based on the inherent race/class bifurcation in that society. As we will see in the following sections, much of this was due to Venezuela's specific historical, social and cultural context.

The Punto Fijo regime was designed to avoid conflict and antagonism, encourage conciliation and negate the polarisation of Venezuelan society along class lines.[15] The system had a number of important achievements in its initial decades. It projected political stability, and had legitimacy amongst most of the people, relative economic growth, and not least, improved educational, health and general living standards for the majority of Venezuelans.[16]

Venezuela long had one of the highest participation levels in elections in Latin America, showing high levels of legitimacy for the system with, for example, 96.5% of electors voting in the 1973 presidential elections, electing Carlos Andrés Peréz for the first time. Furthermore, from the 1960s until well into the 1970s, indicators of social wellbeing made a considerable jump forward. Between 1961 and 1981, levels of illiteracy fell from 50% to 11%, the infant mortality rate ranged between 46.4 per thousand and 35.2 per thousand, and life expectancy at birth rose from 61 years to 69 years.[17] Industrialisation and urbanisation increased substantially during the Punto Fijo period, and popular demands for inclusion were primarily satisfied by increased provision of social goods and increased possibilities for advancement, in other words in Habermasian terms, motivational rewards.

Nonetheless, the regime's main deficits were 'an excessive centralisation, socio-economic inequality, clientelism between State, citizens and organisation, the party domination of institutions and decisions [and] administrative corruption'.[18] The fundamental flaw in the Punto Fijo design was the contradiction between the liberal democratic order on the juridical constitutional level and the reform of a socialist character of the social and economic order.[19] Once the pillar of a limitless oil income fell and the addiction to indebtedness took hold, the contradiction between these two parts became manifest and the model became unsustainable. Both parts of the Punto Fijo equation became irreconcilable, and with it the fragile system of consensus became divided once again along class lines. From the early 1980s onwards, the decline in oil prices and the increases in debt led to the economic foundations of the Punto Fijo state being undermined, prohibiting the distribution of rents to all sectors, and forcing the state to break the populist social pact which had worked in favour of system legitimation up until that time. No longer was it possible to give to one sector without taking from the other. It was no longer possible to conceal the multiple social fractures in the social body of Venezuela with the profits from oil, the product of its physical body. From Black Friday in February 1983, when the government of Luis Herrera Campíns dramatically devalued the bolívar in the face of a slump in oil prices and massive capital flight, the three pillars – the economic, the social and the political – supporting the regime began to crumble.[20]

On the economic level Venezuelans saw their standard of living plummet: between 1990 and 1997, according to the UN, per capita income fell from US$5,192 to US$2,858, and Venezuela's human development index from 0.8210 to 0.7046.[21] Income inequalities increased, as in 1979 the richest 5% of the population earned 41.58 times more than the poorest 5%, but by 1997 that ratio was 53.11 to one.[22] Poverty increased from 17.65% of the population in 1980, with 9.06% living in extreme poverty, to 48.33% in 1997, with a staggering 27.66% of Venezuelans living in extreme poverty.[23] Employment became increasingly informal. In 1983, 41.3% of working Venezuelans were in the informal sector whereas that increased to 48.20% in 1998. The biggest fall was in the public sector – from 22.67% of employment in 1983 to 16.33% in 1998.[24]

Along with these massive falls in the standard of living for ordinary Venezuelans, violence increased. Whereas in 1986, the homicide rate was 8 per 100,000 of the population, by 1999 the number of murders increased to 25 for every 100,000. Of those murders the greatest increase was in Caracas, where the figure increased from 13 per 100,000 in 1986 to 81 in 1999.[25] It is noticeable that the greatest increases in these indices are during years of structural adjustment. The biggest rise in poverty, for example, takes place between 1993 and 1994, when President Caldera began to implement the neoliberal Agenda Venezuela programme, increasing from 41.37% of the population to 53.65%.[26]

Meanwhile with this decline in the personal fortunes of ordinary Venezuelans, a concomitant deterioration in the public domain also took place with public investment declining equally dramatically. Venezuela's tax take fell from 18.4% in 1990 to 12.8% in 1998.[27] Public spending contracted from a high of 37% of GDP in 1982 to 16% in 1998.[28] The *bolívar* devalued about 100% between 1988 and 1993, and inflation remained relatively high by Venezuelan standards, at around 31% annually during the same period.[29]

This economic and social crisis was fundamentally due to the dependence of the Venezuelan economy on oil rent. In 1965 oil accounted for 97% of Venezuela's exports, and by the beginning of the 1990's that figure had only been reduced to 91%.[30] This left Venezuela particularly vulnerable to world oil market conditions, prices falling abruptly in 1986 and 1988 causing critical balance of payments deficits which were financed by borrowing.[31] In 1988 public external debt had reached US$26.6 billion, and by 1998 it was around US$37 billion.[32]

In the context of the increased global hegemony of neoliberal ideology, parts of the Venezuelan economic elite began to press more urgently for reform, while others, dependent on the current system, prevaricated and the systemic defenders of the popular classes actively collaborated or stood on the sidelines, leaving the majority of the population without effective representation.[33] In the end it was the promoters of neoliberal globalisation who won the argument on the day, if not wholly convincingly.

The rise of neoliberalism and the death of a united Venezuela

The deepening political polarisation became most apparent in Venezuela during the second presidency of Carlos Andrés Peréz (1989–93) as he attempted to introduce a neoliberal restructuring programme into Venezuela. The introduction of neoliberal policies by Peréz sparked off the greatest public disorders seen in modern Venezuelan history, which came to be known as the *caracazo* (27–28 February 1989). Peréz brought in a number of International Monetary Fund (IMF) sponsored economic measures, including the raising of fuel costs with a concomitant rise in public transport charges, despite a pre-election discourse to the contrary. This provoked residents of Caracas's teeming shantytowns, and those in many other Venezuelan cities, to come down from the *cerros* (hills) and proceed to loot shops and warehouses, initially for food, but as the disturbances developed for all sorts of consumer goods. Government reaction was initially tame but eventually President Pérez called a state of emergency and left it to the army and police to quell the disturbances. The result was the use of 'massive violence' and an official death toll of 277, an unofficial one running into the thousands.[34] After the *caracazo*, Venezuela would not be the same again as protest became the norm, increasing both in incidence, violence and variety and extending to almost all sectors of society.[35]

Despite the president's admittance of the class nature of the disturbances and the economic measures, and the divisions caused by them, he persisted in their implementation, leading initially to some macroeconomic success. By 1992, however, unemployment, informalisation of employment and poverty had all increased.[36] Meanwhile as the Venezuelan population in general and the popular classes in particular paid the price of economic reform, the governmental and business elites were seen to enrich themselves even further through financial speculation and/or corruption. Dissatisfaction grew and in 1992 Peréz's government was rocked by two unsuccessful coups, the first led by Lt Col. Hugo Chávez on 4 February. While the coups failed, by 1993 Peréz was impeached and under house arrest for corruption, finally going into exile, where he still remains.

This cleared the way for the emergence of Chávez as a political force in the country. By 1997 Movimiento Quinta Republica (MVR) was formed and began to prepare for the 1998 elections.[37] Chávez won the presidential elections of that year with 56% of the votes.[38] As the following section will illustrate, race and class were salient elements needed to explain the results of that election, and would remain so right through the subsequent years of Chávez's presidency. This emergence of race and class as salient issues, have however, a complex background in Venezuelan history going back to colonial times, as the next section will also outline.

Class/race-based polarisation in Venezuela

Despite views to the contrary, racism still exists and operates in Venezuela and this racism has deep roots in the country's colonial past. Furthermore, in Venezuela as in much of the rest of Latin America, concepts of race and class fuse whereby generally speaking it is believed that the darker a person's skin, the poorer that person will be. Before looking at this argument in more detail, we first need to look at the relationship between these two concepts in sociological theory to provide a theoretical background to this contextual discussion.

Racism and class

Miles and Brown, in their book *Racism*, see the concept of 'race' and 'races' as 'socially imagined rather than biological realities'.[39] In a nutshell they see the phenomenon of race and racism as diverse but one that always centres on an ideology based on 'a Self/Other dialectic'.[40] This ideology is twofold they argue. Following Taguieff, the act of racialisation of a given population, attributes that Other with negative attributes ('autoracialisation') while simultaneously and automatically giving the Self positive attributes.[41] Hence, for example, European colonial discourse on Africans portrayed the African as 'less civilised, a barbarian, by virtue of supposedly looking more like a beast and behaving in ways that approximated to the behaviour of a beast'.[42] Conversely, the Self, the European, was seen as being the epitome of civilisation and human development. Conceptualisations such as these they argue seek 'to claim the authority of a natural (and therefore unalterable) difference [and] … is the prelude to exclusionary practices'.[43]

So what is the relationship then between the concept of race and that of class? Miles and Brown argue that the two are interlinked because both perpetuate inequality. 'Racism is a denial of humanity (substituting, as it does, 'races' for 'the human race') and a means of legitimating inequality (particularly inequality explicit in class structures)'.[44] How they interact, however, will depend on the class position of those practicing racism, because '*Erlebnis* (lived experienced of the world) and its consequent problems vary with class position'.[45] Indeed the forms and expressions of racism have had 'varying interaction with economic and political relations in capitalist and non-capitalist social formations',[46] hence any discussion of racism must therefore be 'historically specific [as it is] knowable only as a result of historical analysis rather than abstract thinking'.[47] Consequently discussion on racism in Venezuela and its relationship to class must be looked at in an historical context to be properly understood, which is our task in the next few sections.

Colonial and early Republican contexts

Unlike other parts of the Spanish empire in America, such as Peru and Mexico, Venezuela had no great mineral wealth and had a relatively small indigenous population to work the land, thus offering little by way of financial rewards for its colonists. Colonial Venezuela therefore, remained a poor and peripheral frontier post, with a small and relatively poor elite dedicated to plantation farming, commerce or smuggling.[48] As Venezuela had small indigenous populations relative to the richer colonies of Peru and Mexico, it had to import labour through slavery from Africa, at considerable cost, both human and economic. In the period from the conquest up until 1797, when the African slave trade ended, 100,000 Africans entered Venezuela.[49] These slaves were harshly treated both physically and socially and the black and the indigenous would remain stigmatised within Venezuelan society from thence on.

Nonetheless, Venezuela became one of the more racially mixed colonies of Spanish America, and became quite a diversified society, with a social pyramid with relatively less distance between the top and the base than in other parts of the Empire.[50] This freer structure of Venezuelan colonial society lent itself to a more intimate relationship between the various racial groups.[51] By the end of the colonial era 60% of Venezuelans had African origins and of the 25% classified as white probably some 90% had some African ancestry.[52] A process of miscegenation began therefore in Venezuela from the earliest times of the colony. This would have repercussions on the country's view of itself in later years, as we shall see.

Independence brought little practical change in the living conditions for the masses as a whole, but did usher in changes in the nature and composition of the elites. The end of native Spanish elite dominance, the *caudillo* wars that broke out in the country after independence in 1811 and the Federal War of 1859–63, led to increased *pardo* (mixed European, Indigenous and African) presence amongst elite groups. In general, however, this did not result in any appreciable improvement for the dominated sectors.[53] While republican governments enshrined the principle of equality in successive constitutions, this was more legal aspiration than social fact. In effect Creole (people of European background born in Spanish America) domination became prominent, and as Venezuela developed economically the new Creole elites aligned themselves commercially and diplomatically with outside powers, particularly Great Britain but increasingly the United States. A repressive labour system remained, through a variety of laws and restrictions, with regard to freedom of movement and forced labour. These laws, however, were less successful in Venezuela than in other parts of what was the Spanish empire.[54]

Slavery in the colonial era was replaced in republican Venezuela by positivism as a means to manage race in this new context, in other words it was believed that miscegenation was the path to progress. The most prominent policy in this era was the use of European immigration to 'whiten' and 'civilize' the non-white populations. Those promoting positivist theories 'found the origin of Venezuela's troubles in mingling with blacks'.[55] The answer therefore was in making Venezuela less black, and less indigenous. This policy was placed into a wider framework of aspiration to European and increasingly North American social models, rejecting the indigenous and the African as inferior.

Journalist and veteran Latin America watcher, Richard Gott sees this era in particular in Latin America in terms of a 'white settler' society paradigm.[56] Quoting the Australian anthropologist, Patrick Wolfe, Gott characterises this paradigm as a 'sustained institutional tendency to eliminate the indigenous population', either physically or through policies of assimilation.[57] In Latin America white settlers set out to achieve this by 'simultaneously oppressing two different groups within their territory: they seized the *land* of the indigenous peoples, and they appropriated the *labour* of the black slaves that they had imported'.[58]

Gott goes on to quote the Peruvian sociologist, Anibal Quijano, and his concept of '"colonialidad" or "coloniality"', where societies 'retain or assume the characteristics of colonialism, even when they have become nominally independent'.[59] This resulted in the Latin American white settler elite having a Eurocentric approach to society and nation-building, and a deep mistrust of native and African conceptions of community and society. In consequence the white settler elites of Latin America had more in common with the elites of Europe and North America than their fellow Latin Americans, leading to an 'ingrained racist fear and hatred of the white settlers, alarmed by the continuing presence of the expropriated underclass ...'.[60] Struggles between rich and poor in Latin America therefore not only were class based but also race based, a fact, Gott notes, that 'even politicians and historians of the Left' have ignored, preferring to 'discuss class rather than race'.[61] Venezuela was no exception within this pattern, although it has had distinct nuances due to its individual historical trajectory as noted in this and subsequent chapters.

The rejection of the black and the indigenous continued into the twentieth century through the 'ideology of *mestizaje* (miscegenation), also known as the myth of democracy or racial equality, [which] served to mask racial discrimination and the socioeconomic situation of the Afro-Venezuelan and Indigenous communities'.[62] In this ideology the white European was identified as 'the civilizing agent, making Africans and the Indigenous and their descendants largely invisible'.[63] This ideology also 'denied the existence of social classes', and instead looked to a cultural homogenization, spread primarily through the educational system.[64] This policy of *mestizaje* and the denial of racism within Venezuela continued into the liberal democratic era, known as the Punto Fijo regime, installed definitively in 1958.

With the economic crisis of the Punto Fijo regime, as outlined in the previous section, the vision of a united, non-racial and classless Venezuela lost its mythical power. Racist discourse began to re-emerge amongst the upper and middle classes. The link between class and race became more explicit as Afro-Venezuelan and indigenous people became the scapegoats for Venezuela's economic failure. Ishibashi shows how stereotypes of fecklessness and indolence of Afro-Venezuelans were perpetuated through the Venezuelan media. As Ishibashi puts it: 'The "white" is normally the symbol of the beautiful, the rich, the pure and the sophisticated, while the "black" is the symbol of the ugly, the poor, the impure and the non-sophisticated.'[65] Black people in the Venezuelan media, in advertisements, TV soaps, in the cinema and in beauty pageants, are practically 'invisible'.[66] When they are seen, they are usually associated with partying or the beach, reinforcing the idea of the black as 'feckless', or in a position of providing a service of physical labour.

Class also plays a role in the depiction of blacks in the Venezuelan media, with products directed at the upper classes usually being advertised by white models, while those directed at the popular classes usually using darker-skinned models. As one media photographer admits: 'the darker the [skin] colour, the more [models] are associated with the lowest social classes.'[67] Indeed not only is 'colour associated with [social] classes' but Afro-Venezuelans are also, as we have seen, associated with the 'ugly'.[68] This reinforces the association in the popular mind of the 'west' or the 'white' being associated with the 'superior and civilized' while the rest are 'inferior and savage'.[69]

This phenomenon could also be seen in establishment presentations of the *caracazo* referred to above. To those in power the *caracazo* represented the eruption of barbarism, of primitivism pitted against civilisation.[70] The *pueblo* (people) were a source of barbarism, the government and the elite a force for reason and civilisation; '[t]he nation was split in two'.[71] The *caracazo* symbolised the eruption of the class factor once again into the national political arena and following the logic of our argument, also the question of race.[72] It was these divisions which would contribute greatly to the emergence of Chávez, as shall be explained in the next section.

Race/class divisions and the rise of Chávez

According to Roberts, Chávez's rise signifies 'a repoliticisation of social inequality in Venezuela'[73] with mostly the darker-skinned popular sectors identifying with Chávez and the lighter-skinned middle and upper sectors with opponents of the president. This division was apparent from the initial emergence of Chávez as leader of the 1992 coup referred to above. Using poll data from 1995 and 1998, Venezuelan analyst Damarys Canache finds that it was the poor who mostly supported Chávez's failed coup in 1992 against President Carlos Andrés Peréz, and in a survey in 1995 his support was strongest amongst the lower economic sectors.[74]

This tendency continued in polls carried out before subsequent presidential elections and the recall referendum against President Chávez in 2004. In the 1998 presidential elections, for example, Roberts points to strong support amongst the poor for Chávez, whereas his chief rival Henrique Salas

Römer's appeal was amongst the middle and upper sectors.[75] Canache provides further evidence of this support, showing that in a pre-election survey conducted just before the 1998 presidential elections, 55% of the urban poor declared their intention to vote for Chávez, whereas only 45% of the non-poor expected to back him.[76]

Similarly in the 2000 presidential elections one poll found that 50.5% of socioeconomic sector E intended to vote for Chávez as opposed to 24% for Arias Cárdenas, his principal opponent and co-conspirator in the 1992 coup, while 66.7% of socioeconomic groups A/B intended to vote for the latter.[77] A poll published by Venezuelan polling firm Datanalisis in 2001 found a similar tendency.[78]

Canache, however, predicted that the urban poor of Venezuela would become disillusioned with Chávez and cites poll data to prove this at the conclusion of her study. Nonetheless, poll data posterior to publication of that study reinforces rather than negates the tendency of support for Chávez amongst the poor. In a poll by Greenberg, Quinlan and Rosner in 2004, shortly before the recall referendum held on President Chávez's mandate, 80% of those polled in the A/B/C+ social category intended to vote for his removal from office (Sí) while close to 60% of those in the E social category would vote against (No).[79] Canache bases her prediction on Chávez's failure to deliver promises made to the poor yet when asked for reasons in this poll why they chose to vote in favour of Chávez, 62% said they believed that Chávez helped the poor and almost 60% evaluated the government's *misiones* or social programmes (see Chapter 4) favourably, reinforcing the link between Chávez and the lower class in popular opinion.

More recently still, similar data was found in an Evans/Mc Donough Company Inc./Consultores 30.11 poll published on 29 November 2006, just over a week before the 6 December presidential elections of that year.[80] In this poll 76% of social stratum A/B and 47% of stratum C said they would vote for Manuel Rosales, governor of Zulia state and Chávez's main rival, while 64% of stratum D and 68% of stratum E intended to vote for Chávez. These two stratums made up the majority of respondents, representing jointly 62% of the total. In the event Chávez won that election by 62%, while the turnout was 75% of registered voters. Chávez's support amongst the poor has therefore remained relatively consistent over the eight years since he was first elected in 1998.

While such data supports the thesis that Chávez's support is found mostly amongst the popular sectors, with the middle and upper sectors supporting opponents of the president, an important further argument in this chapter is that there is a racial subtext to this support. While there is no direct poll data to support this thesis, correlations between data on ethnic and class breakdown in Venezuela and the electoral poll data discussed here display marked similarities.

Table 2.1   Class/race polarisation in Venezuela – Poll Data 2000–06 (%)

Year/Social class	A/B	C	D	E	% in election
% social class in overall pop.	5	35	39	21	100
2000	66.7 (Opp)	N/A	N/A	50.5 (Ch)	59.76 (Ch) 37.52 (Opp)
2004	80 (Sí)* 15 (No)*	61 (Sí) 34 (No)	51 (Sí) 43 (No)	38 (Sí) 59 (No)	40.63 (Sí) 59.9 (No)
2006	76 (Opp) 17 (Ch)	47 (Opp) 48 (Ch)	32 (Opp) 64 (Ch)	26 (Opp) 68 (Ch)	38.39 (Opp) 62 (Ch)

Sources: Subero, C., 2000; Greenberg, Quinlan and Rosner, 2004; Evans McDonagh/Consultores 30.11.2006; Consejo Nacional Electoral, 2007.
* Sí refers to the option in favour of removing Chávez; No to the option against.
Key:
Opp = Main opposition candidates: Francisco Arias Cárdenas (2000), Manuel Rosales (2006).
Ch = Hugo Chávez Frías, president of Venezuela.

In surveys done on ethnicity within Venezuela, those who identify as 'Afro-Venezuelan' are in a small minority, of much lesser significance to those who identify as white. For example in the World Values Survey (2007) in Venezuela,[81] 4.2% of respondents identified themselves as Black-Other/Black, whereas 35.8% identified themselves as White/Caucasian White. Nevertheless, the survey also provides a number of intermediate options, such as 'Coloured-Dark' (16.6%) and 'Coloured-Light' (42.7%). Indigenous groups on the other hand represent only 0.5% of the population, but despite their small numbers have important symbolic value.

Apart from the highly subjective nature of such categories (what is the actual physical difference between 'Black' and 'Coloured-Dark'?), not to mention the high probability that those who identify themselves as 'Caucasian-White' have some element of black or Indian blood,[82] the important point to note is that the majority of Venezuelans, approximately 64%, identify themselves as non-white. It is important also to point out that in a social context where the black is highly undervalued, if not despised, the probability of Venezuelans not identifying themselves with that ethnic category is most likely increased.

While at the time of writing it appears that no figures exist providing a breakdown of the racial make-up of each social class in Venezuela, it is instructive to compare social-class breakdown with that of racial categories. As we can see in Tables 2.2 and 2.3, if we compare the total of social sectors

Table 2.2   Social class sectors population breakdown: Venezuela (%)

Social class	A/B	C	D	E	Total
% social class in overall pop	5	35	39	21	100
Total A+B+C and D+E	40		60		100

Source: Greenberg, Quinlan and Rosner, 2004, p. 24.
Note: (A,B,C+). Social strata vary from poll to poll but generally those in A,B and upper C are regarded as in high income brackets; C– in the middle income bracket and D and E in the low income bracket, the poorest income strata.

Table 2.3   Racial category breakdown: Venezuela (%)

Racial category	White	Coloured light	Coloured dark	Black	Indigenous	Total
% race in overall pop	35.8	42.7	16.6	4.2	0.5	100
Totals white/ non-white	35.8	64.2				100

Source: World Values Survey, Venezuela, 1996 and 2000. Categories were self-selected by respondents from presented options.

A+B+C, at 40%, with the total of those who identified themselves as white, at 35.8%, we find a strong similarity in the percentages found pertaining to both those categories. Similarly, if we compare the total of sectors D+E, the poorest social sectors, at 60%, with the total of those who identified as non-white (i.e. black, coloured dark, coloured light and indigenous) at 64.2%, again we find a high level of correlation between both sets of figures. This suggests, although by no means definitively, that there is a strong level of probability that those who identify as white are found in the higher social sectors while those who identify as black, mixed raced or indigenous are found in the D or E social categories. If we then go on further to look at the figures in Table 2.1 above, showing voting patterns in favour of President Chávez, we find similar correlations between percentages in all three sets of figures. In other words, there is a high probability, judging by these figures, that a poorer Venezuelan, with darker skin, will vote for Chávez (see above).

Such support, it has to be surmised, is based on class and race. On the one hand the poor's support for Chávez is based on the fact that he is like them: from a poor background and *pardo* (of mixed indigenous, African and European descent). The figures presented in Tables 2.2 and 2.3 would seem to support this suggestion. Conversely, the rejection of Chávez by parts of the middle and most of the upper classes in Venezuela is precisely due to a rejection of these very qualities: being poor and dark-skinned. This rejection, as we have explained in this chapter, is furthermore based on a deeply rooted historical rejection of the black as being culturally and socially inferior to the white. Hence, despite, as Wright points out,[83] the 'seamier sides of racism' being eradicated during the pre-Chávez period (1958–93), the so-called Punto Fijo era, this association of the black with backwardness remains strong in Venezuela, as we have seen. Thus race and class remain associated in Venezuela despite advancement in eradicating some elements of racism. Indeed class and race is engrained in Chávez discourse, and in the opposition's anti-Chávez discourse, as we shall see in the following section.

Race and class discourse in chavismo

Race and class are central sources of identification for Chávez. Chávez repeatedly emphasises his background as a *pardo* and as a common man. Kozloff quotes Chávez as saying: 'My Indian roots are from my father's side … He [my father] is mixed Indian and Black, which makes me very proud.'[84] He also boasted, according to Kozloff, that his grandmother was a Pumé Indian. Kozloff goes on to report that apart from being *pardo* like 67% of his fellow countrymen and women, 'Chávez was [also] born in extremely humbling conditions in the *llano* [Orinoco plains area of Central Venezuela]: "I was a farm kid from the plains of South Venezuela," he remarked to Ted Koppel on ABC's *Nightline*. "I grew up in a palm tree house with an earthen floor," he added.'[85] Chávez frequently refers to cultural symbols associated with grassroots Venezuelan communities: the *arepa*, a corn bread that is part of the staple diet for ordinary Venezuelans, baseball, the national sport, and occasionally breaks out into a typical Venezuelan song in the middle of a speech.

The Chávez discourse celebrating race and class contrasts greatly with that emanating from opposition elements. Some of this discourse presents deeply subtle forms of racism and classism, whereas others are much more radical. In it the image is projected of a *pueblo* being easily manipulated and incapable of thinking rationally. Pedro Carmona Estanga, for example, leader of peak business organisation, FEDECAMARAS and erstwhile president for forty-eight hours during the coup against Chávez in April 2002, wrote in an article published shortly before the 1998 presidential elections that 'people don't understand the *Constituyente* but simply emotionally follow the candidate that is promoting it'. Francia gives further examples of this, where the vote for Chávez is considered an 'emotional' vote, while votes against him are considered 'rational'.[86] Similarly Julio Borges, leader of political party Primero Justicia (Justice First), qualifies those who vote for Chávez as 'inhabitants' not 'citizens', implying that they acted without thinking.[87] On fieldwork to Venezuela in 2002, I found that some people rejected Chávez because, according to them, Venezuela needed *'gente preparada'*, educated, trained people, this despite the fact that Chávez has a BSc in military science and studied for a masters degree in political science. Such statements tie into Ishibashi's observations regarding the relative 'civility' and 'barbarism' of white and black, light and dark Venezuelans.

Less subtle forms of racism and classism are also found in opposition discourse on Chávez supporters. Supporters of Chávez are regularly referred to as 'hordes' and the pro-government Bolivarian Circles as 'terror circles' by the media according to Reporters Without Frontiers, quoting an ex-government minister, Nora Uribe.[88] In March, 2004, during a high-level international summit in Caracas, opposition television station Globovisión parodied President Robert Mugabe of Zimbabwe as a monkey, prompting six African countries to object.[89] Herrera Salas points to a visceral racism and classism directed towards the president and his supporters by opposition members and media, where the president is routinely referred to as 'Indian, monkey and thick-lipped' or simply as a 'monkey'.[90] More recently, in the 2006 presidential elections, opposition candidate Manuel Rosales offered a prepaid debit card to poor Venezuelans called '*Mi Negra*', meaning 'My Black Lady.' As Sreeharsha reports, Afro-Venezuelans resented both the name and the economic message of this campaign promise as it reinforced negative stereotyping of black Venezuelans.[91]

Some opposition analysts, while recognising this racism and classism within the opposition ranks, blame Chávez for this situation. For Patricia Márquez for example, of the elite Instituto de Estudios Superiores de Administración (IESA) it is Chávez who has 'stirred up the beehive of social harmony'.[92] Yet, Herrera Salas counters, it 'is evident … that [Chávez's] political discourse and the symbolic and cultural practices of the Bolivarian Revolution have emphasised so-called national values, significantly reducing the occurrence of ethnic shame and endoracism in the popular sectors'.[93]

In conclusion, race and class are essential and interlinked elements in discourse amongst *chavismo* and groups opposed to Chávez, which is reflected in electoral contests with the darker poorer sectors voting for Chávez, and the lighter-skinned, better-off sectors against Chávez and for the opposition. Race and class fissures therefore are deeply engrained in Venezuela's social system and this is reflected in its political system.

Conclusion

To sum up, I've attempted to prove three essential points in this chapter. First, that the Venezuelan state failed to secure legitimation according to the Habermasian model, and that this was due to its failure to consolidate gains made on the three levels of society indicated in that model. On the economic level, while great strides were made in general, a failure to move from a dependency situation, particularly on oil revenues, created a fragile economy which was unable to withstand the oil shocks of the 1980s. A failure to create robust systems of taxation, instead preferring to pay for social advances through oil revenues, made the social structures in health and education erected by the Punto Fijo regime, which had achieved notable success, equally vulnerable to the oil shocks. On a political level the institutions created by Punto Fijo, while initially successful, proved too rigid to respond effectively to the challenges of the economic and social emergencies of the 1980s and thus lost the legitimacy gained by them during the boom years. Finally, on the sociocultural level, while there was some success in ameliorating the worse excesses of class/race discrimination in Venezuela, these re-emerged powerfully during the crisis years particularly in the media but also in the distribution of social goods. As we have seen, support for Chávez and for the opposition is polarised along class/race lines, with the darker-skinned popular classes supporting the president and the lighter-skinned middle and upper classes rejecting Chávez and supporting the opposition.

The legitimation gained by the Punto Fijo system was not due to its success in excising the colonialist nature of its economy and society, but rather due to its temporarily obscuring it from view through the largesse of its newfound oil wealth. Its legitimacy therefore was almost entirely dependent on the state's income from oil, and not from the robustness of its institutions and their ability to spread rewards and risks throughout the population.

In effect, Punto Fijo had not gone far enough in breaching the severe fractures, mostly around class and race lines that we found in Venezuela's social structures. These fractures inhibited the generation of 'generalisable interests' and the 'pseudo-consensus' necessary to provide the stability needed for efficient legitimation systems to develop. They affected the economic, administrative (political) and sociocultural levels fundamental to Habermas' theory, inhibiting the possibility of Venezuela developing along advanced capitalist lines. On an economic level successive Venezuelan governments failed to integrate the majorities into the system, leaving large groups of people outside formal employment as unemployed or underemployed.

Similarly on an administrative level only a minority was integrated into the taxation system, which is largely inequitable, thus limiting the state's ability to raise sufficient revenue to finance rational policies which could benefit the majority of citizens. Finally on a sociocultural level the required material rewards and motivations, such as consumption, leisure and career motivations, could not be provided by the state for the majority of its citizens, partially due to a lack of resources, but also, to a lesser extent, because of communicational difficulties due to cultural difference. The result of all these factors is the greater exposure and vulnerability of the Venezuelan state to system crises. This resulted in mass alienation, which previously was dealt with through force, but under the democratic system led to chaos.[94] The result of this mass alienation was the emergence of a strong personalist leader, Chávez, with a discourse based on the extension of democracy to the popular sectors, and parts of the middle sectors, which had felt themselves excluded from the economic, social, political and cultural life of the country. In other words democracy's failures, the failures of its institutions to genuinely reflect and cater for the needs of its peoples, led to gaps emerging between rulers and ruled which favoured the emergence of a populist leader, this time in the form of Hugo Chávez.

The language of crisis was central to the discourse of Chávez, and through that discourse he offered quick and decisive solutions. The following chapters will examine that discourse and those actions more closely in order to show how Chávez offered more inclusiveness and participation in order to seek the legitimacy which the regimes they replaced so clearly had failed to achieve. To begin with in the next chapter the book will go on to examine how Chávez used the illegitimacy of the preceding regime in his discourse to gain power, and the strategies he used to attempt to establish political and cultural hegemony in Venezuela.

Notes

1 CEPAL/ECLAC, 2006, *Anuario Estadistico de America Latina y el Caribe: Estadisticas Economicas.* Available from: www.eclac.cl/publicaciones/xml/3/28063/LCG2332B_2.pdf. Accessed 10 March 2008, p. 124 and p. 186.

2 Ibid., p. 217.

3 Julia Buxton, personal communication, 14 July 2008.

4 Coronil, Fernando, 1997. *The Magical State: Nature, Money, and Modernity in Venezuela.* Chicago and London: The University of Chicago Press, p. 7

5 Ibid., p. 6.

6 CEPAL/ECLAC, 2006, *Anuario Estadistico*, p. 380.

7 UNDP, 2006, *Human Development Report, 2006: Beyond Scarcity: Power, Poverty and the Global Water Crisis.* Available from: www.undp.org. Accessed 10 May, 2008, p. 349. The proportion of GDP devoted to debt declined, however, from 10.6% in 1990.

8 Gamble, A. and Payne, A., 2003, 'The world order approach', in Fredrik Soderbaum and Timothy M. Shaw (eds), *Theories of New Regionalism.* New York: Palgrave Macmillan, pp. 43–63, p. 49.

9 See for example Richard Gott, 2006. 'Venezuela's Murdoch', in *New Left Review* 39 (May–June). Available from: http://newleftreview.org/A2622. Accessed 27 August 2008.

10 Quinta Punto Fijo was the name of Rafael Caldera's house, where the political agreement between the main parties, AD, COPEI and URD, was drawn up after the 1958 coup against dictator Pérez Jiménez. Caldera was the leader of COPEI, the Christian Democratic party.

11 Ewell, J., 1984, *Venezuela: A Century of Change*. Stanford: Stanford University Press, p. 63.

12 Ibid, p. 68.

13 Betancourt, R., 2001 [1956], *Venezuela, Política y Petróleo*. Caracas: Monte Ávila Editores. p. 121.

14 Lombardi, J. V., 1977, 'The patterns of Venezuela's past', in J. D. Martz and D. J. Myers, *Venezuela: The Democratic Experience*. New York: Praeger, pp. 3–26, p. 18.

15 Carvallo, G. and López-Maya, M., 1989, 'Crisis en el Sistema Político Venezolano', in *Cuadernos de CENDES* 10: 47–53, p. 48.

16 Kornblith, M., 1994, 'La Crisis del Sistema Politico Venezolano', in *Nueva Sociedad* 134: 142–157, p. 145.

17 Cartaya V., Magallanes R. and Dominguez C., 1997, *Venezuela: Exclusion and Integration — A synthesis in the building?* International Labour Organisation. Available from: www.ilo.org/public/english/bureau/inst/papers/1997/dp90/index.htm. Accessed 22 August 2003, Chapter 2, no page number.

18 Ibid., no page number.

19 Carrera Damas, G., 1980, *Una nación llamada Venezuela*. Caracas: Monte Ávila Editores, p. 187.

20 Lander, E., 1996. 'The impact of neoliberal adjustment in Venezuela, 1989–1993', in *Latin American Perspectives* 23(3): 50–73, p. 50.

21 OCEI (Oficina Central de Estadistica e Informatica)/PNUD (Programa Naciones Unidas para el Desarrollo), 2001, *Informe sobre Desarrollo Humano en Venezuela, 2000: Caminos para superar la probreza*. Caracas: CDB Publicaciones, p. 92.

22 Lopez Maya, M., 2005, *Del Viernes Negro al Referendo Revocatorio*. Caracas: Alfadil, p. 35.

23 Ibid., p. 36.

24 Ibid., p. 34.

25 Ibid., p. 38.

26 Ibid., p. 36.

27 World Bank, 2001, *World Development Report 2000–2001*. Oxford: Oxford University Press. Available from: www.worldbank.org/poverty/wdrpoverty/report/index.htm. Accessed 14 November 2003, p. 301.

28 Mc Coy, J. L. and Smith, W. C., 1995, 'Democratic disequilibrium in Venezuela', in *Journal of Interamerican Studies and World Affairs* 37(2): 113–179, p. 127; World Bank, *World Development Report*, p. 301.

29 Malavé Mata, H., 1996, *Las contingencias de bolívar: El discurso de la política de ajuste en Venezuela* (1989–1993). Caracas: Fondo Editorial FINTEC, pp. 130–131.

30 Cartaya, Magallanes and Dominguez, Venezuela, Chapter 2.

31 Malavé Mata, *Las contingencias de bolívar*, p. 32.

32 Lander, 'The impact of neoliberal adjustment', p. 51; World Bank, *World Development Report*, p. 315.

33 Civit, J. and España, L. P., 1989, 'Análisis socio-político a partir del estallido del 27 de febrero', in *Cuadernos de CENDES* 10: 35–46, p. 39.

34 Coronil, F. and Skurski, J., 1991, 'Dismembering and remembering the nation: the semantics of political violence in Venezuela', in *Comparative Studies in Society and History* 33(2): 288–337, p. 326.

35 López Maya, M., 2002, 'Venezuela after the Caracazo: forms of protest in a deinstitutionalized context', in *Bulletin of Latin American Studies* 21(2): 199–219.

36 For example, in 1992 unemployment stood at 7.1% as opposed to 6.9% in 1988. Of total employment in 1991, 59.5% was in the formal sector while 40.5% in the informal, as opposed to 61.9 and 39.7% respectively in 1988. Between 1988 and 1991 poverty increased from 46 to 68% and extreme poverty from 14 to 34%. See Lander, 'The impact of neoliberal adjustment'.

37 It was illegal to use the name of the Liberator, Bolívar, for political parties in Venezuela. By using V, the roman numeral for five, the movement's name remained unchanged verbally due to the similarity in Spanish pronunciation of the b and v consonants.

38 Lingenthal, M., 1999, 'Elecciones en Venezuela', in *Constribuciones* XVI(1): 219–235. pp. 222–223.

39 Miles, R., and Brown, M., 2003, *Racism*, 2nd ed. London and New York: Routledge.

40 Ibid., p. 73.

41 Ibid., p. 85.

42 Ibid., p. 37.

43 Ibid., pp. 89–90.

44 Ibid., p. 11.

45 Ibid., p. 105.

46 Ibid., p. 117.

47 Ibid., p. 118.

48 Ewell, *Venezuela*, p. 3.

49 Herrera Salas, J. M., 2005, 'Ethnicity and revolution: the political economy of racism in Venezuela', in *Latin American Perspectives* 32: 72–91, p. 74.

50 Ewell, *Venezuela*, p. 3–4.

51 Wright, W. R., 1990, *Café con Leche: Race, Class and National Image in Venezuela*. Austin: University of Texas Press, pp. 18–21.

52 Ibid., p. 14.

53 Carrera Damas, *Una nación llamada Venezuela*, p. 106.

54 Wright, *Café con Leche*, p. 49.

55 Herrera Salas, 'Ethnicity and revolution', p. 76 citing L. Vallenilla Lanz, 1984 [1930], *Disgregación y Integración*. Caracas: Centro de Investigación Históricas, Universidad Santa María, p. 139.

56 Gott, Richard, 2007, 'The 2006 SLAS lecture: Latin America as a white settler society', Institute for the Study of the Americas, London, *Bulletin of Latin American Research*, 26(2), April: 269–289.

57 Ibid., p. 272.

58 Ibid., p. 273.

59 Ibid.

60 Ibid.

61 Ibid.

62 Herrera Salas, 'Ethnicity and revolution', p. 76.

63 Ibid., p. 77.

64 Ibid.

65 Ishibashi, J., 2003, 'Hacia una apertura del debate sobre el racismo en Venezuela: exclusión y inclusión esteriotipada de personas negras en los medios de comunicación'. Available from: www.globalcult.org.ve/pub/Rocky/Libro1/Ishibashi.pdf. Accessed 20 February 2007, p. 34.

66 Ibid., p. 39.

67 Ibid., p. 48.

68 Ibid., p. 49.

69 Hall, S.,1992, 'The West and the rest: discourse and power' in Stuart Hall and Bram Gieben (eds), *The Formations of Modernity*. Cambridge: Polity Press, cited in Ishibashi, 'Hacia una apertura', p. 56.

70 Ibid., p. 327.

71 Ibid., p. 328.

72 Carvallo and López Maya, 'Crisis en el Sistema Político', p. 48.

73 Roberts, K. M., 2003, 'Social polarisation and the populist resurgence', in S. Ellner and D. Hellinger (eds), *Venezuelan Politics in the Chávez Era: Class, Polarization and Conflict*. Boulder and London: Lynne Rienner, pp. 55–73, p. 55.

74 Canache, D., 2004, 'Urban poor and political order', in J. L. McCoy and D. J. Myers (eds), *The Unravelling of Representative Democracy in Venezuela*. Baltimore and London: John Hopkins University Press, pp. 33–50, pp. 44–46.

75 Roberts, 'Social polarisation', p. 66.

76 Canache, 'Urban poor', p. 46.

77 Subero, C., 2000, 'Clases sociales tienen distinto candidato', in *El Universal Sección Nacional y Política*, 6 April. Available from: www.eluniversal.com/2000/04/06/06102AA.shtml. Accessed 20 June 2003.

78 Datanalisis, 2001, *Escenarios Julio, 2001*, Año IV, número 3, p. 21, Cuadro No 4.

79 Greenberg, Quinlan and Rosner, 2004, 'Venezuela, Resultados Estudio de Opinión Pública Nacional: Junio 23, 2004'. Available from: www.rnv.gov.ve/noticias/uploads/encuesta-greenberg-junio-2004.ppt. Accessed 15 January 2008.

80 Evans/McDonough Company Inc./Consultores 30.11.2007, 'Clima Política Votantes Venezolanos: Presentación de resultados'. Available from: www.rethinkvenezuela.com/downloads/PRESENTACION_ENCUESTA_NACIONAL_NOVIEMBRE_2007.pdf. Accessed 15 January 2008.

81 World Values Survey, 2008, 'Online data analysis, Venezuela – 1996, 2000, sociodemographics – ethnic description'. Available from: www.jdsurvey.net/bdasepjds/wvsevs/home.jsp?OWNER=WVS. Accessed 15 January 2008.

82 As noted by Ewell, *Venezuela*.

83 Wright, *Café con Leche*.

84 Kozloff, N., 2005, 'A real radical democracy: Hugo Chávez and the politics of race'. Available from: www.venezuelanalysis.com/articles.php?artno=1577. Accessed 20 February 2007.

85 Ibid.

86 Francia, N., 2000. *Antichavismo y Estupidez Ilustrada*. Caracas: Rayuela Taller de Ediciones, pp. 109–111.

87 Gomez, E., 2002. 'Sólo la presión social pede liberar conciencias', in *El Universal*, Wednesday 13 February, p. 4.

88 Reporters Without Borders (RSF), 2003. *Venezuela 2003 Annual Report*. Available from: www.rsf.fr/article.php3?id_article=6230&Valider=OK. Accessed 6 August 2003, p.15.

89 Herrera Salas, 'Ethnicity and revolution', p. 85.

90 Ibid., pp. 82–87.

91 Sreeharsha, V., 2006 'Is there a black vote in Venezuela'. Available from:www.slate.com/id/2154688/. Accessed 13 February 2007.

92 Márquez, P., 2004. 'Vacas flacas y odios gordos: la polarización en Venezuela', in Patricia Márquez and Ramón Piñango (eds), *Realidades y Nuevos Caminos en esta Venezuela*. Caracas: Instituto de Estudios Superiores de Administración, quoted in Herrera Salas, 'Ethnicity and revolution', p. 86.

93 Herrera Salas, 'Ethnicity and revolution'.

94 In Venezuela according to Myers the country had experienced only eight months of civilian elected government during its first century and a quarter of independence (1830–1958). Since 1945 alone there have been around ten military interventions into political life in Venezuela, the latest being the April 2002 coup against the Chávez government. Myers, D. J., 1996, 'Venezuela: the stressing of distributive justice', in H. Wiarda and H. Kline (eds), *Latin American Politics and Development*. Boulder, CO: Westview Press, pp. 227–267, p. 229.

3 The leader and the led: hegemonic strategies in the leadership of Hugo Chávez

Introduction

Crisis, as we have seen in the previous chapter, is a central concept in populism, and that chapter documented how Venezuela's social breaches of race and class contributed to the rise of Chávez. This chapter will concentrate on *how* Chávez came to power, that is the strategies used to achieve hegemony, in the Gramscian sense (see Chapter 1). In this way we will be examining not only the political content of the Chávez discourse but also its cultural content and how that contributed to his gaining legitimacy with the majority of the Venezuelan population and thus moving towards hegemony.[1]

Chávez has been identified as an 'outsider' in the sense of an extra-systemic actor who achieves power from outside the traditional party system. However, as Julia Buxton points out, Chávez does not fit that description quite so accurately as while he initially came to public prominence with a 1992 coup attempt, his association with politics, albeit in a clandestine manner, comes from well before this date.[2] Consequently, in this chapter we will look first at the origins of Chávez and the Bolivarian Movement, before going on to examine the coup of 4 February 1992, the emergence and construction of Chávez's discourse and symbolism, and the subsequent transformation of the military Movimiento Bolivariano Revolucionario 200 (Bolivarian Republican Movement/MBR-200) into the electoral and popular civic-military Movimiento Quinta Republica (Fifth Republic Movement/ MVR), which, allied to other leftist movements and parties in the Polo Patriotico (Patriotic Pole/PP – the alliance of parties which supported this first presidential bid), led to Chávez's electoral victory of 1998. The chapter will also examine the more recent attempt at unification of these disparate elements into a unified Socialist party, Partido Socialista Unido de Venezuela (United Socialist Party of Venezuela/PSUV).

In its final sections the chapter will examine the manner in which Chávez set about reordering and refounding the Venezuelan republic through the mechanism of the Assamblea Nacional Constituyente (National Constituent Assembly/ANC) and the resulting Bolivarian constitution of 1999, codifying the leader/people nexus and establishing an incipient hegemony over the Venezuelan state and much of civil society. This hegemony was strengthened amongst the popular classes as the Chávez discourse became centred on attacking the better-off sectors, but alienated some middle groups who abandoned the Chávez coalition and allied themselves with the elites in outright opposition and eventual sedition, creating an antagonistic political polarisation in the country centring on the figure of the president.

'Con Chávez manda el Pueblo'

Clandestine genesis

The return to power of Acción Democrática (AD) in 1958 as part of a civilian/military coup against the military dictatorship of Pérez Jiménez (1948-1958) left the Venezuelan left in the political wilderness due to its exclusion from politics through the Punto Fijo pact. The aggressive Romulo Betancourt anti-communist policy led to many on the left, civilians and military, to revolt against the government.[4] Chávez emerged from this revolutionary leftist tradition, and some members of the Chávez government participated in these movements and insurrections, such as Alí Rodigúez Araque.[5] Contacts were made over the years with various leftist leaders such as famed guerrilla leader Douglas Bravo, and senior members of leftist trade union party La Causa R, such as Pablo Medina, both of whom now firmly oppose the Chávez government. Many leftist intellectuals from that period went on to serve in Chávez's government, such as veteran left politicians José Vincente Rangel and Luis Miquelina amongst others.[6]

The Chávez family not only had connections with the left through brother Adán Chávez, but also the family province of Barinas is situated in the *llanos*, or plains of the Orinoco basin, a long time centre of popular revolt of *pardo* egalitarianism against the hispanicised elites of Caracas and the coast. Chávez's grandfather was Maisanta or General Pedro Peréz Delgado (1881–1924), a colourful guerrilla leader and local caudillo. Maisanta, Ezequiel Zamora (see below), leader of the federalist side in the Federal War (1859–1863) and President General Velasco Alvarado of Peru (1968–1973), all military men and *mestizos* like himself, are central to the identity and beliefs of Chávez.

The military in Venezuela were particularly well placed to sympathise with the problems facing the poorer sectors of society. First, the Venezuelan military had a long history of involvement in Venezuelan politics until Punto

Fijo. Second, the Venezuelan military had a stronger egalitarian tradition than many other armed forces in Latin America. This was partly due to its strong tradition of social mobility for young men from poorer sectors, further added to by liberal educational programmes, such as the Andrés Bello Plan, introduced in 1971 allowing future officers the opportunity to take civilian degrees in Venezuela's universities. Chávez himself was one of the first graduates of this plan and went on to take, but not complete, a masters degree in political science at the Simón Bolívar University in Caracas. Such educational plans facilitated a greater awareness of social situations of the poorer sectors amongst army personnel, especially in a context of crisis, and greater association with civilians.[7]

In 1982 Chávez began to organise the MBR-200 with fellow officers, such as Jesús Urdaneta Hernández and Felipe Acosta Carles, swearing under a symbolic tree to uphold the values of the Motherland and the military and to fight against corruption.[8] The *caracazo* of February 1989 (see Chapter 2), especially the experience of having participated in the massacre of civilians, encouraged many more soldiers to seek out and join the MBR-200, as Chávez himself once pointed out.[9] Contacts with civilian groups, as described above, intensified as disenchantment with the Punto Fijo regime amongst all sectors grew in the wake of the *caracazo*, and these groups more urgently sought solutions and alternatives to the economic decline of Venezuela and the neoliberal programmes being put in place by Carlos Andrés Pérez. The MBR-200 therefore grew within a general context of dissatisfaction with the existing regime and an active seeking of alternatives by most sectors of Venezuelan society.

In the end, an MBR-led coup on 4 February 1992, commanded by Chávez, failed in achieving its objectives in Caracas, but the actions in Maracaibo (led by Arias Cárdenas), and in Aragua and Valencia succeeded, prompting Chávez to request a short television appearance to advise his colleagues to lay down their arms. This brief, instantly famous television appearance by Chávez created a new hero amongst the popular classes. In the speech Chávez advised his colleagues that:

> Unfortunately, for the moment, the objectives we had set ourselves have not been achieved in the capital … new possibilities will arise again and the country will be able to move definitively to a better future … I thank you for your loyalty, I thank you for your courage, your selfless generosity: before the country and you, I alone shoulder the responsibility for this Bolivarian military uprising.[10]

The phrase 'for the moment' (*por ahora*) and its promise of change and Chávez's preparedness to accept responsibility for something that had gone wrong, an unusual occurrence in a country accustomed to politicians evading blame, particularly impressed Venezuelans. '*Por ahora*' and the red beret of the parachute uniform worn by Chávez during the speech became powerful symbols in his growing constituency of supporters amongst the popular classes in the months after the coup, and remain so to this day.[11] A further failed coup in November of the same year, this time amongst the upper ranks of the air force and navy led by Admiral Hernán Grüber, would mortally wound the Peréz government, leading to the president's eventual impeachment and further encouraging pressure for change.

Bolivarian ideology and discourse

But what sort of changes were Chávez and his colleagues looking for when they conspired to capture the Venezuelan state? The military personnel participating in the February 1992 coup justified their action by pointing to the lack of democratic accountability and inclusion in the republic, and of territorial and economic sovereignty. Furthermore they accused the political class of being more concerned with personal gain, through corruption, than the welfare of the people or the republic. The people meanwhile were being placed deeper in poverty, facing increasing crime and related violence, and, as evidenced in the *caracazo*, state-perpetrated violence aimed at eliminating protest. The military were demoralised and delegitimised due to this situation, and due to the perceived corruption and nepotism within its ranks. The insurgents called for a Constituent National Assembly, providing a new constitution and a new model of society in which the 'ultimate purpose of the State is the achievement of collective social welfare of the Nation and the guarantee of respect for the human dignity of all and every one of the members of that Nation'.[12]

Over the following years the MBR-200, and in particular Chávez, refined their thinking and ideology in countless pamphlets and writings, despite their leaders being in prison until 1994, when the government of Rafael Caldera (1994-1999) pardoned them. The MBR-200's ideology was formed in order to provide a system of thinking that was specifically Venezuelan and Latin American, rather than one based on imported ideologies. Spurning the diagnostic of the time purported by Fukuyama and others of the end of history and ideologies, but conscious of the failure of communism and the inapplicability of neoliberalism in Venezuela and Latin America, Chávez and the MBR-200 turned to the thinking and teachings of three major figures from Venezuelan history to form the concept of the 'three-rooted tree': Ezequiel Zamora (see above), and Simón Rodríguez, educator, friend and mentor to the final member of the trinity, the Liberator, Simón Bolívar. Each figure provided a specific element to the new ideology: Zamora the element of rebellion, popular protest and protagonism, summed up in the slogan attributed to him: 'Land and free men! Popular elections! Horror to the oligarchy!'; Rodríguez the requirement for autochthonous ideological originality when he warned that 'either we invent or we commit errors ... America should not servilely imitate, but be original'; and Bolívar, the

Liberator, the symbol of equilibrium between the dualism of rebellion and ideology, force and consent.[13]

Central and crucial to this ideology was the concept of 'el pueblo', the people. Chávez qualified 'popular protagonism as the fuel of history' and only when this protagonism existed was a people truly el pueblo. 'A people exist when they share customs and an effective process of communication exists between them … a collective spirit and a consciousness of the social, or the common existence.'[14] However, '[there] isn't a people in all eras [because to be a people they] must have and share glories in their past [and] … they must have a common will that unites them'.[15] The Venezuelan people specifically, he believed, were a true people, a people who had shown, and were capable once again of greatness:

> [W]e are one of the liberating peoples of the world, we are a people of creators, of poets, of fighters, of warriors, of workers, there's history to prove it, let's honour it, let's honour the spirit of our aborigines, of our liberators, or our women, of our youth …, all of that we have in our veins and in the clay from which we were made, let us show it, it is the moment to show it.[16]

Leadership was vital to achieve the necessary protagonism lying dormant in the people, so that the people would become a people actively struggling. Chávez rejected the notion of the caudillo, the leader/masses model put forward by many of his critics.[17] Leadership must be provided, he argued, in order to galvanise the collective into action, but the leader is but a conduit. The people are an 'unleashed force, equal to the rivers' being channelled by leaders such as Chávez because either 'we provide a course for that force, or that force will pass over us'. Chávez was 'not a cause, but a consequence' and 'an instrument of the collective'.[18] Leadership, he believed, is multiple and is part of a greater movement, in which 'there is a leadership which has been extending on a number of levels, there is a popular force, there are some very strong parties, there are institutions; it would be a sad revolutionary or political process which depended on one man'.[19]

Past and present are indissolubly linked in the struggles of the people to gain their liberation. Chávez saw the present struggle as but a continuation of previous historical popular struggles:

> [We] are in a battleground … where an historical conflict has broken out with fury. Or to be more exact, it has broken out once again after many years of apparent calm, between the forces of domination which have attached themselves to the national body since the conquest, and the liberating forces which have always existed in the bosom of the exploited and deceived majorities for 500 years.[20]

But the past is also a resource for the present, and contemporary Venezuelans are like Janus, having to 'look to the past in order to disentangle the mysteries of the future, to create the formulae to solve the great Venezuelan dream of today'.[21]

Puntofijismo was but another version of the same old model based 'on imposition, on domination, on exploitation, and on extermination'.[22] The most recent incarnations of the model, in the presidencies of Pérez and Caldera

> are inscribed within a transnational political project which, in alliance with powerful national sectors, is increasing its offensive throughout the continent with a fetishistic discourse of the free market, individualist liberty and competition, behind which is hiding the desire to recuperate and consolidate [...] the hegemony of a model of accumulation, threatened for various decades now with a declining rate of utilisation and benefit.[23]

In its stead the MVR and the Chávez government offered an alternative which was fundamentally political and which placed the social above the economic, and which was Venezuelan and Latin American in its ideology and practice.

The Bolivarian doctrine was a doctrine in construction, a heterogeneous amalgam of thoughts and ideologies, from universal thought, capitalism, Marxism, but rejecting the neoliberal models currently being imposed in Latin America and the discredited socialist and communist models of the old Soviet Bloc.[24] The model being proposed, however, was firmly capitalist, not 'savage neoliberal capitalism' but a 'capitalism with another face, with other mechanisms [which] ... is equitable and gets to all Venezuelans, rather than what has occurred in those years ... causing poverty, and the great squalor that exists in Venezuela'.[25]

This Third Way ideological rhetoric became more radicalised, however, as the Chávez government matured and faced down opposition threats. By January 2005 Chávez was talking of 'twenty-first century socialism' which would be different from Soviet Union-style twentieth-century socialism, in that it would be more pluralistic and less state-centred. This socialism would be 'based in solidarity, in fraternity, in love, in justice, in liberty, and in equality' and would mean the 'transformation of the economic model, increasing cooperativism, collective property, the submission of private property to the social interest and to the general interest', created 'from the popular bases, with the participation of the communities'. This socialism was not a dogma, however, but 'must be constructed every day'.[26] The different phases of *chavista* ideology, and the economic policies they entail, will be discussed in more detail in the next chapter.

Structure and organisation

While ideology provided the bedrock of the *chavista* movement in terms of ideas, organisation was essential if the movement was to be a genuine agent for radical change. The movement must be an 'articulatory organisation with the masses, a mobilising and unifying force'.[27] Alliances should be built with heterogeneous social forces, such as workers, resident and neighbourhood communities, students, ethnic minorities, peasants, small and medium business enterprises, sectors of the armed forces, progressive churches, nationalist business sectors, and organised popular forces.

The MBR-200 thus developed an organisational structure with four levels; beginning with grassroots groupings called 'Bolivarian Circles' – essentially self-selected discussion and activity groups, similar to cells. These groups would then elect municipal and in turn regional directorates, which in turn would answer to a five-member National Directorate, again self-selected and led by Chávez, supported by secretariats for each policy area. Assemblies would be held on a regional and national level to arrive at consensus on major policy issues. It was in this way that the MBR-200 decided, in 1997, to abandon abstentionism and participate in the 1998 elections.[29]

The MVR was created originally as a parallel organisation with purely electoral aims allowing for wider membership based on support for Chávez's candidacy. Nonetheless the resounding success of the MVR in winning several electoral contests from 1998 onwards 'led to the MBR-200 not having a role and its eventual disappearance'.[30] Structurally the MVR retained the essential features of the pyramidical organisation of the MBR-200, starting at the bases with Patriotic Circles, rather than Bolivarian Circles, which continued to exist and remained under the control of the president. Ostensibly, the MVR was to be a nationally organised institution with ideological, political and pedagogical aims, with communication channels going both from the top down and vice versa, but there is little evidence to suggest that it went beyond its electoral function.

The MVR, for the purposes of the 1998 elections onwards formed the Patriotic Pole with other political parties, such as Movimiento al Socialismo (Movement to Socialism/MAS), the Patria Para Todos (Motherland for All/PPT), and the Partido Comunista Venezolano (Venezuelan Communist Party/PCV) as 'a wide alliance of alternative forces'.[31] This arrangement continued until President Chávez announced on the 15 December 2006 the formation of the Partido Socialista Unido de Venezuela (United Socialist Party of Venezuela/PSUV), in a speech made shortly after his stunning victory in the December 2006 presidential elections. The main purpose of the new party was to create unity amongst the different forces supporting the Chávez presidency in order to advance in the construction of twenty-first century socialism. In this speech Chávez called for the old parties to 'forget their old structures, party colours and slogans, because they are not the most important thing for the fatherland'. If they chose not to do so and not become part of the new PSUV, then Chávez claimed that was their choice, but they would have to leave the government.[32]

The main purpose of the new party was to forge unity amongst the disparate elements, providing grassroots input into policy and leadership formation, uniting the grassroots and leadership into one single body. The effects of this would be, it was hoped, to counteract the excessive bureacratisation of the movement, with its attendant problems of clientelism and corruption, and pushing forward its autonomisation from the leadership, including Chávez, leaving it less dependent on the president or on any one figure for its perpetuation as a force for the representation of working-class interests. According to the draft statement of principles of the nascent party, the party should be 'born as an expression of the revolutionary will of the people and their political leadership', the purpose of which was to make the slogan 'in order to end poverty you have to give power to the poor' a reality. To this end it 'requires the full and democratic participation of workers, peasants, youth, intellectuals, artists, housewives, small producers and petty traders from the countryside and the city, in the formation and running of all its component organs, in discussion and decision making in regards to programs and strategies, and in the promotion and election of its leadership'. 'In this new party', Chávez announced, 'the bases will elect the leaders. This will allow real leaders to emerge.'[33]

Chavez proposed an organisational scheme similar to that used in the run up to the 2006 presidential election campaign. This would consist of a system of militants organised in base groupings, or battalions, of around 300 cadres, which would then be grouped into larger groupings, mostly organised territorially but some also organised in workplaces. Groups of battalions would elect representatives to formative party events, such as the variety of congresses organised to discuss party programme content.[34]

Organisationally, things did not go quite as smoothly as initially envisaged. Some of the key allied parties refused to dissolve themselves, such as the PPT, the PCV and Podemos (the pro-Chávez section of MAS), being reluctant to abandon years of organising for an uncertain new party structure. Initial grassroots enthusiasm, with around 5.7 million people registering their membership of the new party, became rapidly diluted as the party development process went forward. Old MVR party leadership began to dominate in the evolving structures of the new party, at the expense of the desired activist involvement. Furthermore, a senior member of the party was called before a disciplinary committee of a party that did not in the politico-legal sense exist, not having statutes or disciplinary procedures to speak of, hence creating concerns about pluralism within the new party.[35]

Nonetheless in congresses and in founding documents, radical opinions are being voiced and Chávez has withdrawn his threats to those parties not wishing to dissolve, as well as reiterating promises of grassroots selections of election candidates. The proof of the success of the new party will be in the ability of the grassroots to defeat the 'Bolivarian' party bureaucracy and achieve a genuine renewal of leadership, with pluralist debate and policy making processes prevailing.[36] An acid test for the party in electoral terms was the regional and municipal elections held on 23 November 2008. On a relatively high turnout for such elections of 65% the government party won 58% of the popular vote. Nonetheless, despite winning the majority of governorships, PSUV lost the populous states of Miranda and Carabobo and failed to gain Zulia, an oil-rich opposition bastion. Furthermore, in the mayoral races PSUV lost the capital, Metropolitan Caracas, to the opposition despite running a well-known candidate. Both sides could thus claim victory; the opposition for winning key posts and maintaining 40% of the vote, the government for maintaining its majority share of the vote at just short of 60% and for winning the majority of mayoralties and governorships. How much this was down to the new party or down to Chávez is difficult to say, but proved an adequate result for the PSUV in its first election outing.

'La Constituyente'

While organisationally the *chavista* movement had evolved and changed, the legal background to such changes has been the desire to realise the central tenets and philosophies inherent in the 1999 Bolivarian constitution. As stated previously, the process of change has been seen as essentially political rather than economic or social, and the central mechanism to achieve this change was the refounding of the republic through a National Constituent Assembly, in order to demolish the 'putrid bases' of the old order, the republic of 'bankers, of oligarchs and a people hungry and massacred'.

On assuming the presidency Chávez's first act was to declare a referendum, announced in his inaugural speech in February 1999, and having won that, install a *Constituyente* which was elected on a first past the post system and overwhelmingly dominated by the PP, with 125 seats as opposed to 6 for the opposition. The constitution was drafted in three months, after an intense period of public consultation and discussion, dominated by tensions and opposition from many sectors, particularly those intimately linked with the *ancien régime*. These, as we have seen in the previous chapter, tried to negate the legitimacy of people's motivations in voting for Chávez, arguing that the vote was the product of an emotionalism uninformed by rational thought.

Nonetheless, Tanaka notes that the ANC was constituted with over 50 per cent abstention,[38] while López Maya states that '[the] haste in dealing with such complex and delicate concerns [in the *Constituyente*] generated ambiguities in the final text and resulted in dissatisfaction and tensions', both factors wresting some legitimacy from the final document.[39] Furthermore, despite declaring the previous 1961 constitution 'moribund', much of the 1999 constitution was built on its precepts.[40] The 1999 constitution, however, was approved in a referendum by 71% of the vote, once again, however, with abstention of over 50%. In 2007 a commission was set up and recommended a number of important changes to the constitution, which will be explored below in more detail.

The purpose of the *Constituyente* was as an 'alternative route to power' for the movement, providing the context in which it could grow and consolidate itself, and 'for the great qualitative and quantitative transformations that Venezuela needs'.[41] The process would provide the stimulus necessary for popular participation and political organisation. Through this process the necessary solutions for the social, economic and cultural difficulties of Venezuela would flow. Chávez in his inaugural speech qualified the existing 1961 constitution as 'moribund' and *puntofijismo* an 'ill-fated political model' which will 'die'.[42] The new constitution would instead place the people of Venezuela as the true sovereign of the Nation 'a universal and elemental principle'.[43] An Enabling Law and the Constituent Assembly rather than being a panacea, however, would have 'a fundamental objective which is the transformation of the State and the creation of a new Republic, the refounding of the Republic, the relegitimation of democracy ... It's political, it's macropolitical but it is not economic nor social in the immediate term' which will take time to solve as the problems inherited are 'terrible'.[44] However, in the end the process of the *Constituyente* would lead to the return of the 'collective mentality', to a 'return [of] the idea of utopia to the national mind that is to say, of a country which begins to exist in the collective imagination'.[45]

The *Constituyente* was therefore to be a product of popular participation which would further that participation to make it protagonic, to create the 'active people' discussed above. In the event, García Guadilla finds that the process did have a high level of popular participation from civil society.[46] Furthermore, within the text there were many clauses which furthered the ideal of 'participation and protagonism', through direct democracy mechanisms such as popular assemblies, referendums, recall elections and so on. As López Maya observes, the 1999 constitution provides a different focus on democracy and inclusion than that found in the past in Venezuela, and goes against the grain of neoliberalism, which emphasises the reduction of the political in favour of the economic and procedural (Title I, Chapter VIII).[47] Furthermore human rights were brought up to date and widened (Title III) including for the first time those of the indigenous minorities (Title I, Chapter VIII). Again running against neoliberal thinking, the universal character of social rights was preserved and extended (Chapter V, arts. 86, 87 and 88). The constitution prohibits the sale of shares in the state oil company PdVSA and guarantees state control of the social security system. New institutions were introduced in the form of the electoral and citizen powers, as well as the more traditional executive, legislative and judicial powers.[48]

Yet a number of constitutional clauses strengthened executive power. The presidential period was extended from five to six years, with the possibility of re-election being introduced for one more period. There is increased centralisation with less autonomy for regional and municipal powers, and a one-chamber congress.[49] Álvarez points out that while the innovatory direct democracy mechanisms 'opened channels for direct participation [of the people] at the same time [the constitution] enhanced the power of the national executive' at the expense of the other branches of government and the political parties.[50] Indeed Norden qualified the process which led to the constitution of 1999 and the new powers in the constitution as a coup in all but name, albeit a legal one.[51]

Hegemony nearly secured ...

Fresh general elections, the so-called *megaelecciones* were held in July 2000 under the new constitution, resulting once again in a victory for Chávez and the PP, with the president now being elected until 2006.[52] Opposition up until now had been strong but reasonably contained, complaints centring mainly on procedural aspects of the implementation of the constitution, in particular the appointments to the 'Moral Power' offices, which contradicted the central constitutional principle of popular participation.[53] However, it was the passing of the forty-nine Enabling Laws in November 2001, which introduced presidential decrees in education, finance and public administration,[54] galvanising opposition protest and leading to a mobilisation of the increasingly estranged middle and upper classes against the government by the trade union, business and media leadership, with the active participation of the Catholic Church hierarchy, 'civil society' and old-order political parties. A series of one-day stoppages took place, and accompanying massive demonstrations, culminating in a 'general strike' being called in early April, leading to the almost total paralysis of the all-important oil industry, the brief overthrow of the Chávez regime and the installation as president of the republic of Pedro Carmona Estanga, the heretofore leader of the business association FEDECAMARAS.

During his forty-eight hours in power (11–13 April 2002), Carmona abolished the 1999 constitution and all the public powers, appointing a small governing committee, most of whom were unelected. However, spontaneous popular demonstrations in support of Chávez gained force leading to the restitution of the president and his government to power by the morning of the 14 April (for more information see Chapter 5). A further attempt by the opposition to unseat Chávez took place in December 2002/January 2003 during a crippling strike/lockout which once again closed down most of the oil industry for sixty-three days, leading to a 10.4% contraction of the economy for 2003. The strike, however, was eventually defeated by the government, and the state, as Chávez put it, managed to reimpose its authority.[56] A final attempt, this time legal, was a failed recall referendum against Chávez, a provision provided for by the 1999 constitution, held on 15 August 2004.

United States support for the April 2002 coup,[57] US financial and moral support for the opposition[58] and a plethora of pronouncements of various US officials against Chávez fuelled calls amongst some sectors in Venezuela for a military invasion of the country.[59] Nonetheless, Chávez maintained a consistently strong core of support, winning the 2004 Recall Referendum by 59.09% with an abstention rate of approximately 30%, and a 62.8% win in the presidential elections of December, 2006, with a turnout of approximately 75%, one of the highest in recent Venezuelan history (see Chapter 2).

At the time of writing, Venezuela is beset by a political polarisation symptomatic on the one hand of the success of Chávez's hegemonic strategies, and on the other hand, of the difficulties of including the variety of sectoral demands within the MVR/PP project, and the strength of the opposition counteroffensive to form a new hegemony. Chávez's total negativising of the Punto Fijo period ignored the many social, political and economic advances for the popular classes at that time.[60] Furthermore his attempts to constitute the 'Other' around the concept of the political classes/oligarchy, created two blocs characterised by economic and social position rather than rejection of the old order, alienating, probably for ever, much of the middle sectors.

More recently (2007) a constitutional commission was set up to review the constitution and make suggestions for amendments, further contributing to the existing polarisation between government and opposition, as well as revealing many of the fault lines within the *chavista* movement itself. Led by Luis Britto García, a well known pro-Chávez intellectual, these amendments contained many socially progressive clauses, such as the shortening of the working week, constitutional recognition of Afro-Venezuelans, and elimination of discrimination on the grounds of sexual orientation amongst others. On the other hand they also included clauses centralising powers in the executive more, such as granting powers to the president to decree special military and development zones and to name secondary vice-presidents as needed, extending the presidential term to seven years and eliminating the limit on re-election amongst others.[61] In a referendum on these amendments on 2 December 2007, however, the Venezuelan people rejected the proposals by a close 50.65% to 49.34% in favour. Abstention was high at 43.95% of registered voters, most of these, according to Lander, from the ranks of the president's own supporters.[62]

This was the first electoral loss by President Chávez out of thirteen electoral contests held since first being elected in 1998. The top-down manner in which the amendments were formulated, the presentation of the reform as a Manichean choice between Chávez and US president George W. Bush, and the absence of internal debate on its content, as well as dissatisfaction with the running of the social programmes, increasing street crime, and with corruption within the government, all played their part in assuring that the amendments were defeated. Lander especially singles out the fact that the specific function of the constitutional amendments was to institute 'twenty-first century socialism' within Venezuela, yet there was little debate on the actual content and nature of such a socialist society. In sum, the entire top-down manner in which these amendments were conceived and in which they were to be executed, as well as the enormous complexity of the proposals, went, according to Lander, in opposition to the spirit of participation and popular protagonism which was supposedly at the heart of these proposals, resulting in their defeat.[63]

In the aftermath of the referendum, official responses from Chávez accepted the result willingly, but then apportioned blame to the media, the US conspiracy against the Venezuelan government, and to the Venezuelan people themselves, who were 'insufficiently revolutionary'. Others, not necessarily of the governing parties, but who identified with the 'Bolivarian process', saw the defeat as a direct result of the lack of internal democracy within the *chavista* movement and saw it as an opportunity to widen such democracy and encourage debate and pluralism within the movement.[64]

Chávez learned from some of these errors when he returned to present the key change on re-election to the Venezuelan people in a further referendum on 15 February 2009. In this referendum Venezuelans were simply asked to vote in favour or against eliminating the two-term limit, but this time for all public offices, not just the presidency. This had the double advantage of simplifying the issue for the electorate and making it somewhat attractive to the opposition as well. The government conducted a well-run campaign which resulted in the amendment being approved by 54.86% of the approximately 70% of the electorate who voted. This cleared the way for Chávez to present himself for re-election again when his current term ends in 2012.

Hegemony, neoliberalism and democracy

To sum up, through a skilful blend of 'war of manoeuvre' tactics, such as a coup, a successful series of electoral processes, and a new constitution, and 'war of position' tactics, such as a highly effective antagonistic counter-hegemonic discourse, flawed but effective alliance-building and popular organisation and mobilisation, and the use of symbols of power (the red beret and army uniforms), hope (*por ahora*; Bolívar; utopia) and popular historical struggle (Zamora), Chávez successfully placed himself and his movement in a position of insecure but effective hegemony.

First, in terms of 'war of manoeuvre' tactics, Chávez attempted a coup in 1992, before turning to the electoral path, which, as Francia points out, was 'a military defeat, but a political victory', weakening the Peréz government, establishing Chávez as a popular leader, and clearing the way for his ascent to power through electoral means.[65] Chávez also used a Constituent Assembly to draft a new constitution which strengthened the power of the executive with regard to other state powers, while at the same time introducing elements which allowed more popular involvement in decision-making processes. The *Constituyente* involved extensive popular involvement in the process granting it legitimacy, despite its being compromised to an extent by the speed in which it was implemented and the high rates of abstention in the referendum securing its popular approval. The 1999 Bolivarian constitution was innovative in terms of popular direct democracy and participation, providing extensive social guarantees, despite its strengthening of the executive.

Once drawn up, all public powers required by the constitution were immediately put in place, not always adhering strictly to constitutional requirements, but still providing the country with an entire set of functioning, although imperfect, institutions. This provided the Chávez government with the comprehensive control of the state, the 'primary sources of coercive domination' required to achieve hegemony.[66] Nonetheless the Venezuelan process was by and large transparent, inclusive, and progressive, and therefore legitimate, despite the reservations alluded to above. Furthermore, the process remained predominantly within the law throughout.[67] Opposition freedom of expression was not limited, and despite centralisation tendencies the regions remained important power bases for a variety of opposition figures of national stature, at least until the 2005 regional elections, lost largely by the opposition due to their boycott of these elections.[68]

While these 'war of manoeuvre' tactics achieved the necessary control of the State, hegemony can only be achieved by consent, by 'war of position' tactics as Gramsci advises. Chief among these tactics was the use of discourse to achieve this consent. Chávez used discourses that were antagonistic to the status quo, railing against the traditional parties, condemning their corruption and their self-serving policies. Central to this discourse was the need to start afresh, to refound and rebuild these systems so that they functioned as 'true' democracies.

Chávez therefore built on the 'common sense' of the people, and the inherent resentment they held for the parties, their rulers and state institutions. Moreover, Chávez attempted to take this 'common sense' of the popular classes and, as Gramsci recommends, give them a '"theoretical" consciousness of being creators of *historical* and institutional *values*, of being founders of a State'.[69] Chávez therefore, however imperfectly, has been attempting to genuinely engender and foster 'mass politics', through the wide variety of movements founded by him, including the PSUV, and through innovative participative mechanisms, such as, for example, the communal councils.

Chávez directed his discourse at the informal sectors of the popular classes primarily, although he referred to 'the people' – *el pueblo* -thus rhetorically at least, embracing the totality of the population. He has used tradition and history, or as Laclau put it 'popular traditions' to link leader and people in the construction of the alternative society that he envisaged.[70] In Chávez's discourse *el pueblo* have an essential role; they are sovereign, fighters struggling for their liberation whose spirit must be encouraged by their leaders, and historical subjects who realise their *own* liberation. The people are not the privileged but the downtrodden, economically, socially, culturally and spiritually. Liberation, revolution is an historical force akin to nature which leaders must simply channel and bow down to. Furthermore the leaders must be of 'the people', from 'the people', like 'a fish in the water', as Chávez himself has claimed to be. In the Chávez discourse *el pueblo* are active protagonists in the realisation of their own future.

This phenomenon of the active nature of the people can also be seen in the forms of leadership and organisation found in the Venezuela of Chávez. The MBR-200/MVR has an organised national structure, with militants and local and regional leaderships. Ideological training and discussion takes place, encouraging degrees of critical thought and evaluation. Associated social movements, such as the Fuerza Bolivariano de Trabajadores (Bolivarian Workers Force/FBT) – keep a certain critical distance from the MVR.[72] The Patriotic Pole was an alliance of various political parties which have their own independent historical trajectories and maintain their own internal decision making structures and militants, despite recent attempts to co-opt them into the PSUV. Furthermore there are various factions with different ideological strains within the overall *chavista* movement.[73] This situation, however, is a source of dynamic tension between the centralising forces within the movement, including at times the president himself, and those demanding more autonomy for social movements and more debate.

Certain institutions have delivered judgements which are independent of government, such as the Tribunal Supremo de Justicia (Supreme Tribunal of Justice/TSJ) and the Consejo Nacional Electoral (National Electoral Council/CNE). Government policy promotes self-organisation of local communities to solve local problems, such as the co-operative movement, health committees and communal councils. Overall in the case of the *chavista* movement the evidence points to an organisation caught in a crucible between ideological autonomy and loyalty to a leader and his charisma.

In the Chávez discourse as we have seen, the leader/people relationship is based on activity and struggle on both parts, and not just on the part of the president, to achieve a common goal – a 'concrete utopia' of social justice, fairness and equality. Thus the discourse is delivered within the context of a rejection of neoliberalism and with constitutional guarantees of universal social, economic and human rights. People and leaders are thus linked in a common struggle to create a future, a utopia, which is radically different to that which came before, and not just its opposite. This discursive construction goes against neoliberal precepts as it negates 'the end of ideology' and its replacement by 'common sense' usually conveyed through technocratic assertions and policies. It places politics, not economics, at the centre of its discourse, thus instilling in the people a long-term perspective of struggle to achieve radical structural change. This return of utopia to Venezuelan political discourse acts against the widespread anomie encouraged by the current neoliberal 'reality' being imposed on the region (and the world).[74]

Furthermore, *chavismo* places sovereignty at the centre of its nationalism, once again contradicting neoliberal globalisation discourse. Chávez uses powerful national symbols to reinforce the link between people, national and cultural identity, and himself. He uses clothing, such as the red beret, to convey concepts of power and ideology, and vernacular language, using baseball terminology (the national sport), national cuisine, and religion to convey a sense of identification between leader and people. As we have seen in the previous chapter, Chávez emphasises his poor background, and his ethnic identity as a *pardo*, thus underlining the commonality of origins he has with the majority of Venezuelans. However, Chávez goes further and discusses national metathemes of historical magnitude (nationalism, war, rebellion, social justice), reinforced by the micro-themes mentioned above, with the symbolism of Bolívar constantly accompanying them in word and often in image. Hence Chávez draws attention in his discourse to both structure – be it local, national or global – and agency.

Chávez centred his nationalist discourse on the cultural, on *venezolanidad*, but aligned with a policy of zealously guarding national prerogatives. Thus the government has all but abandoned privatisation, has rejected 'savage neoliberalism' and emphasises ownership of strategic industries, constitutionally guaranteeing State ownership of the national oil industry (Chapter 4). It has pursued an independent foreign policy, cultivating close relations with Cuba, China, Russia, and even Iran, the current *bête noir* of US neoconservatives. He has encouraged and facilitated Latin American unity, and Venezuela has led the development of an oil policy with its OPEC associates, based on output restrictions to maintain 'fair' price levels (see Chapter 7).

Chávez adheres therefore very closely to the hegemonic model put forward by Gramsci, and Laclau and Mouffe.[75] The Chávez government is using force, through its control of the state, but also giving, in its emphasis on ideology, a pivotal role to persuasion and consent. Its willingness to seek out alternative responses to the complexities and demands of globalisation which go beyond textbook IMF/World Bank prescriptions and instead looking to national tradition and leftist ideologies, as well as social-democratic capitalism and now socialism, shows an autonomy of thought and action outside the current global neoliberal hegemony. *Chavismo* has therefore shown itself to be a major block and threat to the implementation of neoliberalism in Venezuela, and indeed in Latin America. Furthermore, this process has quickened and deepened since the presidential win in December 2006, with Chávez's turn to 'twenty-first century socialism', including nationalisations of telecommunications and electricity companies, the granting of new Enabling Law powers to the president by the National Assembly and the process of constitutional Amendments.

More dangerously still, from the elite's point of view, Chávez's mobilisation of the popular classes has provided large sectors of those classes with an 'experience of participation' which has empowered and emboldened them to seek greater social, economic and political participation, contradicting the hegemony of liberal democracy seen as the essential corrolarly for neoliberal globalisation. It is, however, precisely on this terrain that the Chávez movement has run into trouble in achieving hegemony. While much of the anti-neoliberal and nationalistic discourse achieved resonance amongst Venezuelan middle sectors, it has since lost much of this support. Initially this was due to powerful economic logics where the Bolivarian project delivered little benefit to those sectors, although with the recent boom this has changed to a great extent. Indeed according to Buxton, the primary appeal of Chávez was not so much his anti-neoliberalism, but his anti-*puntofijismo* discourse, as it was this which united all sectors of Venezuelan society. The increasing radicalistion of the Chávez project, often in response to opposition attempts at overthrowing the president, has alienated these sectors progressively.[76]

On the other hand, however, much of that rejection is based on equally powerful *anti-logical* emotions based on race- and class-based fears, fears that have been quite successfully whipped up by much of the private media (see Chapter 2). Opposition therefore is extraordinarily active against Chávez, and concentrates on all fronts. The discursive frontier is not clearly drawn as many of the middle sectors, and some parts of the popular sectors, identify much more closely with the Opposition than with Chávez.

How can a government, dedicated to the achievement of equality, counter that irrational fear mentioned above without contradicting the 'logic of democracy'? Sectors of the Venezuelan opposition, and sectors of the Bolivarian movement, have gone beyond reason and dialogue, much of this inspired by their respective leaders, but built upon a very solid but volatile visceral prejudice against their compatriots from opposing classes/races, made worse by consistent denials of this prejudice by many in the opposition camp. It is difficult in such a context to ensure that the 'logic of democracy' is scrupulously followed where such prejudice, added to naked economic self-interest, is translated into sedition and violence. Dialogue is further made difficult by maximalist demands being made by the opposition concentrating on the resignation of the president, the annulment of the entire

Bolivarian project, and the eradication of its movements, as evidenced in the ten-point decree issued by Pedro Carmona in the April 2002 coup, and during the later lockout/strike.[77]

Indeed, Chávez himself has made maximalist declarations by refusing to dialogue with many of those sectors linked to the Fourth Republic.[78] In such a tightly polarised situation, where 'antagonism' goes from the ideological, to the visceral, to violence, it may often be impossible to follow the 'logic of democracy' without resorting to the tactics of 'totalitarianism'. There is an inherent contradiction between the 'logic of democracy' and the logic of 'antagonism', as once the interests of powerful sectors are threatened, democracy in its liberal form at least, as we've seen in the case of many of the opposition strategies against Chávez, becomes a secondary consideration to the 'logic of hegemony'. In this context Chávez and sectors of the Venezuelan opposition have displayed 'totalitarian' tendencies, but only Chávez has balanced them with a determinate programme aimed at democratic inclusion and participation of the popular classes. In this Chávez has shown himself much closer to the 'classic' populist model of a Perón, with its complex structures of popular organisation and participation in furtherance of democratisation. Steve Ellner indeed argues that the *chavista* movement goes further than Peronism in its commitment to ideological debate, with Chávez raising the banner of socialism, its strong identification with the popular classes above a multi-class coalition, the existence of strong sectors of the movement critical of the party's leadership, and the privileging of social movements over political parties, all pointing to a radicalisation which could transcend populism.[79]

Nevertheless, personalisation around the leader, to a greater or lesser degree has led to an increasing reliance on the state as a tool for achieving closure, or 'sutture' as Laclau and Mouffe term it. In the case of Chávez, his refusal to treat with the opposition and many of the sectors which now support them, such as large parts of the middle sectors, has led to a failure to ensure the inclusion necessary to achieve true hegemony in the Gramscian sense of consent. Due to this situation of acute polarisation there is, for the moment anyway, little possibility of regaining those sectors to the government. Thus the Chávez regime sometimes goes against the 'logic of democracy', as Laclau and Mouffe term it, but rarely becomes entirely dominated by the 'logic of totalitarianism'. As Laclau states, there is a mobilisation and self-organisation of previously excluded sectors which has extended the public sphere to a great extent in Venezuela, countering a tendency to bureaucratisation.[80]

Whilst there is a visceral rejection of the President in opposition sectors, there is also an increasing emphasis on 'poverty' and exclusion in its discourse, both in its criticisms of Chávez and in its programmatic pronouncements.[81] This shows that Chávez has to an extent succeeded in moving the discursive 'frontier' to embrace the fundamental social and economic inequalities that any possible future opposition government will have to be seen to address; that in effect a form of 'consent' is being achieved even amongst those sectors. Furthermore Chávez's discursive and programmatic emphasis against neoliberalism continues to make it difficult for opposition parties to declare their intentions in this regard without risking losing votes, forcing them continually to emphasise (and exaggerate) the 'evils' of Chávez and the failures of his government rather than providing concrete programmatic alternatives, thus provoking mistrust or at the very least caution amongst many sectors of the population.[82]

The different sectors of the Venezuelan opposition will find it difficult to achieve hegemony in the Gramscian sense unless it clarifies this ambivalence to neoliberalism. In the present conjuncture, however, unlike in the early 1990s it is much more difficult to construct a coherent, plausible, articulated discourse around neoliberalism due to the increasing weight of evidence being accumulated against its effectiveness as an economic model for Latin American countries, which can also attend to issues of social justice and equality. This is especially so in Venezuela which has had an historically fraught relationship with neoliberalism since the very beginning of its application in Latin America. This is one of the reasons why sectors of the Venezuelan opposition, most of whom would refer to themselves as democratic, have resorted to patently undemocratic tactics to achieve hegemony.

Yet even here Venezuela's opposition sectors have encountered difficulties due to the regional consensus rejecting extra-legal means to achieve power, as evidenced by the division in support in the hemisphere for the April 2002 coup. Any future opposition government will therefore have to carefully navigate between the demands of the increasingly uncertain waters of neoliberalism and globalisation and a wary, impoverished Venezuelan electorate mistrustful of their intentions. Within this context the MVR, or rather the new PSUV, as an organisation ideologically and programmatically opposed to neoliberalism, will in all likelihood continue to find a space in Venezuelan politics, with or without Chávez.

Conclusion

The present chapter has charted and analysed the means by which President Chávez gained power in Venezuela. It has reviewed and examined Gramscian 'war of manoeuvre' and 'war of position' tactics used by the president, and assessed the dangers of authoritarianism which can emerge as groups attempt to achieve hegemony. Following chapters will examine more closely this tension between the authoritarian and democratic tendencies in the Chávez government. While in the present chapter Chávez's strategies to gain political control have been examined, these were prioritised by Chávez in order to clear the way to implement economic and social policies designed to increase popular participation in these areas – as both are equally necessary to increase democracy. In the next chapter therefore we will look at the economic and social policies of *chavismo* and how they further democratic participation, or not. Then we will go on to focus, in Chapter 5, on elements of participation within democratic theory, such as elections, freedom of expression and information, human rights, amongst others, and investigate how these policy areas have fared under Chávez and how they contributed to the government's legitimacy, if at all.

Notes

1   Habermas, J., 1976, *Legitimation Crisis*. Cambridge and Oxford: Polity Press.
2   Buxton, J., 2000, 'Hugo Chávez and populist continuity in Venezuela'. Paper for the Political Studies Association – UK 50th Annual Conference 10–13 April, London, 2000. Available from: www.psa.ac.uk/cps/2000/Buxton%20Julia.pdf. Accessed 6 August 2003.
3   'With Chávez the People Rule'. Campaign slogan for 2000 election campaign.
4   On the same day Betancourt effected the new constitution, the government suspended its guarantees. Carlos Andrés Peréz, then interior minister, and against whom Chávez would effect a coup in 1992 during his second presidential term (1989–93), warned: 'Any insurrectional action, street disturbance, illegal strike will be repressed with severity' (Rodriguez, A., 2001, *Golpes de Estado en Venezuela, 1945–1992*. Caracas: El Nacional, pp. 103–104). Nonetheless, it was said that during the entire Betancourt presidency there were twenty-two coups against him (ibid., p. 104). The two principal coups were known as the *Carupanazo* and the *Porteñazo* during the period May-June 1962.
5   Rodríguez Araque, of the minority PPT party, filled a number of positions in the Chávez government, most notably director of PdVSA and later minister of energy and mines.
6   Others cited by Lopéz Maya are Manuel Quijada, Lino Martínez and Omar Mezza, as well as university figures such as Luis Fuenmayor, Héctor Navarro, Jorge Giordani, Trino Alcides Díaz, and Adina Bastidas. López Maya, M., 2003, 'Hugo Chávez Frías: his movement and his presidency', in S. Ellner and D. Hellinger (eds), *Venezuelan Politics in the Chávez Era: Class, Polarization and Conflict*. Boulder, CO and London: Lynne Reinner, p. 76.
7   Ibid., p. 76.
8   The oath was taken from a quote by Bolívar: 'We will not allow our arms to relax, nor our souls to rest, until we have broken the chains that oppress our people because of the will of the powerful ...' (Chávez Frías, H., 1993, *El Comandante Hugo Chávez a la Nación: Mensaje Bolivariano*. Yare: No publisher, p. 15). The movement was originally called EB-200 or Ejercito Bolivariano-200 (Bolivarian Army-200) 'with objectives strictly limited to the military area'. One of the original founders, Felipe Acosta, died in the *caracazo*. As a result of the *caracazo* the name was changed to MBR-200 and the nature to a 'civic-military movement with political objectives sketched within the insurrectional strategy' (ibid., p. 6).
9   Ibid., p. 16.

10   Chávez cited in Gott, R., 2001, *In the Shadow of the Liberator: Hugo Chávez and the Transformation of Venezuela*. London and New York: Verso, pp. 70–71, my italics.

11   Francia reports that in the carnivals of that year immediately after the coup many of the 'sons of the people came down [from the barrios] disguised as Chávez' and graffiti supporting Chávez began to appear spontaneously Francia, N., 2000. *Antichavismo y Estupidez Ilustrada*. Caracas: Rayuela Taller de Ediciones. p. 83.

12   MBR-200, 1992, *¿Porqué Insurgimos?* Mimeo in CENDES Centro del Estudio del Desarrollo, p. 2.

13   MBR-200/Pirela Romero, Lt Col. A. 1994, *MBR-200: El Arbol de las Tres Raíces*. Valencia, Venezuela, no publishing details.

14   Chávez Frías, H., 1994, *A Dos Años del 4 de febrero*. Yare: No publisher, pp. 3–4.

15   Chávez, 1999, cited in Francia, *Antichavismo*, p. 72.

16   Chávez Frías, H., 2000, *Seis discursos del Presidente Constitucional de Venezuela, Hugo Chávez Frías*. Caracas: Ediciones de la Presidencia de la República, p. 21.

17   See for example Carrasquero, J. V. and Welsch, F., 2001. 'Revolución en democracia o retorno al caudillismo', in J. V. Carrasquero, T. Maingon and F. Welsch (eds), *Venezuela en transición: elecciones y democracia 1998–2000*. Caracas: Consejo Nacional de Ciencia y Tecnología (CONICIT)/Red Universataria de Estudios Políticos de Venezuela-Redpol/CDB Publicaciones, pp. 69–88; Kaplan, M., 2001, *Neocesarismo y Constitucionalismo: El Caso Chávez y Venezuela*. México D.F.: Universidad Nacional Autónoma de México/Corte de Constitucionalidad de Guatemala; Koeneke R. H., 2000, 'Cosmovisión e ideólogos del chavismo', in *Veneconomia* 18(1). Available from: www.veneconomia.com/mensual/mes44.htm. Accessed 16 August 2001.

18   Chávez Frias, *Seis discursos*, pp. 17, 18, 23.

19   Chávez interviewed in Rojas, A., 2004, 'Entrevista: Chávez indica a opposición que violencia pudiera ser su final físico: Seguiremos gobernando con o sin reconciliación', *El Universal*, Sección Política, 12 January. Available from: http://politica.eluniversal.com/2004/entrevista_chavez.shtml. Accessed 12 January 2004.

20   Chávez Frías, *El Comandante*, p. 1.

21   Chávez Frías, *Seis discursos*, p. 8.

22   Chávez in MBR-200, 1996, *Agenda Alternativa Bolivariana: Una Propuesta Patriótica para salir del Laberinto/Presentación de Hugo Chávez Frías*. Caracas: MBR-200, p. 4.

23   Ibid., p. 5.

24   Blanco Muñoz, A., 1998, *Venezuela del 04F-92 al 06D-98: Habla el Comandante Hugo Chávez Frias*. Caracas: Catedra 'Pio Tamayo' CEHA/IIES/FACES/Universidad Central de Venezuela (UCV).

25   Chávez in Croes, C., 1999, 'A mí no me van a cerrar la boca'. *Quinto Día*, 21–28 May: 14–21.

26   Chávez quoted in Wilpert, G., 2007, *Changing Venezuela by Taking Power: The History and Policies of the Chávez Government*. London and New York: Verso, pp. 238–239.

27   MBR-200, no date, *La Importancia de la Asemblea Nacional Constituyente para el MBR-200*. Mimeo in CENDES Centro del Estudio del Desarrollo, p. 5.

28   Ibid.

29   López Maya, 'Hugo Chávez Frías'.

30   Ibid., p. 83.

31   Ibid., p. 84.

32   TeleSUR, 2006, 'Hugo Chávez anuncia la creación del partido único bolivariano en 2007', 16 December. Available from: www.telesurtv.net/secciones/noticias/nota/index.php?ckl=4496. Accessed 21 February 2008.

33   Fuentes, Federico, 2008, 'The struggle for a mass revolutionary party in Venezuela', 28 January. Available from: www.venezuelanalysis.com. Accessed 30 January 2008.

34 Janicke, Kiraz, 2007, 'The battle for the United Socialist Party of Venezuela', 1 December. Available from: www.venezuelanalysis.com. Accessed 30 January 2008.

35 See Lander, Edgardo, 2007a, 'Party disciplinarians: the threat to dissidence and democracy in the United Socialist Party of Venezuela'. Available from: www.tni.org. Accessed 21 February 2008.

36 Fuentes, 'The struggle for a mass revolutionary party'.

37 Chávez in Croes, C., 1997, 'El 4 de febrero no ha terminado', in Quinto Día 7–14 November: 10–16, p. 10.

38 Tanaka, M., 2001, Las Fuerzas Armadas en la Region Andina: No deliberantes o actores políticos? Lima: Comisión Andina de Juristas, p. 155.

39 López Maya, 'Hugo Chávez Frías', p. 85.

40 Viciano Pastor, R. and Martínez Dalmau, R., 2001. Cambio Político y Proceso Constituyente en Venezuela (1998–2000). Caracas: Vadell Hermanos, p. 174.

41 MBR-200, La Importancia de la Asemblea Nacional Constituyente.

42 Chávez Frías, Seis discursos, p. 20.

43 Ibid.

44 Ibid., p. 24.

45 Chávez Frías, El Comandante, p. 11.

46 García-Guadilla, M. P., 2003, 'Civil society: institutionalisation, fragmentation, autonomy', in Ellner and Hellinger, Venezuelan Politics in the Chávez Era, pp. 179–197.

47 López Maya, 'Hugo Chávez Frías'.

48 The Electoral Power is comprised of the National Electoral Power (CNE) as regulating entity, under which is the National Electoral Junta (JNE), the Commission of Civil and Electoral Registry, and the Commission for Political Participation and Financing. The Moral Power is integrated by the Republican Moral Council, comprising the Defender of the People (Ombudsman), the Public Prosecutor, and Comptroller General.

49 Lander, L. E. and Lopez Maya, M., 2000, 'Venezuela: La hegemonia amenazada', in Nueva Sociedad 167: 15–25.

50 Alvarez, A. E., 2003, 'State reform before and after Chávez's election', in Ellner and Hellinger, Venezuelan Politics in the Chávez Era, pp. 147–161. Indeed political parties are not mentioned in the constitution and are only referred to once as 'associations with political ends' (ibid.). Furthermore, state funding for parties was abolished (Lander and López Maya, 'Venezuela').

51 Norden, D. L., 2003, 'Democracy in uniform: Chávez and the Venezuelan armed forces', in Ellner and Hellinger, Venezuelan Politics in the Chávez Era, pp. 93–113, p. 93.

52 Chávez won the vote with 59.76% against that of Arias Cárdenas with 37.52%. There was a 43.69% abstention. The MVR was the largest party in the National Assembly with 44.38% of the vote and 92 seats, followed by AD with 16.11% and 33 seats. CNE (Consejo Nacional Electoral), 2004, Estadisticas Electorales. Available from: www.cne.gov.ve/estadisticas.asp. Accessed 20 January 2004.

53 See PROVEA (Programa Venezolana de Educación Acción en Derechos Humanos), 2001, Situación de los Derechos Humanos en Venezuela/Informe Annual Octubre 2000/Septiembre 2001. Caracas: PROVEA.

54 Enabling Laws are laws made under decree powers given to the president in cases of emergency, and were used many times by previous presidents. Many of these partic-ular laws, such as the Land Law, which could lead to confiscation of non-utilized lands in extreme cases, the Law on Hydrocarbons and the Fishing Law, were sources of grievances for the opposition, due to their having been passed without consultation as well as due to their content.

55 Reuters, Panorama, RNV, 2003, 'Venezuela's economy expected to grow by 6.7% in

2004 according to analysts'. Available from: www.venezuelanalysis.com/news.php? newsno=1143. Accessed 26 January 2004.

56 Rojas, 'Entrevista'.

57 See Aharonián, A. R., 2002, 'Venezuela: Un golpe con olor a hamburguesa, jamón y petróleo'. Available from www.analitica.com/va/politica/opinion/1578534.asp# HOLA. Accessed 10 December 2002; Dissent Voice News Service, 2002, 'The US and the coup in Venezuela'. Available from: www.thirdworldtraveler.com/South_America /US_Coup_Venezuela.html. Accessed 20 January 2004.

58 See Golinger, E., 2006, *The Chávez Code: Cracking US Intervention in Venezuela*. London and New York: Pluto Press.

59 See Venezuelanalysis.com, 2004, 'Rebel Venezuelan ex-military officers ask for a U.S. military invasion of Venezuela'. Available from: www.venezuelanalysis.com/ news.php?newsno=1169. Accessed 15 January 2004.

60 López Maya, M., 1996, 'Neuvas Representaciones populares en Venezuela', in *Nueva Sociedad* 144: 138–151, p. 149.

61 Adapted from Wilpert, G., 2007, 'Venezuela's constitutional reform: an article by article summary'. 23 November. Available from: www.venezuelanalysis.com. Accessed 17 February 2008.

62 Lander, 'Party disciplinarians'.

63 Lander, E., 2007b, 'El referendum sobre la reforma constitucional', 24 December. Available from: www.tni.org. Accessed 18 February 2008.

64 Ibid.

65 Francia, *Antichavismo*, p. 145.

66 Ransome, P., 1992, *Antonio Gramsci: A New Introduction*. New York: Harvester Wheatsheaf, p. 139.

67 Norden, 'Democracy in uniform', p. 93.

68 For example Enrique Salas Römer (ex-governor Carabobo), Enrique Mendoza (Miranda), Manuel Rosales (Zulia), and the latest opposition presidential candidate in the 2006 elections.

69 Gramsci, A., 1971 [1947], *Selections from the Prison Notebooks*. Edited and translated by Q. Hoare and G. Nowell Smith). New York: International Publishers, p. 198.

70 Laclau, E., 1977, *Politics and Ideology in Marxist Theory: Capitalism-Fascism-Populism*. London: New Left Books.

71 Ellner, S., 2003, 'Hugo Chávez y Alberto Fujimori: análisis comparativo de dos variantes de populismo', in *Revista Venezolana de Economia y Ciencias Sociales* 10(1): 13–37, p. 20.

72 Ellner, S., 2003, 'Organised labor and the challenge of Chavismo', in Ellner and Hellinger, *Venezuelan Politics in the Chávez Era*, pp. 161–178.

73 Ellner, 'Hugo Chávez y Alberto Fujimori', p. 28.

74 París Pombo, M. D., 1990, *Crisis de identidades colectivas en America Latina*. Mexico D.F.: Plaza y Valdes.

75 Laclau, E. and Mouffe, C., 2001, *Hegemony and Socialist Strategy: Towards a Radical Democratic Politics*, 2nd ed. London and New York: Verso.

76 Buxton, J. D., 2008, 'The Bolivarian Revolution as Venezuela's post-crisis alternative'. Paper presented at the 2nd Global International Studies Conference, Ljubljana, Slovenia 2008. Draft version.

77 Carmona Estanga, P., 2002. 'Decreto del Gobierno Provisional de Pedro Carmona Estanga', in *Observatorio Social de América Latina* III(7): 27–28.

78 This discourse however was qualified. See Chávez, *A Dos Años*.

79 Ellner, S., 2008, *Rethinking Venezuelan Poltics: Class, Conflict, and the Chávez Phenomenon*. Boulder, CO: Lynne Rienner, p. 172.

80 Laclau, E., 2005, *On Populist Reason*. London: Verso, p. 61.
81 For example, presidential candidate for the 2006 elections, and governor of Zulia, Manuel Rosales, announced 'that the social area will be the backbone of his government program [and] explained that his government plan [would] include really fair allocation of oil revenues by means of two axes – minimum wage for all unemployed and direct contribution to the underprivileged' (*El Universal*, 8 August 2006, 'Rosales's candidacy formally announced'. Available from: http://english.eluniversal.com/ 2006/08/09/en_pol_art_09A762409.shtml. Accessed 22 February 2008.
82 In a poll conducted in January 2004, the largest percentage of those surveyed, 38.7%, described themselves as non-aligned politically, the so-called 'ni-ni's' while 25% described themselves as pro-Chávez and 33% anti-Chávez. *El Universal*, 2004. 'Datanálisis asegura que 38,7% de los venezolanos no objeta ni apoya a Chávez'. *El Universal* Sección Avances, 9 January 2004. Available from: www.eluniversal.com/ 2004/01/09/09A1432526.shtml. Accessed 9 January 2004.

4 Populism, globalisation and the socioeconomic policies of the Chávez government

Introduction

In previous chapters, democracy's lack of legitimacy due to social divisions along race/class lines and to economic dependency on industrialised countries were all identified as key aspects in the emergence of populism. Previous democratic regimes in Venezuela, preceding the emergence of Chávez, failed in the long term to establish policies aimed at lessening these social fissures thus losing popular legitimacy. Chávez exploited this lack of legitimacy and presented an alternative model seeking to democratise the political space, furthering participation of the popular classes and thus gaining the legitimacy denied the previous *puntofijista* regime. Central to this strategy was the use of discourse dividing the social space along antagonistic lines – *el pueblo* versus the oligarchy and *partidocracia*.

This chapter will go beyond discourse in the strictest sense to examine the socioeconomic policies of the Chávez government, analysing and assessing to what extent these provided it with the legitimacy denied previous governments. To do this, the chapter will use a structure drawn from Susan Strange's book *States and Markets* based on four areas of political economy – finance, production, security and knowledge. Strange's structure is one of the best-known and most accessible IPE frameworks.[1]

Strange's framework of analysis for international political economy is based on four basic values: (i) wealth; (ii) security; (iii) freedom; and (iv) justice. Each society, she maintains, gives different weighting to each of these values, which in turn affects the balance between the state (authority) and the market in that society. Strange's analytical framework is based around a number of key questions, which can be summed up in the question: *Cui bono?* Who gets what? Who benefits? Who loses?

In order to answer this question Strange encourages us to investigate who has power and what the source of that power is. Power, she argues, may not necessarily lie within the state, but in other structures such as international organisations (IOs), transnational corporations (TNCs), NGOs, and the media, amongst others. It is necessary therefore to abandon state-bound views of power and concentrate instead on its distribution in the four essential structures in which the values of wealth, security, freedom and justice are constructed: finance, production, security and knowledge. We must ask ourselves who has control over these four structures when seeking out the ownership and source of power.

What does Strange mean by each of these four structures? The financial structure is, in a nutshell, credit availability and currency values. This structure has the power to 'allow or deny ... people the possibility of spending today and paying back tomorrow, the power to let them exercise purchasing power and thus influence markets for production, and also the power to manage or mismanage the currency in which credit is denominated, thus affecting rates of exchange with credit denominated in other currencies'.[2] Governments and banks share these powers, and the structure is both local, because currencies are local in origin, and global, due to the technologisation of transactions and financial markets.

The production structure is, according to Strange, '... the sum of all the arrangements determining what is produced, by whom and for whom, by which method and on what terms'.[3] Thus, under this heading what is examined is labour, industrial production and wealth, in other words 'what creates wealth in a political economy'.[4] This structure has been influenced by two great changes which now affect most of the states of the world: a change to a demand-led market economy, in other words capitalism, and more recently, a change from production geared to national markets to one geared to global markets.

The security structure in political economy, she asserts, 'is the framework of power created by the provision of security by some human beings for others' and is usually built around the institution of the state in each country, and globally in association or in competition with other states.[5] The security structure, however, does not simply entail protection from 'sudden unnatural death', but also from hunger, disease, disablement and other hazards, and involves the distribution of security amongst the different groups in society – in other words in this context we mean 'human security'.[6]

Finally, '[the knowledge structure] comprehends what is believed (and the moral conclusions and principles derived from those beliefs); what is known and perceived as understood; and the channels by which beliefs, ideas and knowledge are communicated – including some people and excluding others'.[7] Furthermore, '[it] determines what knowledge is discovered, how it is stored, and who communicates it by what means to whom and on what terms'.[8] This power is diffused and unquantifiable, and has been subject to changes in the provision and control over information and communication systems, in the use of language, and in the fundamental perceptions of and beliefs about the human condition which influence value judgements, and consequently political and economic decisions and policies.[9]

The Chávez government's programme

Steve Ellner identifies three stages of the Chávez presidency, and a possible fourth.[10] These are:

1   a moderate period (1999–2000) which emphasised the political over the socioeconomic;
2   a more radical state (2001–04), characterised by anti-neoliberalism, ruling out privatisation for example, and by the confrontation against an insurgent opposition refusing to recognise the government's legitimacy;
3   the emergence of the outlines of a new economic model (in 2005) made possible by the weakening of the opposition as they were defeated in their different insurgent attempts to unseat Chávez and by the rise in oil prices;
4   a possible new phase from Chávez's victory in the 2006 presidential elections based on economic and organisational changes, encapsulated in the constitutional amendments proposed by the president.

Each stage was accompanied by 'the intensification of conflict, the exit of moderates, the consolidation of power, and the radicalisation of goals'.[11]

When Chávez came to power, after five years of government under ex-COPEI patriarch, Rafael Caldera, Venezuelans were worse off than ever. Poverty had increased, land remained in the hands of a tiny minority, and unemployment and underemployment had increased, with almost half of those employees working in the informal sector.[12] Inflation remained high, minimum salaries did not cover basic needs, and per capita income had fallen dramatically.[13]

The Caldera government also had left a legacy of neoliberal reform. It implemented some privatisations, in the banking, telecommunications, steel and transport sector. It removed price and exchange controls in 1996, but then had to apply a banded system of exchange rate control on the *bolívar* (Bs) in order to attempt to control capital flight brought on by a severe banking crisis.[14] It removed pro-employee legislation, such as retroactive severance payments, and in the social security sector. It pursued a double strategy on oil, of high output and increased private foreign investment, the so-called *apertura* or opening, leaving oil prices at around US\$10 a barrel in 1997–98.[15]

Chávez, however, saw the source of Venezuela's problems as political and not economic: 'Inflation, hunger, insecurity, education, poverty, all that forms a problematic mass, the cause of which is … the exhaustion of the political model'.[16] The answer, therefore, was to be found first in the implementation of profound political change, through a Constituent Assembly (*Constituyente*), and then through the restoration of an interventionist state working alongside the market; that is, to paraphrase Adam Smith, the visible hand of the state accompanied by the invisible hand of the market.

The Bolivarian economic model is, according to Chávez, 'humanist, self-managing, and competitive'. *Humanist* first, because the *human being* would be central to policy, while the *state* 'regulates, stimulates, and promotes the economic process', and the *market* fulfills 'the laws of supply and demand, [but is] not ... monopolised or oligopolised'.[17] In this way, Chávez declares, the Bolivarian economic model is closer to the Third Way model of Tony Blair, or Bill Clinton, than a socialist or capitalist state.[18]

Second, the Bolivarian project envisages an economy which is *self-managing*, that is that it is a democratised economy, with alternative organisational forms flourishing, such as co-operatives and other types of association. Finally, it is to be a *competitive* economy, insofar as it can reach high levels of productivity and so compete with foreign products. As Rodríguez summarises it, the Bolivarian economic system is one 'in which there would be an active intervention of the state, co-existing with the forces of the market, within which there is an important place for non-traditional forms of economic association such as co-operatives, and which is capable of achieving a high level of competitiveness and productivity'.[19] Rodríguez stresses that it is not, as many in the Opposition contend, a Marxist proposal, despite much of the leftist discourse and symbolism of Chávez and others in the Polo Patriótico. Rather it is 'a quite general and not very new general proposal',[20] which 'distances itself from the traditional economic proposals of the extreme left'.[21]

Indeed, on gaining power in 1998, Chávez sent a strong signal of continuity to the international financial community by retaining in the finance portfolio Caldera's minister, Maritza Izaguirre. As a result there was little change in finance management. The currency exchange arrangements were maintained, even as public spending was increased. In the new constitution of 1999 there was no great change in fiscal policy regulations, which Kelly affirms remained consistent with the capitalist principles of the 1961 constitution.[22] Indeed, she concludes that while there is a strong emphasis on social rights and entitlements (see 'Security' below), the constitution also includes important orthodox economic principles 'that could even signal a shift somewhat to the right'.[23]

This orthodoxy changed in 2001 when the government introduced a series of forty-nine special laws, the most contentious of which were in the areas of land reform, in oil policy and in fishing. These laws were seen to be sufficiently radical by the Venezuelan elites, and by the US, for them to launch a series of illegal and legal attempts to unseat Chávez, including the opposition coup against him in April 2002, the oil strike ending in February 2003, and the recall referendum of August 2004. This political uncertainty led to disastrous falls in economic growth, and corresponding rises in poverty, unemployment and inequality. It did, however, contribute to the severe discrediting of the opposition for the majority of Venezuelans. With its victory in the recall referendum in particular, the government regained the confidence to plough ahead with a new set of measures signaling a new phase in its development.

The introduction of the mission programmes in 2003, in health in particular, signaled the beginning of the emergence of this new model. Furthermore, new experiments in worker cooperatives and co-management were introduced in the production apparatus. The government also began in 2005 to expropriate companies and hand them over to the workers to run. Land reform intensified, tax collection was strictly enforced, popular participation was encouraged through novel mechanisms for decision-making on key issues effecting communities.

By January, 2005, in a speech given to the World Social Forum in Caracas, Chávez announced that Venezuela would move towards a new 'socialism for the twenty-first century'. Wilpert, reviewing Chávez's speeches on the concept, outlines the president's vision of twenty-first-century socialism.[24] It would be a socialism which would transcend capitalism, but also the statism of twentieth-century socialism; which would be humanist and based on solidarity; and which would be based on full democracy, that is participatory and protagonistic democracy, but also a democracy of the means of production towards a communal system of production and consumption. This vision, according to Chávez's view, should not be dogmatic, nor should it follow a particular recipe, but rather should be a socialism which is constructed on a daily basis.

Most analysts concur that the central problem of Chávez's concept of twenty-first-century socialism is that it is based too much on ideals and has little actual programmatic content. Álvarez claims that only Hugo Chávez can know what the actual details of twenty-first-century socialism are, but that it will certainly be more radical that what came before.[25] Wilpert states that what is needed is an 'institutional definition or at least a set of defining features'.[26] Lander and Navarette see it as based on the concept of 'endogenous development' with 'associative forms of property and control, such as cooperatives and co-management ... stimulated through diverse types of micro and small credits granted by state-funding entities' reliant on state purchasing of the products and services produced.[27]

The introduction of the constitutional amendments proposals put forward by a presidential commission in 2006 could have been a signal for the beginning of a new phase, the actual construction of twenty-first-century socialism in Venezuela. Many of the elements had already been introduced, as seen above, and other moves, such as the nationalisations of the telecommunications company CANTV, as well as the new agreements with private oil companies in the Orinoco oil fields were further moves in that direction. The defeat of the referendum, however, has cast uncertainty on how this next stage will advance.

The following four sections will use Strange's four structures to examine the Chávez government's policies in these areas more closely. In the section on 'Finance' we will look at taxation policy, oil revenue, international debt, currency values, country risk and credit availability. In 'Production' we will examine a number of policy areas related to work, income and modes of production, including employment and income, trade unions, agricultural and non-agricultural production, economic growth and trade policy. In 'Security' we primarily concentrate on social policy areas, most notably health. In 'Knowledge', we look at education, but also at how policy in production, the media and other areas help the Chávez government to ensure that strategic knowledge is kept within the state or spread to the popular sectors. By examining policy in these four areas we will seek to answer Strange's simple question: *Cui bono?* Who gains, who loses? We will therefore seek to establish not only if there has been a transfer of wealth from the rich to the poor within Venezuela, but also how the Chávez government is seeking to alter the position of Venezuela within the wider international framework of globalisation.

Finance

Taxation policy

No great changes were announced in taxation policy in the initial period of the Chávez government, although it did pursue a policy of modernisation of the tax-collecting agency, the SENIAT, and introduced the Plan Evasión Cero, or Zero Evasion Plan to reduce tax evasion. Some of the intial rise in tax take can be attributed to the re-introduction of the Banking Debit Tax (Impuesto Débito Bancario/IDB) and the introduction of a further tax on financial transactions, but most of it is due to the overall take as a percentage of GNP.

In 1998, the last year of the Caldera government, tax take was 10.33% of GDP, but in 2005, under Chávez, it was 14.63%. Improvement in internal collection (that is primarily income tax and sales tax) was most notable, with an increase from 5.96% to 9.65% of GDP in the same period. However, there is a pronounced reliance on sales taxes at 45.6% of tax take in 2007.[28] Nonetheless, VAT was set at a reduced rate of 9% (from February 2007) down from the previous 14% and there were plans to eliminate it altogether by 2009, making up for the shortfall by increasing the enforcement of tax collection and charging increased taxes on capital, as well as on gambling, and reforming both income tax and capital tax, but in the face of financial crisis the government reversed this decision and raised the VAT rate to 15% in March 2009.

Income tax on people and companies (Impuesto sobre la renta/ISLR) on the other hand stood at 35% of tax take in the same year,[29] which nonetheless showed an overall increase from 2% of GDP in 1999 to 3.2% in 2006.[30] As a result, non-oil tax revenue went from 10% of GDP in 1999 to 12% in 2006,[31] but remained well below the Latin American average of 18.5% (1999–2003).[32] Overall therefore, the Chávez government improved the tax take, and diversified it, to a certain extent, away from reliance on oil revenues, but it did not significantly restructure it.

Oil revenue

The government took a number of steps to ensure greater state control of oil revenue. At a legal level, the constitution ensures that PdVSA remains in state hands, but does leave the door open for private sector involvement in its filial companies or strategic associates.[33] This was the legal context in which the Chávez government then took greater control over the oil industry in three moves.[34] First, the defeat of the management-led oil stoppage in February 2003 provided the government with the legal pretext to remove upper and middle management layers and 18,000 oil workers who participated in the strike. The old neoliberal guard within PdVSA was finally removed allowing for greater government control of the company and the industry. Second, in 2005 the government changed thirty-two 'service agreements' with oil companies working in marginal oil fields into joint ventures with majority PdVSA stakes, thus increasing government control and revenue within these oil fields. The third move, in 2007, was changing the existing Orinoco Belt joint ventures into PdVSA-controlled projects, once again increasing government control and revenue.

While these moves secured government control of the internal oil sector, the government also pursued an aggressive diplomatic offensive to push up the oil price. This policy consisted of renewed coordination with other OPEC countries, and large non-OPEC oil producers such as Mexico and Russia, to establish production quotas. The purpose of this policy was to maintain stable prices and thus stable revenue from oil.

Both these policies bore financial fruits for the government. The OPEC strategy contributed to oil price rises from $8.43 in 1998, to a price of $92 for Venezuelan crude at the time of writing (March 2008). While the OPEC policy has not been entirely responsible for this rise – international tension in the Middle East in particular providing an important impetus to price rises – the repeated insistence from oil-purchasing countries to abandon them shows they still have an impact.

These historically high oil prices, coupled with the increased control of the state over the oil sector, saw state income from oil rise dramatically. In

1999 oil revenue stood at $6 billion but by 2005 the Venezuelan state received $25 billion dollars in revenue from PdVSA alone out of total earnings of $85,730 billion.[35] Oil income for the Venezuelan state went from 5.79% of GDP in 1998, the last year of the Caldera presidency, to 15.89% of GDP at the end of 2006.[36] This increased revenue also helped finance increased social spending.

International debt

The Chávez government, however, scrupulously maintained debt repayments and indeed increased them from 18.6% of total spending in the Caldera presidency (1993–1998) to 22.0% in the period 1999–2003.[37] External debt has remained relatively constant throughout the Chávez presidency, with a tendency to increase in more recent years. According to ECLAC (the Economic Commission for Latin America and the Carribean), gross external debt stood at $37,016 billion in 1999 and rose to $40,456 billion in 2003 and $52,949 in 2007.[38] Nonetheless, despite these rises Venezuela's debt is lower relative to other Latin American countries.[39] Average debt repayments during 1999–2003 were approximately US$3,480 million per year,[40] but payments have been lowered in the years since, standing at $2,900 billion in 2006.[41] Nonetheless, despite this lowering in repayments, the prompt payment policy is in keeping with the government's intention to maintain Venezuelan sovereignty in economic decision-making, by removing cause for the international financial community to involve itself in Venezuelan affairs. Venezuela has insistently rejected interference from the IMF for example, and is one of the few Latin American countries free from IMF loans.[42]

Currency values and country risk

Wide variations can be found in the main macroeconomic indicators, yet the government strived to keep these within internationally accepted limits, despite opposition activity affecting them. International reserves were maintained at reasonably high levels, except during the coup and strikes of 2002, when they reached historic lows.[43] The *bolívar* was devalued from Bs.650/US$1 in the first trimester of 2000 to Bs.1,920/US$1 in the first trimester of 2004, when currency controls were put in place to stem capital flight.[44] In 2007 a new *bolívar* was introduced, the *bolívar fuerte* (strong *bolívar*) at a conversion rate, as of March, 2008, of 2.14 *bolívares* to the dollar, one new *bolívar fuerte* being equal to 1,000 old *bolívares* (BCV, 2008). Nonetheless, in all likelihood the Venezuelan *bolívar* is overvalued by around 30% relative to the dollar, making imports cheaper relative to locally produced products, hence affecting production policies and inflation.[45]

Country risk also oscillated according to the political situation, reaching a high of 1406 basis points in February 2003, just after the strike, to be reduced to 596 on 22 December 2003, thus reducing interest rates on new loans taken out by the state.[46] Similar figures were maintained in the preceding years, with 580 basis points as of March 2008.[47]

Inflation between 1999 and 2007 was on average approximately 20%, with a low of 12.5% in 2001, a high of 31.2% in 2002, the year of the opposition coup and the most recent rate standing at a relatively high 22.5%.[48] Nonetheless historically speaking these are quite low figures for Venezuela, with average inflation between 1989 and 1998 at 52.5%.[49] At the time of writing, the current Venezuelan rate of inflation is, however, the highest in the region.[50] Such a high rate has knock-on effects, most notably in terms of purchasing power for the country's poor.

Credit availability

One of the first moves of the Chávez government was to 'democratise' credit availability. The government opened a variety of popular credit agencies, such as the People's Bank (Banco del Pueblo), providing small loans for small and medium-sized businesses, and the Women's Bank (Banco de la Mujer) having a similar function, but this time exclusively for women. Between 2001 and 2003, the Women's Bank and the People's Bank gave out 70,000 micro-credits between them.[51] However, there is little evaluation of the effectiveness of these schemes, and some evidence of high default levels.[52] The government also requires private banks to reserve 3% of their credit portfolio for micro-credits. According to Wilpert, private banks alone provided $500 million such credits in 2005.[53] This availability of micro-credits to people in the popular classes has facilitated the expansion of the popular economy, a central policy for the democratisation of the means of production as we shall see in the next section.

Production

General production policy

As previously stated, in the initial years of the Chávez government there was little change to the basic production apparatus as the government set about implementing profound political change. The constitution of 1999, the result of that process, has a number of important sections on production, some outlining the parameters of legislation on issues such as employment and social security rights, while others attempt to define the limits of the private and public spheres.

Chapter V of the constitution outlines much of Venezuelans' social and family rights. In particular, Articles 89 to 97 deal with workers' rights, guaranteeing existing rights (Article 89) restricting the working day to a maximum of eight hours and the working week to 44 hours (Article 90), guaranteeing the worker a 'sufficient salary which will allow him or her to live with dignity' (Article 91) and the right to social provisions based on time served, overturning the removal of that right by the Caldera government (Article 92). Job security, protection against unfair dismissal, and trade union rights, including the right to strike, are also guaranteed (Articles 93–97).[54]

As we noted also in the previous chapter, the constitutional amendments proposed by the presidential commission would have had a profound effect on the production apparatus if they had been passed, most especially the suppression of the right to private property and the move to a socialist model of production, with more state control of the economy given constitutional status. These proposals were defeated, however, in the December 2007 referendum.

The constitution has a number of articles that set out the type of productive system pertinent to Bolivarian Venezuela. These articles protect private property and activity, whilst forbidding monopolies and oligopolies and encouraging social-type business associations, such as small and medium-sized businesses, cooperatives, family businesses, credit unions and other such economic units (Articles 112; 113; 115; 308). Article 113 allows the state to licence private contracts to exploit resources pertaining to the state. In Title VI, Chapter 1, the constitution reserves the right of the state to use tariffs to protect national companies, and guarantees equal treatment for national and foreign capital. It places a duty on the state to ensure 'food sovereignty', giving protection and resources to national agriculture, and discouraging 'latifundismo' or land concentration in favour of smaller productive units (Articles 305–307). These general provisions provide the framework within which economic growth should develop, the results of which we shall see in the next section.

Economic growth

Economic growth, initially, was severely affected by political instability and some say, government policy. Total average GNP growth stood at 3.2% in 1999/2000 to fall to −9.4% in 2002/2003.[55] Goods production also suffered, with manufacturing being particularly damaged, going from 3.9% growth in 1999/2000 to −10.6% in 2002/2003 and services from 3.4% to −4.9%, with commerce being particularly hit.[56] Most of these figures show the influence of the April 2002 coup and the later strike of the same year.

The situation changed dramatically, however, once the oil strike was defeated. The Centre for Economic Policy Research (CEPR) shows that the Venezuelan economy grew on average by 11.85% in the period 2004–2007,[57] one of the best performing economies in the region and with predictions of continued growth in 2008 of 7% to 8%. The CEPR report also maintains that while much of this growth is attributable to the high prices of oil on the international markets, government policy is its chief engine, particularly its expansionary fiscal policies. It therefore does not concur that the economy is heading for a bust in the event of oil prices declining, as argued by Rodríguez for example (see Conclusions below).[59]

Nonetheless, the current situation in terms of the overvaluing of the currency and inflation is making it difficult for Venezuela to diversify its economy away from oil. Indeed, Álvarez, concludes, oil has 'been the principal dynamo of the economic results'.[60] He notes a 44% increase in oil revenue between 2005 and 2006, revenue increasing from 51% of total income in 2000 to 56% in 2006. Similarly, oil exports have grown from 77% in 1997, the year before Chávez was elected to power, to 89% in 2006.[61] At the time of writing this dependence on oil is one of the chief problems facing the Chávez government which economic policy so far has failed to remedy.

Employment and incomes

For the bulk of workers, employment, underemployment and pay remain at difficult though improved levels. Between 1999 and 2001 unemployment hovered between 16% and 10%, rising to 16.2% in the second semester of 2002 to fall again to 9.3% in the first semester of 2007, according to official figures.[62] The proportion of workers in the informal sector remained substantial although with a tendency to fall: in 1999 52.4% of the economically active population (EAP) was in informal employment but this was reduced to 44.3% in the first semester of 2007.[63]

To achieve these figures the government tried a number of approaches. In its first four years it announced a number of employment plans but with little effect on the figures.[64] Then in February 2004, the government initiated the latest, Mission *Vuelvan Caras* (Turning Heads), planning to incorporate a million Venezuelans by July of that year into training and reactivate idle business infrastructure to provide them with employment.[65] In the event Provea reports that between 2004 and 2007 the Mission, renamed Mission Che Guevara in September, 2007, trained around 836,138 people, but few of those actually found work in the labour force.[66]

Incomes, in general, tended to fall during the Chávez presidency. According to CEPAL, in 2006 Venezuelan workers earned 84.8% of the real average wages earned in 2000.[67] Despite this overall lowering of wages, the minimum urban salary saw a steady and progressive rise from Bs120,000 in 1999 to Bs614,790 in 2007.[68] Nonetheless few people actually receive the minimum wage, according to PROVEA; 51.6% of workers earned less in the first semester of 2006 and Labour Ministry checks found that 40.12% of businesses inspected did not pay the minimum wage.

Moreover, the cost of the basic basket of food remained consistently above the minimum salary for most of the lifetime of the Chávez government, however PROVEA does report that the minimum salary as of June 2007, was

21% above the cost of the official basic food basket (Bs614,790 versus Bs508,621). While recognising the importance of this, PROVEA warns that as 51.6% of employed people do not actually receive the minimum wage, along with the 9.5% of unemployed who receive no salary at all, 61% of the working population could not cover the price of the official food basket.[69] In effect only 27% of all Venezuelan workers earned more than the minimum wage. High levels of inflation and the devaluation of the Bolivar also had a negative impact on the affordability of the basic food basket. Moreover, private analysts put the cost of the basic food basket much higher.[70]

State / trade union relations

Labour relations between the Chávez government and the main trade union confederation, the Confederación de Trabajadores de Venezuela (Venezuela Workers Council/CTV) have been tense, to say the least. The CTV, alongside the main business association, FEDECAMARAS, were at the forefront of opposition campaigns to remove Chávez from office. Both these organisations led a series of work stoppages, most notably the 'indefinite' strike of 8–11 April 2002, which culminated in a *coup d'état*. A further stoppage took place later that year lasting throughout December and into early February 2003, bringing the country's oil industry to a virtual standstill.

The confrontation between the CTV and the government, however, was not entirely surprising. The CTV had been declining as a potent force in Venezuelan politics due to many allegations of corruption, a patchy record in defending workers' rights against various neoliberal attempts to curtail them, and declining trade union membership.[71] Chávez had repeatedly stressed the need to 'democratise' the trade unions, as the constitution required in Article 95, and eventually a referendum calling for such democratisation was held in December 2000. While the government won the referendum, with a very low turnout (almost 77% abstention), the existing CTV leadership of Carlos Ortega as president and Manuel Cova as vice-president won the subsequent elections, although under highly questioned circumstances.[72]

Re-elected and revitalised the CTV leadership launched an all-out campaign to discredit the government and remove it from office, in alliance with FEDECAMARAS, the media, opposition political parties, the Church, and an assortment of 'civil society' (i.e. middle and upper class) groupings. Whilst the CTV and its allies managed to mobilise substantial numbers of people to strike against the government, this was achieved through intense media campaigns (see Chapter 5), the locking out of staff by company management, and promising to pay staff that went on strike – promises that were not always upheld. Nor were these strikes unqualified successes: poorer areas of Caracas, informal workers, transport sectors, and electricity sectors, as well as many areas in the interior of the country continued to work as normal. The strikes failed in their objective, specifically to remove Chávez from office, and indeed the government emerged from them revitalised while the opposition became exhausted and discredited. Nonetheless the economic impact of the strike was significant. According to a National Assembly report, almost US$8 billion was lost to the economy.[73]

Since these occurrences the leadership of the CTV has changed and its seditious behaviour has been dropped. Furthermore a new labour confederation, the Unión Nacional de Trabajadores (National Worker's Union/UNT), has emerged, more in tune with the government's social and economic vision, but nonetheless attempting to establish autonomy from it. Chávez, however, does not see such autonomy as being necessary, stating baldly on one occasion that 'Trade unions cannot be autonomous, we have to put a stop to that!'[74] (For more on trade unions see the section on 'Associational autonomy' in Chapter 5).

Agricultural production

Under the Land Law introduced in 2001, 3,499,890 hectares approximately have been transferred up until the end of 2006, according to official sources. Of these 1,900,000 hectares were from land deemed idle which was then reclaimed by the state to be distributed.[75] While most of this land has been transferred to private small and medium farmers, some have been transformed into cooperatives or mixed 'socialist' enterprises, with 51% of ownership resting in state hands.

Investment has been strong in agriculture from both private and state sectors, with the former investing more. Private investment in agriculture grew from 0.50% of GDP in 1998 to 2.48% in 2006, while public investment in the same period went from 0.03% GDP to 0.60% GDP.[76] Subsidies are being provided for certain key agricultural products and private-sector banks are required to provide loans to encourage cultivation of these products as well.[77] The state-owned Venezuelan Agriculture Bank (Banco Agrícola de Venezuela) was also created to provide loans to small and medium farmers.

Nonetheless these efforts have yet to achieve their stated aim of food sovereignty. While the government has been successful in reclaiming and redistributing land, and while there has been strong investment in this process, it has not been so successful in making this land productive. Food production has increased only by 1.8% between 1996 and 2005 and only 1.5% between 2005 and 2006, according to the government.[78] Shortages in many important products, such as milk, sugar and beef, have been common. Imports of agricultural products have soared; private sources claim food imports rose almost threefold between 2002 and 2006 – from $1,350 billion to $3,044 billion – contradicting much lower government figures.[79]

Non-agricultural sector

Private-sector production has been severely affected by the political situation in Venezuela, especially considering that the major business organisation FEDECAMARAS and associate business groups, such as FEDECOMERCIO (representing major retailers) and to a lesser extent FEDEINDUSTRIA (representing national industrialists), were at the forefront of campaigns against the Chávez government. Industry maintains that the Chávez government has been detrimental to industrial activity. One report noted that in 1997, two years before Chávez came to power there were 11,640 industries which generated 467,000 jobs, while at the end of 2003 there were only 260,000 jobs in industry. Furthermore, that industry which did continue producing did so at 50% of capacity. Reasons for recession given by businessmen were political instability and low demand.[80]

Since 2004, however, economic activity has recuperated and, according to the US-based CEPR, private-sector growth has been stronger than state-sector growth, with the former at around 12.3% of real GDP in 2006, with construction, finance and communication growing particularly well. Finance for example grew by 39.2% in 2006 as opposed to manufacturing growing by a much more modest 10.4%.[81]

Most sectoral state policies are directed at the small and medium-sized business sectors, by providing credits and following a policy of state buying of Venezuelan products and services. On gaining power the new government set in motion reviews of the legislation on the privatisation of electricity, aluminium, telecommunications, petrochemicals, and gas in order to ensure that these deals complied with national goals.[82] Privatisation was halted and the government announced the launching of new state-owned telecommunications and airline companies in 2004, in line with its policies of state ownership of strategic services. This was furthered in 2006 with the nationalisation of key strategic companies, CANTV, the privatised telecommunications company and Caracas Electricity, the power company for the capital. It is important to note that the Venezuelan state paid the market rate for both these companies and their takeovers were negotiated with their US owners.

In effect therefore, as PROVEA notes, there are five different types of state involvement in company ownership and management in 'socialist' Venezuela. These are:

1   Enterprises 100% owned by the state, such as the aforementioned CANTV and Caracas Electricity, not to mention, of course, the state oil company, PdVSA.
2   Mixed-controlled companies, with joint state-worker management, such as the aluminium processing plant, Alcasa.
3   Worker-controlled companies, such as CNV, which makes valves and the paper manufacture, Invepal. These are companies which were about to

close and were instead expropriated by the state. They are 51% owned by the state, but the workers effectively control their decision-making structures.

4 Business-run enterprises but with state help.

5 Cooperatives. SUNACOOP, the state body responsible for cooperatives, state that there are 215,000 cooperatives registered, but only about 70,000 are actually operating. This sector is actually retracting as regulatory frameworks, designed to counteract misappropriation of funds, take effect; between 2003 and 2007, the number employed was reduced from 570,395 people to 185,817 people.[83] Cooperatives are financed by the state and it is normally the state which buys their services.

Provea identifies some problems with increased state involvement in production, particularly strong evidence of politicisation of employment.[84] Another problem identified by the UN's ECLAC shows a reduction in foreign direct investments. In 2007, Venezuela attracted $646m of foreign investment compared with Colombia and Peru which pulled in $9bn and $5.3bn respectively. Even small economies such as El Salvador and the Dominican Republic attracted more than Venezuela, with about $1.5bn each.[85] That said these different experiments in ownership and co-management provide important diversity in the economy, and examples of different methods to democratise the workplace.

Trade policy

In international trade, Venezuela has consistently resisted the Free Trade Agreement of the Americas (FTAA), concentrating instead on trade agreements with other Latin American countries, such as the entry of Venezuela into MERCOSUR (the common market of the South[86]) in July 2006, as well as seeking to fortify joint negotiating agreements on the FTAA with Brazil and Argentina. Venezuela has also entered into a number of cooperative trade agreements with other Latin American states. Venezuela and Cuba also initiated the ALBA, the Bolivarian Alternative for the Americas trade and association agreement. Venezuela under Chávez has pursued a policy of diversification of trade, not only encouraging inter-Latin American trade, through its membership of MERCOSUR for example and through ALBA, but also actively pursuing trade with Asia, particularly China and India, and the EU, Canada and Russia, in an attempt to lessen its reliance on trade with the US. Nonetheless, the US and Colombia remain Venezuela's main trading partners.[87]

Security

As stated at the outset of this chapter, by security what is meant is human security, that is human welfare, as opposed to military security. Wilpert identifies four phases in government social policy strategy: the first, during 1999, was characterised by the implementation of the armed forces-led Plan Bolívar 2000;[88] the second phase, lasting from 2000–2001, consisted of the launching of the government's long- and medium-term poverty reduction programmes, of macroeconomic reform, urban and rural land reform, the creation of Bolivarian schools, and support for micro-credits and coopera- tives; the third lasted from December 2001 to May 2003, where due to the unsettled political and economic situation the government experienced many setbacks in implementing their policies; the latest phase, dating from May 2003, consists of an all-round offensive on the part of the government on poverty and exclusion through the vehicle of the various *misiones* ('Missions'). Since then, the *misiones* element of the Chávez government's social policy has been widened and deepened to create a parallel structure to the existing pre-Chávez bureaucracy.

Plan Bolívar 2000 took as its base line the notion that human security was synonymous with national security and that the armed forces could play an important role in the provision of that welfare. As a result the military partic- ipated in providing transport, house-building and repair, policing, and food distribution, disaster relief, school construction, road-building, and more. Twenty thousand homes were built, 10,000 rebuilt and soldier-aided mega markets sold 112,000 tons of food each month in poor regions at discount prices.[89] Over two million people received medical treatment. Nearly a thousand inexpensive markets were opened, over two million children were vaccinated, and thousands of tons of rubbish were collected, just to name a few of the programme's results.[90] The plan was criticised for being poorly managed and having little transparency, resulting in charges of corruption against the officers in charge of the programme. Wilpert argues, however, that given the context of recession and the major disaster of floods and landslides in Vargas state, as well as the seriousness of the problems, the lack of resources, and the government's focus on reforming the constitution, Plan Bolívar 2000 still had an important positive impact on the poor of Venezuela.

In the second phase of social policy identified by Wilpert , the govern- ment initiated its medium to long-term policies such as the Land Law, and the credit giving schemes (see above).[91] However, not only did the govern- ment work to distribute land in the countryside, it also worked on urban land reform. Local communities were required to elect land committees to facili- tate the transfer of title deeds to the occupants of slum dwellings, as well as work on the transformation of their neighbourhood. According to Wilpert

5,600 active land committees were established facilitating the transfer of titles to 126,000 families by mid-2005.[92]

As we saw in Chapter 2, the government launched a number of social *misiones*. The impact of these *misiones* overall has been notable, however, statistics are again hard to come by or unreliable, according to PROVEA. While education will be covered in the following section, 'Knowledge', below, this section will look at the flagship 'Into the Neighbourhood' (*Barrio Adentro*) Mission, as well as various Missions on access to food, employment, housing and identity initiatives amongst others.

Barrio Adentro has established health clinics in the poorest areas of Venezuela covered mostly by Cuban medical personnel as part of Venezuelan-Cuban cooperation agreements under ALBA. By 2007, 2,441 new clinics had been built, with a cumulative number of consultations of over 225 million, from its inauguration by President Chávez in 2003. Under this Mission, the government claims that health coverage has increased from 3.5 million Venezuelans in 1998 to 20.5 million in 2007, with the number of doctors increasing from 1,628 to 19,571 during the same period, an increase of 1,102%.[93] *Barrio Adentro* III aims to redress the long historical neglect, including by the current government, of the existing hospital system. An associated Miracle Mission (*Misión Milagro*) provides eye operations for children in Cuban hospitals, and claims to have made over 51,000 interventions, many of them in neighbouring Latin American countries.[94]

Whilst government figures on the achievements of the Missions are extremely positive, a report issued by a number of social organisations in 2007, however, found that access to health remained quite low. Constitutional guarantees of access to health had not been regularised into a governing law. The report found very low levels of coordination between the various organisations delivering health care in Venezuela, such as the above-mentioned Missions, the existing state hospital system, the social security health system, and the private sector. Shortages in equipment and medicines were noted in the new Mission network of community clinics as well as in the existing state system. In general, *per capita* spending has been much lower than that recommended internationally, despite the large rises in spending claimed by the government, and inequities in access to medicine based primarily on income. Immediate action was recommended to redress these shortcomings, starting with a new law ensuring constitutional guarantees are implemented.[95]

The government's principal policy on access to food, Mercal Mission, provides low-cost food stuffs through a state-run store network of 15,743 distribution centres and sales points, benefiting 10 million people and distributing 4,600 tonnes of food daily, according to the government.[96] Community kitchens and other schemes come under this Mission as well, with the community kitchens providing free meals, shelter, educational programmes and basic health care to about 600,000 Venezuelans suffering from extreme poverty.[97]

In employment, Mission Turn Heads (Misión *Vuelvan Caras*) builds on the work of the educational *misiones* by helping their graduates find work (see above) and on land, Mission Zamora encourages families to return to the land as well as providing land for poor families, through land redistribution (see previous section). The Mission Guaicapuro ensures that constitutional rights granted to indigenous communities are put into effect.

The Housing Mission seeks to guarantee the right to housing within a context of low achievement on the part of the Chávez government in solving the pressing housing problems of Venezuelans. The housing deficit in Venezuela is considered to be in the region of 2,800,000 dwellings, according to the Housing Ministry, including replacing existing inadequate or badly situated stock and required new-build.[98] PROVEA estimates that almost 13 million Venezuelans do not live in adequate accommodation, with around 100,000 families joining that number every year.[99] The government's response to this problem have taken various manifestations, but the most recent is the Mission Habitat, launched in 2004, and a new law governing mortgages and state support for home purchasing.[100] In 2006, the government built 56,069 dwellings in total, over 5% more than in the previous year and continuing an upward trend from the low point of 2003. To date, according to PROVEA, over the eight years of the Chávez government (1999–2007), the state has built 193,369 dwellings,[101] nowhere near the quantity needed, a fact admitted by the president on a number of occasions.[102]

Novel mechanisms to solve the housing problem included the signing of a number of agreements to supply housing from the governments of China, Iran, Brazil and Uruguay. Others, following the precepts of the 'participative and protagonic' involvement of Venezuelans in decision-making processes central to the government's political philosophy, has been the involvement of communities through Community Housing Organisations (OCVs) in coordinating and carrying out building activities.

Finally, the Identity Mission aims to ensure that everyone obtains legal identity documents. According to government statistics by February 2007 approximately 21.5 million Venezuelans, or immigrants in irregular citizenship situations, had received identity cards as a result of this Mission.[103] Its importance rests not only in being recognised by the state, but also in terms of access to government services, access to employment and, not least, the right to vote.

Knowledge

The social polarisation characteristic of Venezuelan society previous to Chávez was also reflected in the knowledge structure. One of the difficulties the

Chávez government has faced since coming to power has been in recruiting trained personnel for government. Much of the university sector, a mostly middle-class bastion, remains implacably opposed to the government, and much of their expertise goes to opposition groups. Large parts of state bureaucracy are staffed by sectors hostile to the government. In PdVSA 18,000 management and senior staff took part in the December 2002 strike/lockout. As was noted above, the private sector, particularly larger capital and transnationals, were actively involved in opposition to the government in the form of strikes and other actions.[104] The private media (see Chapter 5) was also at the forefront of the opposition. Finally much of the international community, lead by the US, was also active in supporting the opposition, and many foreign-owned transnationals took part in the strikes.

Whilst the privatisation process had not been as thorough in Venezuela as in other Latin American countries, key sections of the productive apparatus with strategic significance, such as telecommunications, were already in private foreign hands. All these sectors possessed substantial parts of the knowledge structure in Venezuela, and were often actively using their access to it to bring down the government.

The government responded in a number of ways to this adverse situation facing it. First, in education, one of the main planks of the Chávez government's policy is the Bolivarian Schools scheme, first for primary schools and then extended to secondary level, seeking to raise the standards and variety of education and tackle scholarly desertion and even malnutrition. These schools provide day-long tuition with more cultural and sports activities,[105] and they provide children with breakfast, lunch, and a late afternoon snack, regular meals that many poor children often did not receive before. Wilpert states that these schools now serve about 700,000 children or about 17% of all elementary-school children.[106] In general, as a result of government educational policies, the percentage of children in kindergarten went from 53.4% in 1999 to 65.8% in 2006; in primary school from 89.7% in 1999 to 99.5% in 2006; in secondary school from 27.3% to 41%.[107]

Second, it introduced a raft of Missions on education which would help train personnel, more sympathetic to the Bolivarian project, to staff the bureaucracies. The most important of these were Missions Robinson, Ribas and Sucre. Mission Robinson I covers basic literacy and II the completion of primary education. Official sources state that by 2004 over 1.3 million Venezuelans benefited from the programme and that by 2005, Venezuela was 'illiteracy free'.[108] Rodriguez and Ortega, however, using Household Survey Data found that the reduction in illiteracy was moderate 'at most' and given that, expensive.[109]

Mission Ribas aimed to provide schooling to the estimated five million adult Venezuelans who dropped out of secondary education. According to official figures, by April 2007 1,193,478 people had participated in the

Mission with 421,581 graduates.[110] This project is notable also as scholarships of approximately $100 are made available to those most in need, as is the case in Mission Sucre. This Mission, according to official figures, had 383,281 cumulative participants by January 2007 with 81,086 active scholarships awarded. Many of these students were being educated in so-called 'university villages' in smaller towns and cities, bringing third-level education to the people and avoiding migration to the cities. In March 2007, for example, I visited a shopping centre transformed into one of these 'villages' in a town in Miranda State. In total according to the government forty-five of these 'villages' were inaugurated by January 2007.[111]

The government also sought to increase university access for poorer sectors. Enrolment in third-level education increased from 668,109 in 1999 to 1,074,350 by 2006.[112] The government also launched the Bolivarian University to tackle the fall in the admission rates for poor people to universities, standing at only 19% in 1998. The university began its first classes in October 2003 and at the time of writing has five campuses throughout the country. The university is aiming to reach a total enrolment of 100,000 students, but data on actual numbers attending is hard to come by.[113] The university gives classes in medicine, journalism, law and environmental studies,[114] and one of its clear objectives is to contribute 'to the change of the Venezuelan state'.[115] Related to this need to staff the bureaucracies, substantial numbers of personnel for the government were found amongst left-wing academic circles to staff upper management in state bureaucracies.

Third, as we have seen above, the government strengthened its hold over PdVSA, not only in terms of ownership, but also in terms of data-processing and holding. The company responsible for all PdVSA's data-processing needs, INTESA, was found to have close links to the US defence and intelligence industries when the contract was cancelled after the oil strike in 2003.[116] Renationalisations of the largest telecommunications company, CANTV, electricity services and other strategic services ensures protection of data in these sensitive areas.

Fourth, through agreements with Cuba, the government used Cuban personnel to staff some Mission programmes, such as *Barrio Adentro*, where many Venezuelan medical personnel were unsympathetic and unwilling to work. Increased cooperation with other Latin American states, such as Argentina, and further afield in Asia, was used to replace the lost investment and technology traditionally sourced from the US. The government also used state radio and television, and funded and encouraged community-based media to counteract negative coverage from the private media (see Chapter 5). One other initiative of interest, according to Wilpert was the government's decision to change the software used in government departments to free, as opposed to Microsoft-owned software, hence escaping from the 'trap' as Chávez called it of intellectual property.[117]

The overall impact of government socioeconomic policies

First of all, it is important to point to the positive outcomes of the government's economic and social policies. In all four areas, the Chávez government sought to maintain state involvement in key elements of each of the four structures, and so maintain indigenous control of these elements, whilst simultaneously promoting private enterprise and foreign investment from non-traditional sources (i.e. non-US). The government looked to maximise the variety of forms of ownership, increasing credits for previously excluded sectors. In this way, the Chávez government attempted to tip the balance between the state and the market in favour of the former, while favouring more participation of the popular classes.

In the finance structure, the Chávez government maintained tax rates to a large degree, while collection rates were improved substantially. It maximised its control of tax revenue from oil to finance social spending. Simultaneously, it attempted to improve macroeconomic indicators, and pursued a policy of maintaining high foreign reserve levels, and prompt payment of debt. In this way it hoped to keep international financial markets content as the government pursued its long-term strategies, and keep international financial institutions (IFIs) at arms length, particularly the IMF.

In production, the government abandoned privatisation, keeping control of key production apparatuses, such as the oil industry, in the hands of the state and renationalising strategic companies in telecommunications and power. It promoted different ownership types, such as cooperatives and state-owned co-managed enterprises, and put government business towards these newly created enterprises. It pursued a policy of diversification of foreign investment and trade towards Europe and other areas of the South, particularly within Latin America, but also to Asia, most notably China.

In human security, the Chávez government increased social spending significantly, especially in education, and on its Missions. It sought to provide universal coverage and increase popular participation in the structures by which these social goods were provided. These programmes were financed by national resources, led by the national government, and executed through parallel structures from the established bureaucracy and implemented largely through presidential decrees.

The Chávez government sought to reorder the balance in the knowledge structure, which was primarily in private, corporate hands, by encouraging alternative media outlets, increasing access of the popular classes to third-level education and regaining control of key areas of the economy, such as oil and telecommunications.

Thus the government pursued an intensive populist redistributive policy in all four structures, aimed at counteracting the growing dominance of the globalised market, particularly the transnational agents of that market. This

was achieved by an increased protagonism of the state and increased participation of the Venezuelan people.

The results of these policies have been largely positive, at least since 2004.
Economic growth has been amongst the highest in the region, with an
average of 11.85% between 2004 and 2007.[118] Total social spending in
Venezuela has increased substantially during Chávez's tenure in office.
According to the CEPR, total social spending went from 9.4% of GDP in 1999
to 13.6% in 2006. Furthermore, the CEPR stresses that this does not include
social spending by the state oil company, PdVSA, which in 2006 represented
7.3% of GDP, bringing total social spending in that year to 20.9% of GDP. In
effect real social spending per capita has increased threefold since Chávez was
voted into office in 1998.[119] In 2008 social spending accounted for 57% of
total public spending or 18.6% of GDP.

Most areas of spending have increased: official statistics state that
spending on education as a percentage of GDP stood at 5.1% in 2006, as
opposed to 3.4% in the last year of the Caldera government (1998), and
indeed is the highest in a decade.[121] Spending on health has increased from
1.8% of GDP in 2000 to 7.71% in 2006, although most of this spending is
from outside the regular budget, which accounts for only 1.75% of GDP, the
bulk of resources going to the Missions and deriving from PdVSA and other
extra-budgetary sources.[122] Housing, however, still receives low public
support, increasing only from 1% of GDP in 1998 to 1.6% in 2006. Spending
on housing as a percentage of social spending is slightly less than in 1998,
which stood at 11.8% as opposed to 11.6% in 2005 and 2006.[123]

This social spending has had an important impact on social indices.
United Nations Development Programme (UNDP) Human Development
Index statistics show that between 1998 and 2005, Venezuela's international
HDI ranking increased from 0.770 to 0.792.[124] According to official figures
the national HDI index rose from 0.7056 in 1997 to 0.8786 in 2006.[125]
Income poverty was reduced from 44% of the population in the second
semester of 1998 to 31% in the second semester of 2006 and extreme
poverty fell from 17.1% to 9% in the same period.[126] Taking non-cash-based
measures into account it may have been reduced even further. Weisbrot and
Sandoval estimate that health benefits alone could have lowered the rate by a
further 2%.[127] Inequality, measured by the GINI coefficient, also fell, from
0.4865 in 1998 to 0.4200 in 2006.[128]

Venezuela compares well with the rest of the region in both spending and
results. According to CEPAL, the Latin American average for the percentage of
social spending to GDP was 15.9% in 2004–2005, as opposed to Venezuela's
total spend of almost 21% in 2006; average spending on education in the
region for the same period was 4.3% as opposed to Venezuela's 5.1% in
2006, and average health spending was at 3.4% as opposed to Venezuela's
7.71%.[129] Similarly, average poverty levels in the region stood at 35.1% in

2007, with 12.7% in absolute poverty, as opposed to Venezuela's levels of 30.2% and 9.9% respectively in the same year.

An important complaint of liberal commentators, such as Rodriguez and Álvarez,[130] is that the advances in the Venezuelan economy are fuelled by oil. While this is true, it is also true that the entire region has benefited from a worldwide commodities boom in recent years.[131] Economic statistics from CEPAL show a huge boom in mining activity for example, with a growth of 26.8% in 2003, 9.6% in 2004 and 7.7% in 2005.[132] Peru, with one of the higher growth rates in the region, and one of its neo-liberal 'stars', has seen its mining-sector exports grow fourfold from around $1,262 million in 2002 to $4,427.6 million in 2005, providing an explanation for a large part of that growth.[133] In 2005, gold alone took up 17.1% of the value of Peruvian exports and copper 10.7%.[134] The value of Peru's exports of primary products in 2005, accounted for 82.9% of all exports, almost as high as Venezuela's at 90.6%.[135] Yet growth rates are not as impressive as those of Venezuela's, with a 6.9% average during the years 2004–2007,[136] as opposed to 11.85% reported above for Venezuela in the same period. Moreover Peru's social spending in 2004–2005 was 8.9% unlike the much higher levels in Venezuela of 21%. Poverty reduction, in Peru, as a result was not as dramatic as in Venezuela, falling from 54.8% in 2002 to 44.5% in 2006, a reduction of 10.3%, as opposed to Venezuela's reduction of 18.4% during the same period.[137]

While this brief comparative exercise does not pretend to be particularly scientific nor exhaustive, it does point to the need for a comparative context in discussing Venezuela's efforts in economic growth and poverty reduction, which is largely absent from most critics' reviews of its performance in those areas.

Weisbrot and Sandoval discount liberal warnings of an economic crisis looming for Venezuela.[138] Revenue has exceeded spending for most of the years of growth, allowing Venezuela to have a balanced budget, for example, in 2006. The government has conservatively estimated oil prices in its budget setting, and Venezuela has a large amount of currency reserves to draw on in the event of a downturn. Weisbrot and Sandoval, however, do identify, along with Rodríguez, inflation and currency overvaluation as being the major problems facing Venezuela in the future, but because of 'its large current account surplus, large reserves, and low foreign debt, the government has a number of tools available to stabilize and reduce inflation – as well as eventually bringing the currency into alignment – without sacrificing the growth of the economy'.[139]

Finally it should be noted that it is difficult to measure to what extent the Chávez government is responsible for failing to achieve its economic and social objectives in the earlier period (2001–04), due to the (often seditious) nature of the opposition campaign against it. Conversely, the oil boom has without a doubt contributed an inordinate amount to the current upswing in growth and reduction in poverty. Nonetheless, it is spurious to claim, as Rodriguez and Álvarez do, that government policy has had either no effect, or only negative effects on the economy, or on poverty. Nor does either analyst recognise the wider achievements of the Chávez government of reasserting Venezuelan economic sovereignty over the production apparatus.[140]

But these quantative considerations must also be balanced with more qualitative indicators showing increased popular participation in each of the four areas surveyed. In human security alone, the Pan American Health Organisation, in its review of the *Barrio Adentro* Mission, shows an exponential growth in popular participation in governance of the Mission. By 2006 there were 8,951 health committees operating in Venezuela. These committees have an average membership of eleven members, elected by the community, charged with identifying the principal health problems in the community, prioritising them and defining the principal actions which the community must carry out to resolve them and to support the work of local health clinics. Health committees must also liaise with and participate in local communal councils.

This experience is not, as with previous experiences, subordinated to bureaucaratic government structures. The health committee, as one member reports, has been 'the pioneer of everything ... no government entity comes around here to tell us what there is to do ... If it were not for the Health Committee we would not be united as we are at the moment 99 per cent, which is a very beautiful thing'. The result is an instance of autonomous popular political participation which identifies health needs, makes demands of the state to satisfy them and monitors the implementation of these measures.[141] As we have seen, the expansion of cooperatives, worker-controlled enterprises and other forms of social ownership in Venezuela are providing similar participative experiences within the economy.

This is not to say that Venezuela's economy and social policy efforts do not face problems. In terms of the economy, Wilpert identifies three interrelated economic problems: the persistent and increasing dependence on oil for revenue, which in turn funds much of the social programmes; the resultant 'Dutch disease' whereby oil undermines other productive sectors, as under a market system it is cheaper to import goods than to produce them; finally, the applicability of the emerging Bolivarian model outside of an oil-rich nation such as Venezuela, with implications for its long-term sustainability.[142]

Similarly in the social policy area, as in general government policy execution, PROVEA identifies inefficiency in the execution of government policy, lack of coordination between government agencies, improvisation in policy-making, constant changing and rotation of ministers, with often entire new teams being brought along with the new appointees, and, corruption, with a ministerial anti-corruption commission investigating 370 reported cases in 2007.[143] Moreover, Wilpert points to the vulnerability of many social policies as they were introduced through presidential decree rather than parliamentary law, prejudicing their institutionalisation. He also points to the problem of the use of patronage favouring government supporters.[144] While problems such as lack of coordination between ministries, corruption or patronage predate the Chávez era, there is little evidence of a concerted strategy to confront these problems, particularly that of corruption. Others, such as the frequent changing of ministers are as a direct result of the president's own style of governing. These problems are increasingly undermining government support and causing increased frustration amongst the citizenry, including the government's own supporters.[145]

Populism and Bolivarian Venezuela's socio-economic policies

In Chapter 2 we saw how a lack of legitimacy on the part of states to address structural inequalities leaves a gap open in democracies between what Canovan called 'the politics of redemption' and 'the politics of scepticism'.[146] Populist leaders enter through that gap to take power, using strong anti-status-quo discourses to attract support, especially from the popular classes. The failure of ISI policies linked to populism in the 1980s led to that gap being widened and Latin American populaces seeking forms of government which reflected more accurately their desire for participation. In Chapter 3 we saw how Chávez used anti-status-quo discourses to make direct links between himself and the people.

Many analysts identify the Chávez government's socioeconomic policies as being typically populist. Rodríguez for example,[147] claims that they are typical populist macroeconomics, as identified by Rudiger Dornbusch and Sebastian Edwards.[148] Álvarez also concludes that the 'so-called "twenty-first century socialism" will … probably be a radical version of the old and failed recipe of regulations and controls which all of Latin America tried from the 1930s until the 1980s'.[149] In making these judgements, however, both analysts fail to place *chavismo* in context. The Venezuela of the twenty-first century is not Latin America of the 1980s. For a start, over two decades of neoliberal policies, have led, in the majority of cases, to more inequality in Latin American countries and less sovereignty on the part of governments in the region to tackle this growing inequality. This, in turn, has had a knock-on effect on democracy in the region, widening the gap between 'the politics of redemption' and the 'politics of scepticism', as we saw above. The crisis of the 1980s and 1990s in Venezuelan politics and institutions, as explained in Chapter 2, showed the total inability of the Venezuelan elites to tackle this problem in an effective way. Chávez emerged through that gap in response to this failure and as such is a product of Venezuela's particular historical trajectory.

As Ellner points out, furthermore, there are a number of important differences between past populist experiences in the region and Chávez.[150] First, we find a government attempting to widen participation in a more profound and comprehensive manner, promoting community initiative and involvement in policy-making. Land committees, health committees, neighbourhood housing committees and a plethora of other community participation mechanisms not mentioned here, have deepened the democratic involvement of the popular classes in the allocation of scarce public goods.

Second, the Chávez government has gone further than most populist governments in challenging the economic power of the elites, both in terms of ownership and execution. The Land Laws and the expropriation of idle companies, 'reflect the Chávez government's rejection of private property as an absolute right devoid of social responsibilities'.[151] The promotion of alternative forms of distribution and production, such as the Mercal food store network and the different forms of worker-run companies and cooperatives, offer competition to privately run enterprises.

Third, unlike previous populist regimes which emphasised multiclass coalitions, the Chávez government directly challenges middle and upper sectors by prioritising the popular classes both in terms of discourse and policy. As we have seen, social spending has increased dramatically, accompanied by the participatory processes mentioned above, giving new levels of power to the popular classes.

Finally, and importantly, few critics have articulated how any government can NOT follow expansionary policies at the height of a massive oil boom. An equally valid question is if it is possible to build socialism, with its demands for equality and fairness, in the midst of an oil boom driven by market forces.[152] In the Bolivarian revolution there is a concerted effort, through the state, to reconcile these contradictions, by reasserting national sovereignty in policy-making in order to reorder to some extent the structural inequalities compounded by globalisation, without turning its back entirely on the opportunities globalisation presents. Once again there is a strong connection between the leader and the people brought about by these policies, but these links are motivated by ideology as well as through policy.

The Venezuelan government puts inequality at the centre of its political discourse. The Venezuelan state, under the Chávez government actively operates in the market, of goods, services and ideas, to tip the seesaw of market and state to a more balanced equilibrium. The issue of national sovereignty was central to this strategy and it is here that we can understand the origin of the fierce resistance of the 'knowledge-rich' middle classes, many of whom are already deeply integrated into transnational sectors closely linked to the core country economies, especially the US.[153] The Chávez government, therefore, intervened on behalf of ordinary workers, independent 'informal' workers, small businessmen, peasants and indigenous people, in order to further their interests and hence the national interest, reinforcing Venezuela's sovereignty and economic independence in an increasingly globalised world. In this way, it sought to strike a balance not only between the state and the market within Venezuela, but also between the global market and the national market, and the global international structure and Venezuela's national strategic requirements as an independent sovereign nation.

Whether the Chávez project is sustainable in the long term depends greatly on the evolution of the Bolivarian experiment. Much depends, as both Wilpert and Ellner point out, on eradicating the state's 'institutional fragility, inefficiency and corruption'.[154] Furthermore, as Marxist critic Heinz Dietrich asserts, this can only be possible with the democratisation of the Bolivarian movement, renovating its structures to ensure pluralistic debate which can critically evaluate the success and failure of policy strategies and so map out the best way forward.[155] The continued success of the government's socioeconomic policies is equally dependent on such a process.

For most of Chávez's tenure the opposition has only sought the destruction of the Chávez government and has refused to cooperate in a public-spirited manner with it, denying its legitimacy. While this has abated to a certain extent, in that outward use of illegal strategies have been more or less abandoned, the rejection of Chávez still remains constant. Scrutiny of the government's policies in the economic and social areas by an impressive array of analysts linked to the opposition, some of them referred to here, is increasing, building up a strong case against them. Equally, criticism is increasing on the left. Only with reform, rooting out inefficiencies and corruption can this case be answered effectively and in this way the survival of this particular attempt to contest neoliberal hegemony in Latin America be guaranteed.

Conclusion

In this chapter I have attempted to provide a comprehensive review of the socioeconomic policies of the Chávez government up to 2007, eight years after coming to power, using a framework derived from Strange's *States and Markets*. This review has shown the following key characteristics of this policy: a strong policy of redistributivism with a high level of popular participation processes accompanying and guiding its delivery through social policies and a stronger role for the state in the economy with the diversification of management structures, from entire state ownership of key sectors, to co-management of expropriated companies and co-cooperativism, amongst others. Through redistributivism and participation the Chávez government sought to secure its legitimacy and confront the global hegemony of neoliberal globalisation to create a new more socially conscious state form, not only within Venezuela but also within the Latin American region. In this way *chavismo* represents an important ideological challenge to the neoliberal project in one of the regions of the world where it has matured most. In response, one of the chief accusations in the counter-attack by the global neoliberal hegemony against the Chávez government was its alleged anti-democratic nature. It is to that element we turn in the next chapter.

Notes

1 Strange, S., 1994, *States and Markets*, 2nd ed. London and Washington: Pinter.
2 Ibid., p. 90.
3 Ibid., p. 64.
4 Ibid.
5 Ibid., pp. 45–46.
6 Ibid., p. 47.
7 Ibid., p. 117.
8 Ibid., p. 121.
9 Ibid., p. 120.
10 Ellner, S., 2008, *Rethinking Venezuelan Politics: Class, Conflict, and the Chávez Phenomenon*. Boulder, CO and London: Lynne Rienner, pp. 109–139.
11 Ibid., p. 139.
12 In 1998, two-thirds of the population lived below the poverty line, half of these in extreme poverty. There was an extreme concentration of landownership, with 70% of agricultural land in the hands of just 3% of proprietors and the country was not self-sufficient in food production. Unemployment stood at 11% and an estimated 49%, or 4.3 million of the economically active population, was employed in the informal sector, where wages were on average 45% of the salaries of formal sector workers. EIU (Economist Intelligence Unit), 1998, *Venezuela: Country Profile*. London: EIU.
13 Inflation stood at 99.9% in 1996 and at an average of 58% throughout the entire Caldera presidency (1993–1998). BCV (Banco Central de Venezuela), 2004, *Información Estadística*. Available from: www.bcv.org.ve/c2/indicadores.asp. Accessed 27 July 2004. In 1997, the minimum salary was Bs75,000 while the value of the basic basket of goods was Bs168,778 (OCEI (Oficina Central de Estadistica e Informatica)/PNUD (Programa Naciones Unidas para el Desarrollo), 2001, *Informe sobre Desarrollo Humano en Venezuela, 2000: Caminos para superar la probreza*. Caracas: CDB Publicaciones, p. 165). Per capita income stood in 1997 at US$2885, as opposed to US$4910 in 1993, the year before Caldera came to power (ibid., p. 92).
14 41% of Venezuelan banks had passed into foreign hands by 1997, the State telecommunications company CANTV, the steel industry, and VIASA, the state airline (which has since disappeared) were all privatised.
15 Buxton, J., 2003, 'Economic policy and the rise of Hugo Chávez', in S. Ellner and D. Hellinger (eds), *Venezuelan Politics in the Chávez Era: Class, Polarization, and Conflict*. Boulder, CO and London: Lynne Rienner, pp. 113–130.
16 Blanco Muñoz, A., 1998, *Venezuela del 04F-92 al 06D-98: Habla el Comandante Hugo Chávez Frias*. Caracas: Catedra 'Pio Tamayo' CEHA/IIES/FACES/Universidad Central de Venezuela (UCV).

17 Ibid., p. 612.
18 Ibid., p. 19.
19 Rodríguez, F., 2003, 'Las consecuencias económicas de la revolución bolivariana', in *Revista Nueva Económia*, 19 April: 85–142, p. 91.
20 Ibid.
21 Ibid., p. 92.
22 Kelly, J., 2000, 'Thoughts on the constitution: realignment of ideas about the economy and changes in the political system in Venezuela', prepared for delivery at the 2000 meeting of the Latin American Studies Association, Hyatt Regency, Miami 16–18 March. Available from: www-personal.umich.edu/~mmarteen/svs/lecturas/lasa2000/kelly2.htm. Accessed 3 August 2004. The Central Bank, for example, remains independent and rules are included to ensure fiscal responsibility and monetary control, although Chávez attempted to eliminate it in the constitutional amendments proposed and defeated in 2007 in a referendum on the issue.
23 Kelly, 2000, No page reference. Article 299, for example, established the socio-economic system of Venezuela as based on 'social justice, democratisation, efficiency, free competition, protection of the environment, productivity and solidarity'. Article 311, insists that ordinary income must cover ordinary spending. Article 318 establishes Central Bank autonomy and Article 319 the norms that it must adhere to (*Constitución de la Republica Bolivariana de Venezuela*, 1999. Available from: www.constitucion.ve. Accessed 10 June 2008).
24 Wilpert, G., 2007, *Changing Venezuela by Taking Power: The History and Policies of the Chávez Government*. London and New York: Verso.
25 Álvarez, A., 2007, 'Venezuela 2007: Los Motores de la Revolución se alimentan con Petróleo', in *Revista de Ciencia Política: Edición Especial 2007*, pp. 265–289. Available from: www.scielo.cl/pdf/revcipol/v27nEsp/art16.pdf. Accessed 10 June 2007, p. 266.
26 Wilpert, *Changing Venezuela by Taking Power*, p. 240.
27 Lander, E. and Navarette, P., 2007, *The Economic Policy of the Latin American Left in Government: Venezuela* – Briefing Paper 2007:02. Amsterdam: TransNational Institute. Available from: www.tni.org. Accessed 5 June 2008, pp. 31–32.
28 SENIAT (Servicio Nacional Integrado de Administración Aduanera y Tributaria), 2004. *Bolétin Mensual No. 39*. Available from: www.seniat.gov.ve. Accessed 19 July 2004; SENIAT, 2007, 'Informe de Recaudación Gerencia de Estudios Economicos Tributarios Diciembre 2007'. Available from: www.seniat.gov.ve. Accessed 27 February 2008, p. 28.
29 Ibid.
30 Weisbrot, M. and Sandoval, L., 2007, *The Venezuelan Economy in the Chávez Years*. Available from: www.cepr.org. Accessed 5 June 2008, p. 8.
31 Ibid., note 18.
32 Rodríguez, 'Las consecuencias económicas', p. 30.
33 *Constitución Bolivariana*, 1999, Article 303.
34 Wilpert, *Changing Venezuela by Taking Power*, pp. 222–223.
35 Lander and Navarette, *The Economic Policy of the Latin American Left*, p. 26.
35 MEF, 2006, 'Gobierno Central Presupuestario 2006'. Available from: www.mf.gov.ve/archivos/2000020201/Presentaci%F3n%20GCP%20A%D1O%200 06.pdf. Accessed 5 June 2008.
37 Rodríguez, 'Las consecuencias económicas', Table 6, pp. 16–18.
38 ECLAC, 2008, *Estudios Economico de America Latina y el Caribe, 2007–2008*. Available from: www.eclac.cl. Accessed 25 August 2008, Table 1: Principales Indicadores Economicas, p. 4.

39   Wilpert, *Changing Venezuela by Taking Power*, p. 84.

40   Own calculations based on BCV, *Información Estadística*, 2004.

41   BCV (Banco Central de Venezuela), 2008, *Información Estadística: Reservas Internacionales y Servicio de la Deuda Pública*. Available from: www.bcv.org.ve/cuadros/2/231.asp?id=32. Accessed 10 June 2008.

42   Wilpert, G., 2004, 'IMF says Venezuela's economy will grow 8.8% in 2004'. Available from: www.venezuelanalysis.com/news.php?newsno=1257. Accessed 27 April 2004. The article quotes finance minister Tobias Nobrega responding to IMF growth predictions for 2004: 'Venezuela is overcoming its financial difficulties independently of the IMF and it is doing this by applying the opposite of what is recommended by the well-known but limited IMF recipes.' Indeed the feeling was mutual: the IMF was one of the first organisations to welcome the coup-installed government of Pedro Carmona Estanga (See Union Radio, 2002, 'FMI ofrece colaboración a nuevo gobierno venezolano', Friday 12 April. Available from: www.unionradio.com.ve. Accessed 10 June 2008).

43   Reserves stood at US$14,849 million in 1998, the year before Chávez came to power, and fluctuated from a low of US$9,823 million in February 2002, reflecting a period of intense political activity which culminated in the April 2002 coup, to a high of US$23,453 million in May 2004, the latter figure primarily due to the currency controls implemented shortly after the ending of the strike/lockout of 2002/03, to stem capital flight. In 2007, total international reserves stood at $34,286 billion, an historic high reflecting the high price of oil and increased state revenue (BCV, *Informacion Estadistica*, 2008).

44   BCV, *Información Estadística*, 2004.

45   Weisbrot and Sandoval, *The Venezuelan Economy*, p. 16.

46   Rivas, E., 2004, 'A Venezuelan miracle?' Available from: www.venezuelanalysis.com/articles.php?artno=1098. Accessed 3 February 2004.

47   BCV, *Información Estadistica*, 2008.

48   SISOV/ Sistema Integrado de Indicadores Sociales de Venezuela, 2008. 'Indicadores; Precios; Tasa de Inflación'. Available from: www.sisov.mpd.gob.ve/indicadores/. Accessed 10 June 2008. Own calculation based on figures for Metropolitan area of Caracas, 1999–2003.

49   Lander and Navarette, *The Economic Policy of the Latin American Left*, p. 43, note 10.

50   CEPAL, 2006, *Anuario Estadistico de America Latina y el Caribe: Estadisticas Economicas*. Available from: www.cepal.org. Accessed 10 May 2008, p. 295.

51   Wilpert, G., 2003. 'Mission impossible? Venezuela's mission to fight poverty'. Available from: www.venezuelanalysis.com/articles.php?artno=1051. Accessed 11 November 2003.

52   One report from 2004 estimated that bad debt in all the different government social banks was in the region of 37% of all loans. O'Donoghue, P. J., 2004. 'Flagship government non status banking system losing bad debt battle'. Available from: www.Vheadline.com. Accessed 14 July 2004.

53   Wilpert, *Changing Venezuela by Taking Power*, p. 77.

54   *Constitución Bolivariana*, 1999.

55   Of this oil activity went from 3.2% to −10.7%, and non-oil activity from 3.0% to −8.0%.

56   BCV, *Información Estadística*, 2004. Taking 1984 as base year.

57   Own calculations based on data from Weisbrot and Sandoval, *The Venezuelan Economy*, p. 7.

58   Carlson, C., 2007. 'Venezuela enters fifth consecutive year of growth'. Available from: www.venezuelanalysis.com. Accessed 8 March 2008.

59 Rodríguez, F., 2008, 'An empty revolution: the unfulfilled promises of Hugo Chávez', *Foreign Affairs* 87(2) March–April. Available from: www.foreignaffairs.org/20080301faessay87205/francisco-rodriguez/an-empty-revolution.html. Accessed 10 June 2008.

60 Álvarez, 'Venezuela 2007', p. 268.

61 Ibid., p. 269.

62 SISOV, Sistema Integrado de Indicadores Sociales de Venezuela, 2008, 'Indicadores: Producción, Empleo y Precios'. Available from: www.sisov.mpd.gob.ve/indicadores/EM0301800000000/. Accessed 10 June 2008.

63 Ibid. 'Necesidades y Demandas de Trabajo: Ocupados en el Sector Informal'. Available from: www.sisov.mpd.gob.ve/indicadores/EM0200900000000/. Accessed 10 June 2008. PROVEA, however, maintain that this may have been due to change in the definition of 'informality'. See PROVEA, 2007, *Informe Anual 2006–2007*. Available from: www.derechos.ve.org. Accessed 10 June 2008, p. 109.

64 PROVEA, 2003, *Situación de los Derechos Humanos en Venezuela: Informe Annual Octubre 2002/Septiembre 2003: Las muertas de abril*. Available from: www.derechos.org.ve/. Accessed 9 January 2004, p. 123.

65 MINCI (Ministerio de Communicación y Información de Venezuela), 2004, *Gestión del Gobierno*. Available from: www.minci.gov.ve/logros.asp?t=1. Accessed 24 July 2004.

66 PROVEA, *Informe Anual 2006–2007*, p. 111.

67 CEPAL, 2007, *Economic Survey of Latin America and the Caribbean: Statistical Apendix*. Available from: www.eclac.cl. Accessed 11 June 2008, Table A-28, p. 315.

68 SISOV/Sistema Integrado de Indicadores Sociales de Venezuela, 2008, 'Indicadores; Salario Minimo'. Available from: www.sisov.mpd.gob.ve/indicadores/EM0400300000000/. Accessed 11 June 2008.

69 PROVEA, *Informe Anual 2006–2007*, p. 110.

70 Ibid., pp. 118–119.

71 See Ellner, S., 2003, 'Organised labor and the challenge of Chavismo', in Ellner and Hellinger (eds), *Venezuelan Politics in the Chávez Era*, pp. 161–178.

72 Ibid., p. 172.

73 AN (Asamblea Nacional)/OAEF (Oficina de Asesoría Económica y Financiera), 2003. 'Impacto de la Huelga General sobre las perspectivas Economicas y Fiscales para 2003 en Venezuela'. Available from: www.oaef.gov.ve/publicaciones2/Informes/Analisis/2003/Finanzas/ia%200303-054%20impacto%20del%20paro%20civico.pdf. Accessed 3 August 2004, p. 3.

74 PROVEA, *Informe Anual 2006–2007*, p. 123.

75 Ibid., p. 203. The process however has not been without conflict, as much land deemed to be in public hands was claimed by private landholders. PROVEA reported in 2004 that approximately twenty peasants were murdered by unknown agents, presumed to be acting for landholders (see PROVEA, *Situación de los Derechos Humanos en Venezuela*, p. 238). In PROVEA's 2007 report, violence against peasants has been reduced, and arrests and prosecutions of perpetrators have increased, but the threat remains including that of kidnapping (PROVEA, *Informe Anual 2006–2007*, p. 214).

76 Ibid., p. 205.

77 Ibid.

78 Ibid., p. 55.

79 Ibid., p. 56.

80 Acuerdo Social, 2004. 'Sector Privado – Indicadores Sabía usted que …'. Available from: www.acuerdosocial.com/index.asp?spg_id=33. Accessed 8 July 2004.

81 Weisbrot and Sandoval, *The Venezuelan Economy*, p. 7.

82 Buxton, 'Economic policy and the rise of Hugo Chávez', p. 124.

83 PROVEA, *Informe Anual 2006–2007*, p. 110.
84 Ibid., pp. 115–116.
85 Robert Plummer, 2008, 'Chávez in pre-election cash spree', 26 May. Available from: www.news.bbc.co.uk. Accessed 3 June 2008.
86 MERCOSUR (Mercado Común del Sur) is the 'Common Market of the South' including Brazil, Paraguay, Uruguay and Argentina as founding members, with Venezuela due to become a full member once ratified by parliaments of founding members. Bolivia and Chile have associate status.
87 See Chapter 7 for a more detailed discussion on Venezuelan trade policy
88 Wilpert 'Mission impossible?'.
89 Gable, D., 2004, 'Civil society, social movements, and participation in Venezuela's Fifth Republic'. Available from: www.venezuelanalysis.com/articles.php?artno=1103. Accessed 9 February 2004.
90 Wilpert, 'Mission impossible?'.
91 Ibid.
92 Wilpert, *Changing Venezuela by Taking Power,*
93 Ibid., pp. 27–28.
94 Ibid.
95 Observatorio Comunitario por el derecho a la Salud, 2007. *Derecho a la Salud en Venezuela 2007: Situación del Derecho a la Atención Sanitaria.* Available from: www.derechos.org.ve/Informe_derecho_Salud_2007_.pdf. Accessed 28 April 2008.
96 See government website for Mercal Mission at www.mercal.gov.ve.
97 Wilpert, *Changing Venezuela by Taking Power,* p. 142.
98 PROVEA, *Informe Anual 2006–2007*, p. 219
99 Ibid., p. 220.
100 Wilpert, *Changing Venezuela by Taking Power,* p. 137.
101 PROVEA, *Informe Anual 2006–2007*, p. 220.
102 Wilpert, *Changing Venezuela by Taking Power,* p. 138
103 MINCI (Ministerio del Poder Popular para la Comunicación y la Información), 2007, *Misiones Bolivarianas Caracas: Coleción Temas de Hoy.* Available from: www.minci.gov.ve. Accessed 21 November 2007, p. 51.
104 Most of the main private banks and transnationals, such as McDonalds, took part in the December 2002/February 2003 strike/lockout. Fieldwork observation.
105 Most Venezuelan public schools, as indeed in many other Latin American countries, have *turnos* or two intakes of children in the morning and afternoon.
106 Wilpert, *Changing Venezuela by Taking Power,* p. 122.
107 PROVEA, *Informe Anual 2006–2007*, pp. 89–92.
108 Wilpert, *Changing Venezuela by Taking Power,* p. 124.
109 Rodriguez, F. and Ortega, D., 2006, 'Freed from illiteracy? A closer look at Venezuela's Robinson Literacy Campaign'. Available from: http://frrodriguez.web.wesleyan.edu/. Accessed 10 March 2008.
110 MINCI, 2008, 'Nueve años de revolución: estadisticas de los aspectos sociales' – Presentación. Available from: http://minci.gob.ve/especiales/22/40274/. Accessed 11 June 2008.
111 All statistics, MINCI, *Misiones Bolivarianas Caracas*, p. 25.
112 MINCI, 'Nueve años de revolución'.
113 PROVEA, *Informe Anual 2006–2007*, pp. 92–93.
114 Wilpert *Changing Venezuela by Taking Power,* , p. 128
115 Ibid., p. 219.
116 Ibid., p. 98.
117 Ibid., p. 102.

118 Weisbrot and Sandoval, *The Venezuelan Economy*, p. 7.
119 Ibid., p. 9.
120 SISOV, 2009, 'Indicadores: Total / Gasto público social como porcentaje del PIB', www.sisov.gov.ve. Accessed 9 April 2009.
121 PROVEA, 2007, p. 86.
122 PAHO (Pan American Health Organisation), 2006, *Barrio Adentro: Derecho a la Salud y a la Inclusión Social en Venezuela*. Caracas: Organización Panamericana de Salud. Available from: www.ops-oms.org.ve. Accessed 10 March 2008, p. 15.
123 SISOV, 2008, 'Indicadores; Gasto público en vivienda como porcentaje del gasto social'. Available from: www.sisov.mpd.gob.ve/indicadores/VI0301600000000/ Accessed 11 June 2008.
124 UNDP, 2000, *Human Development Report 2000*, p. 179; and UNDP, 2007, *Human Development Report 2007*, p. 230. Available from: www.undp.org. Accessed 11 June 2008.
125 MINCI, 'Nueve años de revolución'.
126 Weisbrot and Sandoval, *The Venezuelan Economy*, p. 10.
127 Ibid., p. 9.
128 MINCI, 'Nueve años de revolución'.
129 CEPAL, 2007, *Social Panorama of Latin America 2007: Briefing Paper*. Santiago: ECLAC. Available from: http://eclac.cl/ Accessed 10 March 2008, p. 24.
130 Rodríguez, 'An empty revolution'; Álvarez, 'Venezuela 2007'.
131 UNCTAD (United Nations Conference on Trade and Development), 2007, *Trade and Development Report 2007*. Available from: www.unctad.org. Accessed 12 March 2008, p. 7.
132 CEPAL, *Anuario Estadistica de America Latina y el Caribe*, p. 93.
133 Ibid., p. 219.
134 Ibid., p. 214.
135 Ibid., p. 186.
136 CEPAL, 2007, *Preliminary Overview of the Economies of Latin America and the Caribbean: Statistical Annex*. Available from: http://eclac.cl/publicaciones/xml/4/31994/Statistical_Annex.pdf. Accessed 11 June 2008, Table A-2, p. 156, own calculations.
137 Ibid. Own calculations based on poverty statistics provided in Table 1, p. 11.
138 Weisbrot and Sandoval, *The Venezuelan Economy*.
139 Ibid., p. 2.
140 Wilpert, *Changing Venezuela by Taking Power*, p. 69.
141 Organización de Panamerican de Salud, 2006. *Barrio Adentro: Derecho a la salud e inclusión social en Venezuela*. Caracas: OPS. Available from: www.paho.org. Accessed 2 September 2008, pp. 40–43.
142 Ibid., pp. 102–103.
143 PROVEA, *Informe Anual 2006–2007*, p. 22.
144 Wilpert, *Changing Venezuela by Taking Power*, pp. 147–148.
145 Ibid., pp. 23–24.
146 Canovan, M., 1999, 'Trust the people! Populism and the two faces of democracy', in *Political Studies* XLVII: 2–16.
147 Rodríguez, 'An empty revolution'.
148 Dornbusch, R. and Edwards S. (eds), 1991, *The Macroeconomics of Populism in Latin America*. Chicago: University of Chicago Press.
149 Álvarez, 'Venezuela 2007', p. 274.
150 Ellner, *Rethinking Venezuelan Politics*.
151 Ibid., p. 132.
152 Thanks to Julia Buxton for these observations.

153 Blanco Muñoz, *Venezuela del 04F-92 al 06D-98*, states for example that 'the immense majority of our great team of Venezuelan economists today subscribe to neoliberalism', p. 618.
154 Wilpert, *Changing Venezuela by Taking Power*; Ellner, *Rethinking Venezuelan Politics*.
155 Dietrich, H., 2007, 'Derrota estratégica en Venezuela; peligro mortal para Bolivia y Cuba', 3 December. Available from: www.aporrea.org. Accessed 10 March 2008.

5 Democrat or authoritarian? Democracy in Bolivarian Venezuela in comparative perspective

Introduction

So far in this study, we have seen how historical structural fractures in Venezuela created the conditions which led to a crisis of legitimacy for the Punto Fijo political system (Chapter 2). This legitimacy crisis caused gaps to widen between the Venezuelan people and governments, facilitating the emergence of Chávez. In power, Chávez has sought legitimacy through economic, social and political policies which increase participation and therefore help secure hegemony (Chapters 3 and 4). These polices, however, as Laclau and Mouffe suggest, may lead to forms of 'totalitarianism' which negate the 'logic of democracy' inherent in the widening of popular participation.[1]

Chávez has been repeatedly accused of authoritarianism, principally by opposition leaders but also by many foreign supporters of the opposition and even amongst some on the left. In this chapter, we will examine more fully this dichotomy between democracy and authoritarianism in the Chávez government. Specifically we will seek to answer two key interrelated questions: to what extent is the Chávez presidency democratic, and to what extent has it achieved legitimacy?

Furthermore, in order to provide a broader context in which to seek answers to these questions, it is useful to bring in a comparative element to the discussion. Chávez has sometimes been compared with another Latin American president branded as both populist and authoritarian, Alberto Fujimori of Peru (1990–2001). Both presidents have been accused of authoritarianism, yet both presidents came to power through democratic means. Both presidents furthermore based their discourse on a celebration of the 'people' against a corrupt and corrupting system. Both therefore raise questions about concepts of democracy and authoritarianism within the context of populism.

To facilitate the comparison therefore this chapter will use a framework based on ideas on democracy found in Rueschemeyer et al. and Dahl, which encompasses five key policy areas generally accepted as indicative of democracy: electoral law and practice, presidential authority and institutional autonomy, human rights, media freedom and the right to information, and associational autonomy.[2] At the end of this examination we should have a clearer picture of the Chávez government's attitudes and behaviour in these areas enabling us to evaluate the extent of the president's democratic legitimacy. First of all, however, let us look more closely at the theoretical basis of our comparison between Fujimori and Chávez.

Fujimori and Chávez as *democraduras*[3]

There is a substantial literature referring to the democratic/authoritarian hybridity of the Fujimori government. Sinesio López wrote of the Fujimori government as a 'formal dictatorship in constitutional democracy' in other words a '*democradura*'.[4] Mauceri wrote of it as an 'autocratic democracy'.[5] Conaghan refers to *fujimorismo* as a hybrid that combines 'some of the formalities of a democratic system with non-democratic practices'.[6] Similar ambivalence is found in discussions on the Chávez government. Cameron recommends comparison with 'Juan Perón in Argentina or Alberto Fujimori in Peru'.[7] Freedom House rated both Peru and Venezuela as 'partially free' in 1999, with a rating of 5 for political rights and 4 for civil liberties for Peru, and 4/4 for Venezuela, a score which remains unchanged today.[8]

Most comparisons made between Fujimori and Chávez emphasise their supposed shared authoritarianism. Tanaka states, for example, that: 'Fujimori as much as Chávez [took] advantage of institutional reforms which, while they were formally democratic, constitute authoritarian governments in practice'.[9] More specifically, these accusations centre on two areas: human rights and institutions. Attacks on the media are emphasised, as are the use of threatening and insulting language against the opposition. The 'colonising, substituting, closing and eliminating' of institutions, the minimal role given to parties, and the use of the armed forces for support have all been cited as dangers to the independence of institutions.[10] Grompone[11] and McClintock[12] both regard the Fujimori regime as authoritarian, while Naím and Caballero regard Chávez similarly.[13] In both cases the norm amongst opponents of these presidents is to refer to them in language pertinent to authoritarianism: 'dictator', 'tyrant' etc. Donald Rumsfeld, secretary for defence for much of the US presidential administration of George W. Bush (2000–2008) famously compared Chávez with Hitler.

Yet, both governments also display traits that can only be identified as democratic; both presidents were elected with large majorities, both introduced new constitutions which were approved by the people in referendums, both went on to be re-elected with large majorities under the new constitutions. Chávez indeed has won three presidential elections (1998, 2000, 2006) and a recall referendum against his rule (2004). Under both presidents Peru and Venezuela had institutions normally associated with democracies; courts, elected assemblies, full universal suffrage, political parties, 'free' media, etc. In polls Venezuelans have expressed some of the highest levels of satisfaction with their democracy in Latin America. In the annual report published by the repected Chilean polling firm Lationbarómetro in 2007, 59% of Venezuelans surveyed pronounced themselves satisfied with their democracy, the second highest in the region after Uruguay with 66%, and well above the regional average of 37%.[14] Similarly, poll ratings for Fujimori were consistently high, particularly during his first term as president. Surely under such circumstances these rulers could not be judged 'dictators' or 'tyrants' as the above-mentioned critics charge?

Measuring democracy: a theoretical framework

Rueschemeyer et al. conceived of democracy as based on three principles: (i) regular, free and fair elections of representatives with universal and equal suffrage; (ii) responsibility of the state apparatus to the elected parliament; and (iii) freedom of expression and association as well as the protection of individual rights against arbitrary state action.[15] If a regime ranked near zero in the first two dimensions it was, according to the authors, an *authoritarian* regime, if in all three, *totalitarian*.

A democracy would be considered restrictive if the stipulated conditions are met to a large extent but: (i) significant sectors of the population are excluded though suffrage restrictions; (ii) responsiveness of government is significantly reduced, through say military interventions or political pacts; and/or (iii) limitations of the freedom of expression and association significantly narrow the range of articulated political parties, for example, though their prescription.[16] Furthermore, Reuschemeyer et al. lay emphasis on the centrality of the need for participation of the marginalised and excluded in the political process as a fundamental part of the democratisation process.[17]

Dahl also considered that the following 'institutions' must be present to establish effective participation in a democracy: (i) elected officials; (ii) inclusive suffrage; (iii) right to run for office; (iv) freedom of expression; (v) alternative information; and (vi) associational autonomy.[18] Thus a comparative framework based on these writings would look something like that shown in Table 5.1.

In the following sections, using this framework, we will analyse these key policy areas for both governments. To avoid overextending our examination we will limit it to the first five years of both presidencies, 1990 and 1995 for Fujimori and 1998 to 2003 for Chávez, but with further information on

Table 5.1   *Democracy and participation*

Rueschemeyer et al. (1992)/Dahl (1989)	Policy area
1 Free and fair elections of representatives with universal and equal suffrage	a Electoral law and practice
2 Responsibility of the state apparatus to the elected parliament	b Presidential authority and institutional autonomy
3 Freedom of expression and association as well as the protection of individual rights against arbitrary state action	c Human rights d Media freedom and the right to information e Associational autonomy

Chávez offered after that cut-off date to provide added support to the main arguments.

Authoritarianism and democracy in the governments of Fujimori and Chávez

a) Electoral law and practice

A number of elections and referenda were held during both presidencies, however, due to space considerations this section will concentrate on the general elections held in Venezuela in 2000 and in Peru in 1995, with a brief update in the case of Venezuela. In both cases these were the first major elections for each president under new constitutions (see following section). In both cases also there were accusations of electoral fraud. However, these accusations were much more acute and sustained in the case of the 1995 elections in Peru. Furthermore, the Peruvian elections were held as part of a process of change which was initiated under the auspices of a self-coup (*autogolpe*) and in the aftermath of a prolonged guerrilla war.[19]

Two key conditions governed the 1995 Peruvian elections – the control by the Armed Forces of large swathes of territories through emergency powers granted due to the Sendero Luminoso War and the centralisation of development project funds in the presidency and directed at key electoral areas. According to Montoya, 47% of the Peruvian population lived (in 1995) in emergency zones, under the control of the armed forces, encompassing almost 21% of the electorate, mostly in rural areas.[20] This situation allowed the government to 'discourage' opposition party militants from campaigning in these areas as well as using peasants organised under military controlled vigilante groups (*rondas campesinas*) to campaign for the government.[21] It also allowed Fujimori to use his position as head of state within these areas to recruit state officials, political authorities and, above all, sectors of the armed forces, as his campaigning agents.[22] The position of the army as distributors of food and construction aid, on which many peasants in these areas relied, enabled them to put pressure on locals to vote for Fujimori.

Schady develops this last point further.[23] He identified a concentration of resources in the ministry for the presidency and the use of development programme funds as being key tools used by Fujimori to gain votes. Such expenditure was directly attributable to the president according to polls and the president spent large amounts of time opening projects funded by such expenditure in these key electoral areas.[24]

In the event Planas noted severe discrepancies in the voting pattern for congressional seats in the 1995 elections.[25] Almost 40.80% of votes cast in the congressional elections were cast as spoiled votes, as opposed to 8.72% spoiled in the concurrent presidential vote. The spoiling of these votes was never satisfactorily explained, having been attributed to technical problems by the Electoral Board, and subsequently pursued little by the opposition.[26] Planas notes, like Montoya, that the root of the problem lay in 'the management of institutions and state concerns to guarantee the continuity in power of Fujimori leaving very little room for pluralism and political liberty for those sectors opposing the regime'.[27] In other words these elections, instead of marking the beginning of a new democratic era, marked a continuation and deepening of the authoritarian dynamic which had started with the *autogolpe* of 1992.

Nevertheless the OAS in the executive report of its electoral observation mission, while acknowledging most of these complaints and the particular conditions under which the elections were held, voiced little criticism of the process.[29] In general, the OAS felt that complaints were dealt with adequately, and that many of the other problems noted such as delays in the setting up of polls and getting the vote started were normal problems and 'were not a widespread factor that could have compromised the outcome'.[30] Furthermore, the vote for the government was impressive with 62.4% of votes for Fujimori and 52.10% of votes going to the president's movement Cambio-90-Nueva Mayoría. Few questioned the clear support given to the president by the electorate and the unquestioned legitimacy that this entailed. The 1995 elections were the final test of the full return to democracy in elections that were 'more or less clean'.[31]

The Venezuelan 2000 elections were also held in an atmosphere of considerable mistrust. Kornblith reports a situation of 'judicial, institutional and organisational advantage in favour of government candidates, and insecurity for the rest of the participants'.[32] Many of the institutions designed to guarantee fairness and equity, including the Supreme Tribunal of Justice (TSJ), the Attorney General, the People's Defender, and the National Election

Council (CNE), were chosen by congressional committee rather than with the popular participation that the constitution required, creating an atmosphere of insecurity with regard to legal guarantees.[33] Furthermore, a number of serious technical and electoral roll problems were detected before the elections scheduled for the 28 May, heightening the tension and mistrust already palpable since the election of Chávez in 1998.

Nonetheless, the Chávez government accepted a court ruling brought by a number of NGOs to postpone the elections to 30 July, and took advantage of the intervening time to change the composition of the CNE and correct the technical problems. The OAS noted that the deficiencies and difficulties were rectified 'creating credibility and confidence in the new electoral authorities' and that actions on the part of NGOs, the People's Defender and the Attorney General inspired 'a climate of transparency and confidence in the electoral process, which in the Mission's opinion, is an indication of the strong democratic political culture that prevails in Venezuela'.[34]

Furthermore, some commentators who questioned the legitimacy of the vote, such as Miriam Kornblith, cited above, had clear links to the opposition. Kornblith was attached to AD, one of the two main *puntofijista* political parties and led the pre-Chávez electoral council in Venezuela. In general during the Punto Fijo era electoral fraud was extremely common and much easier to carry out as elections were not automated then, as was the case in the 2000 vote.[35] Kornblith's claims that there was electoral fraud in 2000 must be treated cautiously therefore, especially considering that the OAS concluded that the 'electoral process culminating in the July 30 vote must be considered valid overall'.[36]

Therefore, we have a similar situation in both elections in that critics of the government contradict the OAS's findings. The evidence suggests that in Peru, however, the elections were held in an atmosphere where the full power and weight of the state was used much more comprehensively to ensure the re-election of Fujimori. In Venezuela, greater doubts remain if there had been an attempt to skew the election results in favour of the government, as Kornblith maintains. Furthermore, a robust and vigilant opposition, media and civil society campaign and the vigilance of the international observation organisations guarded against any attempt there may have been to ensure a fraudulent outcome on behalf of the Venezuelan government. Media coverage was 'critical of the government and the election authorities' and broad freedom of expression and assembly were found,[37] as opposed to Peru where much of the media was 'unambiguously aligned with the [Fujimori] administration'.[38] In 2000, Chávez did not yet have the full weight of the state behind him as he did not have the time advantages of Fujimori to establish himself as completely in power, and Fujimori had comprehensively crushed the opposition in the 1992 self-coup.[39]

Fujimori's greater grip on power is reflected in the greater scale of the reported fraud in Peru 1995, and the effective disenfranchisement of large sectors of the population in the emergency areas due to the coercion of poorer sectors by the military. In Venezuela, on the other hand, reports indicate that there was little or no intimidation of electors to vote in favour of the governing party, allowing people to effectively vote freely, indeed the OAS reports that 'military personnel demonstrated … a generally co-operative and friendly attitude towards voters and other players in the process'.[40] Nonetheless, abstention rates in Venezuela were exceptionally high for most of the 1990s, a trend that has continued under Chávez, virtually disenfranchising large proportions of the population.[41] Moreover, manipulation of electoral rules to favour governing parties was commonplace during the Punto Fijo era and has been availed of equally by the Chávez government.

In sum, while there is disquiet about the manner in which both elections were held, there is little doubt that the results were a reflection of the will of the people. Both presidents were extremely popular before the respective elections and had high levels of legitimacy with the population. However, comparatively speaking the evidence suggests that there were greater levels of political pluralism and electoral fairness in the 2000 elections in Venezuela than in Peru 1995.

Subsequent elections in Venezuela repeated this trend of questioning of election procedures and results by the opposition as opposed to general, if often qualified, acceptance and approval of these elections by international observers. One of the most bitter of these was the recall referendum called by the opposition against Chávez in 2004. In the referendum 59.25% voted No to removing Chávez from office, while 40.74% voted in favour, with 30.02% abstention. Immediately the opposition disputed the result, citing exit polls claiming a victory for the opposition, fixing of the electronic voting machines, and disparities between the numbers who signed the petition in favour of recalling the president and the numbers that actually voted for it in some areas. These claims were synthesised in a paper presented by opposition linked academics Ricardo Haussman of Harvard and Roberto Rigobon of the Massachusetts Institute of Technology (MIT).[42] The Washington-based Center for Economic and Policy Research, however, comprehensively refuted the Haussman/Rigobon report as being deeply flawed methodologically and totally unsubstantiated.[43] In the event, international observers such as the Carter Centre and the OAS did not accept opposition accusations of fraud and the elections were generally considered to be fair and free.[44]

By the 2006 presidential elections this opposition attitude had changed quite considerably. A unified opposition candidate was agreed, Governor Manuel Rosales of Zulia State, with full opposition participation in the campaign. Chávez won the contest handsomely, with 62.84% of the vote, as opposed to Rosales's 36.9%. The elections also had one of the lowest abstention rates in recent Venezuelan history with only 25.3%. Furthermore, Rosales immediately accepted defeat. This caused the European Union Election Observation Mission to report:

> The electoral process complied in general with international standards and with national legislation as regards the management of the electoral administration and the electronic voting system. The high turnout in the Presidential Elections, and the peaceful environment in which they were held, together with the candidates' acceptance of results, open the way forward to improvements in the confidence that the general public has in the electoral processes, as well as their quality, and to dialogue between the main institutional and political stakeholders in the country.[45]

In general therefore, despite opposition claims, international observation missions from the US (Carter Centre), the Americas (OAS) and Europe (the European Union) have consistently accepted the generally free and fair nature of elections in Venezuela, despite misgivings on some procedures and the use of state resources in campaigning.

b) Presidential authority and institutional autonomy

One of the principal points of comparison between Fujimori and Chávez, according to critics, is in their dominance of institutions in order to use them for the perpetuation of power. According to this view, both presidents pursued similar policies of centralisation of power in the hands of the executive at the expense of other branches of government. This section will review the writing of new constitutions, the independence of the judiciary, and the situation of the military, among other issues, to measure the extent of institutional autonomy in both countries.

The Fujimori government, according to Grompone, sought from the beginning to establish an authoritarian regime based on social control, restrictions on mobilisation and limited pluralism.[46] Fujimori introduced a raft of legislative decrees granting the president and the armed forces wide powers in the anti-subversive war, thus paving the way for the self-coup of April 1992. Through the self-coup, Fujimori centralised power further, clarified his authoritarian intentions, and received the apparent support of the public in doing so.[47] It was international, not national pressure, which forced Fujimori to hold elections for a Constituent Assembly (CCD) that eventually resulted in the constitution of 1993.

The CCD was strongly pro-Fujimori, the majority of opposition parties having boycotted the elections. It gave increased power to the executive, by establishing the possibility of re-election, and making congress a unicameral legislature with a reduced number of representatives (from 240 to 120). Tanaka notes, however, that the 1993 constitution is not exactly a tool 'made to measure for an authoritarian government'.[48] The CCD also put forward mechanisms encouraging popular participation and 'direct democracy'. Hence, the 1993 constitution allowed only one immediate re-election and established mechanisms of citizen consultation such as a referendum, or public protection such as a Public Defender or ombudsman, as well as a Constitutional Court. '[T]hese things turned against the government when it tried to perpetuate itself in power', prompting the government to destroy 'the same institutional order created under its hegemony'.[49] Thus, Grompone can argue correctly that Fujimori's 'authoritarian project did not lose its unity of purpose and its direction'.[50] Fujimori never had, nor developed, a constitutional, democratic conviction and the constitution was treated as an obstacle to the perpetuation of the regime's power, rather than fundamental to its survival. The self-coup of April 1992, not the constitution of 1993, was the true measure of Fujimori's commitment to democratic institutions.

In the case of Venezuela, a similar situation seemingly developed at first sight, prompting Tanaka to maintain that 'in both cases we have authoritarian and anti-party leaders who impose constitutions strongly marked by participative and modernising mechanisms, which finally resulted in being counterproductive for them'.[51] The Bolivarian constitution of 1999 was written up by a Constituent Congress strongly dominated by members elected on the government's ticket, but many of whom have since passed into the opposition.[52] Public participation in its deliberations was very high and quite successful.[53] It strengthened areas such as human rights, justice, and citizen control of public life. New regulatory bodies such as the Defender of the People to protect human rights and represent citizen concerns to the state were created, and democracy was extended through the establishment of referendums, recall referendums, and constituent assemblies amongst other innovations.

Yet a number of constitutional clauses, similar to those in the 1993 Peruvian constitution, strengthened executive power. The presidential period was extended from five to six years, with the possibility of re-election being introduced for one more period. There is increased centralisation with less autonomy for regional and municipal powers, and a one-chamber Congress. Álvarez points out that while the innovatory direct democracy mechanisms 'opened channels for direct participation [of the people] at the same time [the constitution] enhanced the power of the national executive' at the expense of the other branches of government and the political parties.[54] Constitutional amendments presented to, but rejected by, the people in 2007 were framed in a similar vein, with centralisation of power in the executive accompanied by socially progressive policies on popular participation (see Chapter 3).

In both situations the end result was the sweeping away of the old order and the installation of a new one. Yet the crucial difference in the approach of the two presidents is that Fujimori achieved his new order through a coup, which then was copper-fastened and legalised by the constitutional process, while Chávez effected his new order through legal means. Norden, therefore, can justifiably state that Chávez achieved radical change 'through the rules and procedures of Venezuela's existing constitutional democracy ...'.[55] This was certainly not the case with Fujimori.

In itself, the strengthening of executive power through constitutional change was not unusual in a Latin American or a global context, and the innovative provisions provided a balance to those favouring the executive. Difficulties arose, however, in the implementation of these provisions and, in the Peruvian case especially, with the passing of legislation which contradicted the spirit and sometimes the letter of the *Carta Magna*. Fujimori, on executing the self-coup, sacked thirteen Supreme Court judges, the Attorney General, and hundreds of lower level judges and prosecutors. The judges were replaced by provisional judges; by early 2000, 70% of judges and prosecutors remained provisional.[56] This situation affects the security of the judges and thus the quality of their work, as they are aware that they can be removed at any time for whatever reason. In Venezuela, judicial personnel were to be renovated by a new appointments procedure, which continues in operation but progress has been slow. While in 2003 approximately 25% of judges' positions were secure, this increased to only 50% by 2007.[57] Appointments, moreover, did not always follow established legal procedures.

In Peru, the Constitutional Court was dissolved in the self-coup and was not replaced until 1996, despite a requirement to do so in the 1993 constitution. It lasted only one year, as three of its magistrates who voted against Fujimori's second re-election were sacked and never replaced.[58] The Attorney General, Blanca Nélida Colán, was seen to be extremely partial to the government, dropping or actively blocking human rights and corruption cases brought against it.[59] In Venezuela, on the other hand, Supreme Court judges were immediately appointed but, along with the Public Powers (the Attorney General, Chief Comptroller, and the Public Defender), by committee instead of with the public involvement as required by the new constitution. The appointments were, however, ratified by the National Assembly as the constitution requires. Nonetheless, these appointments were seen to favour the government due to the perceived use of clientelism in their appointment and have little public confidence. In general, however, there is separation of powers in Venezuela, in that the president cannot name public powers, as is the case in the United States where the president can name Supreme Court judges, nor dismiss any of the public powers at will, as happened in Peru during the self-coup and when members of the Constitutional Court were dismissed.

With regard to the armed forces, as we have seen Fujimori became the only public representative with power of appointment over the military, allowing him and Vladimiro Montesinos (head of SIN, the Peruvian intelligence agency, and in effect co-president with Fuijimori) to monopolise that institution. Similarly in Venezuela, the President became responsible for all promotions from colonel or naval officer upwards, and thus the only elected representative with power over the armed forces, as well as being commander in chief. Promotions, therefore, rested exclusively in the hands of a party leader and thus a single political group, promoting alliances between that grouping and the armed forces.[60]

Furthermore, in Peru the military participated to an 'unprecedented degree in government decision making ... accompanied by a weakening in the institutional prerogatives of the military'.[61] In Venezuela it is argued that a similar situation exists, but there ordinary soldiers have been given the vote and take part in highly publicised developmental schemes, such as Plan Bolívar 2000, and the running of popular markets. Higher ranking officers are put in charge of important ministries or state agencies, such as the Economy Ministry and the national oil company, PdVSA.[62] Many military have been elected to government office; nine of the twenty-two Chávez-linked governors elected in the 2004 regional elections were military.[63]

The Venezuelan model, therefore, emphasises peacetime uses of military skills and experience and de-emphasises differences between the military and civilians. Indeed, as Wilpert observes, while there has been a militarisation of civilian functions there has been an equal process of 'civilianisation' of military functions. Wilpert cites Chávez as saying that he wants: 'The participation of the Armed Forces in the development of the country and the participation of civil society in the development of the Armed Forces'.[64] There is not therefore a strict separation between military and civilian roles, nor is there is a great degree of civilian control over the military. Furthermore, this deep involvement of the military in the affairs of state in both countries can lead to military corruption, though in Peru this was largely in the illegal economy of drugs and gun-running, while in Venezuela it is primarily in the misuse of state funds.

To conclude, Tanaka expresses the opinion that the authoritarian dynamic pursued by Fujimori after 1995 was likely to be repeated by Chávez after his election triumph in 2000.[65] Whilst there are some similarities in the authoritarian dynamic of both presidencies, in the Venezuelan case there was a clear will on the part of the government to have existing institutions replaced by new ones, however imperfect they may be.[66] In Peru, in contrast, much legislation encouraging deinstitutionalisation was by presidential decree and there was a marked reluctance to install many of the institutions required by the 1993 constitution. The Peruvian Congress, after April 1992, rarely rejected a presidential decree, whereas the Venezuelan government has repeatedly seen proposed legislation hotly contested in the National Assembly, at least until 2005 when the opposition boycotted the assembly elections, leaving the parliament almost entirely dominated by *chavistas*. Chávez has only used decree powers when granted to him by the National Assembly, in 2001 and in 2008, and then in only specific, though admittedly wide, areas. Fujimori, on the other hand, used decree laws incessantly. Between, February 1991 and December 1992 alone, 923 laws were passed through presidential decree, effectively installing a neoliberal economic model in Peru.[67]

The impartiality and effectiveness of institutions in Venezuela is questioned, but they do not act as blatantly in favour of the government as Peruvian institutions did for Fujimori. For example, in Venezuela, the judiciary, the CNE and other state institutions have delivered decisions which have not been favourable to the government. Institutional autonomy is far from the democratic ideal in Venezuela, but it is debateable if, as the opposition insists, they are completely controlled by Chávez. Rather, the institutions are subject to the pressures of a highly polarised society, where few can remain independent from the main political currents confronting each other.

The difficulty is that by using a zero-sum strategy in insisting on the removal of Chávez from office as the only remedy to Venezuela's difficulties, and promoting and using unconstitutional means to achieve that aim, further polarisation and politicisation of democratic institutions is encouraged making it even more difficult to ensure their impartiality. Few people involved in public life can avoid taking sides in the ideological battle between both political groups. The threat of subversion, be it active subversion seeking the government's overthrow, or passive, as in blocking government-inspired change, only serves to undermine the construction of autonomous institutions. The opposition, despite their professed support for institutionality, have shown existing institutions little respect. For the Venezuelan government, involved in a hegemonic struggle against powerful adversaries, not least of all the United States, ensuring impartial institutions, apart from historical, technical and logistical difficulties, could be tantamount to surrendering power. This situation gives further impetus to the more authoritarian elements within the government coalition.

c) Human rights

Human rights in Peru and Venezuela during the presidencies of Fujimori and Chávez are similar in an important way in that both developed in a context of conflict and struggle; however, the natures of these conflicts are radically different. On the one hand, the conflict in Peru was between a leftist subversive guerrilla organisation, Sendero Luminoso, working from outside the state, with no institutional or sectoral support (although with initial popular support in some areas), to undermine and destroy the state as it stood. In Venezuela, on the other hand, the conflict is between the national government, controlled by Chávez and his political movement and allies, and the opposition, composed of much of the business, trade union, media, cultural, religious and academic sectors, elements of the armed forces, and an ideologically diverse group of political parties and movements. The threat to the central government in Venezuela, therefore, comes from both within and outside the state and seeks to take control of the state and its structures, through legal and illegal means.

Human rights in the Peruvian case, therefore, developed in a context of violent struggle, indeed war, especially during the earlier Fujimori years, and were consistently abused by both sides. In Venezuela, on the other hand, human rights have developed under Chávez in a context of mostly peaceful hegemonic struggle between two nearly matched opponents, both of whom use the concept as an essential but contradictory element in their discourse.

Human rights violations in Venezuela as a result have not been as severe as those in Peru, although this does not signify their absence.[68] In Peru, during the war against Sendero Luminoso, Peruvian citizens, especially those living in the poorest areas of the country, suffered drastic curtailments of their human rights. Draconian anti-terrorist laws were passed by all of the democratically elected governments since the restoration of democracy in 1980. Fujimori intensified the draconian tendencies of the state, especially after the self-coup of April 1992, providing the security services, especially the armed forces, with the legal means that they had always demanded to deal with the insurgency as they saw fit, with little regard for formal legal proceedings and minimum guarantees.[69]

In 1992 alone, the year of the self-coup, 3,101 people died in violence of which 42% were the responsibility of the armed forces; there were 286 reports of forced disappearances and 114 extra-judicial executions.[70] The Fujimori government has been accused of involvement in a number of notorious massacres of innocent civilians, and of torture. Chief among these are the kidnappings, torture and assassinations of ten students and a professor of the University 'La Cantuta' on the 12 September 1992 and the massacre of fifteen people at a dinner in Barrios Altos in November 1992. At the time of writing Fujimori is being tried in Peru for these massacres, as well as for corruption charges. Impunity for state agents was assured by a systematic passing of a series of laws, which resulted in the colonisation of the judicial system and the exclusion of the security forces from any possible court action.[71] Chief among these was Law 26479, passed in June 1995, which explicitly excluded from prosecution for human rights abuses those who were involved in 'the struggle against terrorism' from 1980 onwards.

Under Chávez, flagrant violations of human rights of a violent nature, specifically due to the actions of national security agencies under the control of the central government are not as numerous, nor as coordinated, if at all, as in Peru under Fujimori. Nonetheless, the figures for deaths at the hands of the security forces are relatively high for a nation in peacetime. According to statistics provided by PROVEA, a total of 852 people died as a result of security force actions between 1998 and 2003, an average of approximately 170 people per year. Most of these deaths, 80%, were as a result of executions by state security forces.[72]

Many of these deaths, however, were not the direct responsibility of the central government. In the period 2003–04 for example, out of a total of 231 deaths reported, 55 or 23.8% were at the hands of central government agencies, 120 or 52% were at the hands of regional police forces, and 27 or 11.7% were by municipal police forces. The rest (28 or 12.5%) were as a result of joint operations between various combinations of these entities.[73] The central government agencies referred to here are the CICPC, the 'forensic police' charged with investigating high-level crimes such as murders, robberies etc. (32 deaths), the armed forces (FAN) (10 deaths), the GN (National Guard) (11 deaths) and DISIP, the political police (2 deaths). More recent data has shown a decrease in these figures but not to any dramatic extent. In the latest figures available at the time of writing, 165 people died at the hand of the security forces, of which 19.39% were the responsibility of security agencies controlled by central government, the rest of state and municipal police forces.[74] Despite the fact that control of many of these latter agencies passed to the government from the opposition in this period, there was little change in these figures pointing to structural shortcomings within these forces rather than because of party political control. Also it should be pointed out that during this period, up until 2005, the government did not have complete control over many of the central government crime agencies such as the CICPC and DISIP.

Nonetheless, as one of Venezuela's foremost human rights campaigners Liliana Ortega of COFAVIC (Committee of Families of the Victims of the Events of February and March, 1989) points out, the state has a responsibility to ensure prosecution of those responsible and to devise strategies to prevent such deaths recurring. For Ortega, it is this impunity which is the chief obstacle to human rights and justice in Venezuela: 'There is great impunity in Venezuela because there is an institutionality which permits it, which tolerates it, which promotes it. It is for this reason that investigations into crimes do not bring results.'[75]

While these structural failings are a permanent feature of the Venezuelan state and are not necessarily exclusive to the Chávez era, they do point to a contradiction between a strong government discourse against human rights abuses and its failure to stop such practices.[76] Moreover, figures for such deaths under the previous Caldera presidency compare favourably with those we have just discussed under Chávez. During that period, 1993–98, a total of 675 deaths at the hands of the security forces were reported, an average of approximately 135, considerably lower than the deaths reported above (170 per year) during Chávez's first five years in office, and which, as we have seen have not improved greatly in more recent years.[77] It is thought, however, that the passing of a new Police Law in April 2008, after a long period of community consultation, may go someway to solve these problems. The law provides for an integrated national police system, greater respect for human rights, more social control over the police with a strong element of community controlled policing, strengthened disciplinary provisions, and a stronger focus on the victim amongst other measures.

A notable case of deaths blamed on the central government, but later found to be untrue, were those which took place during a large opposition march on 11 April 2002, the day the opposition coup was launched against the government, when nineteen people lost their lives and over a hundred were injured. The opposition claimed that those who died on 11 April were 'their deaths', and that these in their totality were due to President Chávez.[79] It is generally believed, however, that shooting came from both sides and that many of the deaths were as a result of opposition sharp shooters placed in strategic locations.[80] PROVEA also points to incoherence on the part of the opposition in its discourse on human rights. During the forty-eight hours in which the opposition was in power, under Pedro Carmona, between 11–14 April, the *de facto* government committed various human rights abuses, including extra-judicial killing, unauthorised detentions and torture.[81] In the following days, seventy-three more people lost their lives before the restoration of Chávez to the government.[82] Clearly then, elements of the opposition used human rights for discourse purposes, but contradicted this discourse in practice to a much greater degree than the Chávez government.

Human rights violations in Venezuela therefore are characterised by two fundamental contextual points: (i) a hegemonic struggle between a central government and an elected and non-elected opposition with its own popular and structural power base; and (ii) the use of human rights as a central discursive pillar of that hegemonic struggle which neither side fully translates into effective policy. Both sides of the conflict have been responsible for human rights violations, though ultimately it is the government's responsibility to ensure that those responsible are brought to justice. Impunity is a result of government inaction and a historically defective institutional system, and both sides of the conflict have benefited from it. The opposition, with many allies in the international community, is constantly and actively vigilant in identifying, publicising and repudiating any human rights violations on the part of the national government. It does not, however, highlight those cases that have been the responsibility of anti-government elements, and immediately blames the government for all victims without hesitation.[83] Furthermore many opposition members responsible for human rights violations are defended by the opposition, including those who participated in the coup.

The Venezuelan government has grave responsibilities with regard to human rights violations, but it has not violated human rights, nor is it currently capable of doing so, to the same degree nor with the same consistency or purpose as the Fujimori government. There are structural commonalties, such as the tendency to impunity, which were exacerbated by actions and/or inaction of both governments. Nonetheless, the degree to which human rights abuses took place in Peru must be put in the context of the magnitude of the security emergency which the Fujimori government faced on coming to power, not to mention the human rights abuses of previous democratic regimes. Chávez did not face the challenge of a vicious guerrilla war, thus it is difficult to measure the extent of human rights abuse between both governments equitably. However, it is debatable if the human rights abuses Chávez has been accused of are any greater than those perpetrated by previous Venezuelan governments and indeed sections of the opposition. Human rights violations in Venezuela are therefore a result of the inadequacies of the Venezuelan state, inadequacies which the Chávez government has failed to correct, but are not state policy directed by the government, unlike in the case of Fujimori.

d) Media freedom and the right to information

Freedom of expression and the freedom of the press are often placed together as synonymous, yet as Lichtenberg argues they can sometimes be contradictory.[84] Free speech entails that people are able to communicate without interference and that there are many people communicating, or at least many ideas and points of view being communicated.[85] The autonomy of editors, publishers and media owners, however, is often in reality a property claim disguised as a claim for free speech.[86] What is important for freedom of speech is the 'multiplicity of ideas and sources of information', while other considerations such as non-interference are secondary.[87]

Habermas describes an ideal-type 'public sphere' as a realm of social life where the exchange of information and views on questions of common concern can take place freely so that public opinion can be formed, and consequently policy and society as a whole can be developed.[88] In other words, free expression and a diversity of voices are necessary to allow the public to inform itself freely and thus take an active part in public debate and policy formation. Yet in Fujimori's Peru and in Chávez's Venezuela the situation according to many critics is far from this paradigm and much closer to the 'propaganda model' of Herman and Chomsky.[89]

This model contains the following 'essential ingredients [...] or set of news "filters" ...: (i) the size, concentrated ownership, owner wealth, and profit orientation of the dominant mass-media firms; (ii) advertising as the primary income source of the mass media; (iii) the reliance of the media on information provided by government, business, and "experts" funded and approved by these primary sources and agents of power; (iv) "flak" as a means of disciplining the media; and (v) "anticommunism" as a national religion and control mechanism. These elements interact with and reinforce one another.'[90] The Venezuelan and Peruvian media broadly follow these 'ingredients' with some modifications to reflect local conditions.

It is not uncommon for Fujimori and Chávez to be compared in terms of attacking freedom of expression and freedom of the press.[91] However, while many of these reports provide quite accurate information, they often do not provide a broader context from which to judge the behaviour of the media and therefore the government's attitude to it. The main point of comparison between Peru and Venezuela is the media's colonisation by sectors dominated by or sympathetic to a specific political identity. In both cases there has been coincidence between media and business sectors. A crucial difference, however, is that in Peru the coloniser was the Fujimori government, and its particular brand of neoliberalism, while in Venezuela it is mainly sectors opposed to the Chávez government, many of which promulgate a pro-US, market friendly, liberal democratic agenda.

A second difference was the more autonomous role of the media in opposition campaigns in Venezuela, as opposed to the direct interference of state agents in media output in Peru. In both cases, however, collusion results in a willing ideological colonisation, characterised by five strategies used mostly in favour of the coloniser, but sometimes against it by some sections of the media:

1   discrediting the adversary by using disqualifying, insulting language and/or inaccurate and misleading information;
2   distorting or withholding of information;
3   the use of abundant cascades of propaganda;
4   international campaigns in supranational organisations; and,
5   economic pressures and physical intimidation.

In Peru, shortly into Fujimori's first term, the media got a reminder of old-style authoritarian control strategies. During the April 1992 self-coup the armed forces raided and occupied newspapers, news magazines, television and radio stations as well as foreign press agencies, detaining journalists and influencing and censoring content.[92] After the self-coup the Fujimori government withdrew such tactics and instead began a campaign of 'economic harassment' of the media using the tax agency (SUNAT), import duties on paper and withholding of government advertising as implements to ensure conformity with government policy.'[93] Fujimori therefore 'combined neoliberal economics and close relations with the military to bring about the management of information'.[94]

Conaghan reports that in general the Fujimori government ignored the little investigative reporting that took place against its policies.[95] 'Political scandals are revealed by the press, abuses are denounced by the opposition, and policies are challenged. But much of this political discussion is either ignored by authorities or 'processed' by institutions in ways that do not fundamentally resolve or clarify issues ….'[96] The end result of these strategies was a climate of self-censorship becoming predominant throughout the media, with only a few exceptions showing independence.[97] Most of the television channels were actively or predominantly pro-government, especially América Television, Frecuencia Latina and Panamericana, as well as the state-owned Channel Seven.

The Peruvian media during the Fujimori period displayed most of the 'filters' of Herman and Chomsky's propaganda model. The emergence of the so-called *vladivideos* at the end of the Fujimori regime revealed the personal and financial connections between media proprietors and people in or involved with the government, especially Vladimiro Montesinos (filter 1).[98] The Peruvian media, as seen above, were receivers of 'flak' (filter 4), and were dependent on government advertising and wary of losing private advertising due to government pressure (filter 2). Furthermore Conaghan reports that 42% of television news content consisted of pronouncements and activities of government officials (filter 3).[99] Sustained campaigns of vilification of prominent media or opposition personalities, or in favour of particular government policies, were often developed. The intention of these campaigns was to instil a fear of a return to terrorism and hyperinflation, in effect the Peruvian equivalent of Herman and Chomsky's fifth filter, the use of anti-communism as a control mechanism.[100]

With regard to Venezuela, Lugo and Romero argue that during the Punto Fijo era there was a media–state pact of 'symbiotic dependence', and the 1998 election was fought under its rules.[101] That pact fulfilled to a large degree Herman and Chomsky's propaganda model, and the Venezuelan media still operates under its parameters. Media outlets are owned by 'wealthy families with serious financial stakes in defeating Chávez'.[102] Furthermore, these families owe their wealth and its continuance to a system that closely interlocks them into business and political circles through reliance on government subsidies and advertising, and private-sector advertising from companies who often are equally reliant on the state for support (filter 1; filter 2). During the Punto Fijo era the media was the stage on which political discourse was played out, giving it a crucial role in the political process, but one particularly dependent on political and state actors for news (filter 3). Furthermore, there were few actors of any weight who were not involved with the pacts which constituted that political arrangement. 'Flak' was sometimes used by the government to keep the media in line: Presidents Carlos Andrés Peréz, Rafael Caldera, and Jaime Lusinchi all used state instruments or outright censorship to discipline the media (filter 4).[103] Finally, anti-communism was a trademark of the Punto Fijo pact and this was reflected, and still is reflected, in the media (filter 5).

The relationship between the media and President Chávez initially was ambivalent. It is commonly thought that the Venezuelan private media were supportive of Chávez initially, however, Lugo and Romero state that the media 'maintained the appearance of objectivity and rarely manifested openly its partisanship' during this period and Villamediana shows that much of the coverage was very hostile to him.[104] Chávez on assuming power broke the 'symbiotic' pact referred to in Lugo and Romero and quickly tried to implement his own agenda.[105] His confrontational discourse with the main organisations of entrepreneurs and business, such as FEDECAMARAS, and against the media itself, as well as government inability to supply advertising and subsidies as traditionally done, led the media to abandon any attempt to find compromise with the government and eventually seek its downfall. As there was no unified approach from opposition sectors on how to overthrow Chávez, nor on whom or with what model to replace him, the media became a space for consensus-seeking amongst the opposition, and not between government and opposition as it had hitherto acted. Confrontation with the government, rather than consensus, has become the political language of the day, and the media placed itself in the front line of that battle. The media indeed has become 'a counter revolutionary element' in the process of the hegemonic power struggle of *chavismo* against the establishment.[106]

The Venezuelan media therefore went through three stages in its relationship with Chávez in the time period under study: (i) balance; (ii) hostility; and (iii) seditious rebellion. In the final stage the media have twice played key parts in combined business, opposition and trade union efforts to overthrow the Chávez government. During the April coup the media created a climate of intolerance and instability through non-stop broadcasts of opposition mobilisation and incessant negative commentaries on the behaviour and personality of President Chávez and his government with sometimes little regard for veracity or fact. It took an overwhelmingly partisan role in the coup, obstructing the government and its supporters from making its case, facilitating opposition seditious activities and blacking out news of the government's return to power.[107] The de facto government of Carmona meanwhile closed community radio stations, arresting and torturing some of their workers. 'The Venezuelan population saw their right to receive information violated ... and the spokespeople of the constitutional government and sectors which demanded the restitution of the rule of law saw their right to express themselves broken.'[108] Such strategies continued or were amplified during the so-called *paro cívico* or lockout/strike led by FEDECAMARAS and the CTV from December 2002 to early February 2003.[109]

The government and/or its supporters, however, have also done their part to limit freedom of expression and the right to information. Attacks on journalists, leading sometimes to death, bombings of newspaper offices, verbal attacks on the media by the president, accusations of criminal misdeeds of individual journalists by state media agencies, and an abusive use of mandatory state broadcasts, are among the strategies used by the government or pro-government factions to limit freedom of expression. Nonetheless these justified complaints must be put into the broader context of contemporary Venezuelan society to be understood properly.

Chávez repeatedly won elections and had high poll ratings, even in the most difficult years, yet this statistically important group of people did not see their views being reflected in the media, and were indeed regularly insulted by it.[110] Some of the journalists, who have been particularly targeted with attacks, are also suspected of having participated in the coup, and in general of conducting a sustained and legally questionable campaign against the government. Nevertheless, most journalists are caught in the crossfire between media owners and government, although some of the more prominent anti-government journalists are in reality political actors, such as Patricia Poleo, Ibeyise Pacheco, Marta Colomina, some of whom visited Washington regularly prior to the coup.[111]

Yet, despite frequent calls to the military to intervene, seditious activities, suspected violent activities, and campaigns of misinformation, no journalist or media worker has been put in prison, nor had the government until recently used any of its considerable power over the media to give it 'flak'. While many journalists have suffered attacks, these have been on both sides and could be seen as victims of the profound political polarisation found in the country, which has been contributed to both by government and by the media and opposition. Furthermore it has been demonstrated that the opposition too is capable of subterfuge and violence. It is not beyond speculation that opposition sympathisers intent on discrediting the government could have perpetrated some of the more prominent attacks on journalists and media outlets.[112]

As pointed out above, the use of the media in both Peru and Venezuela is much closer to Herman and Chomsky's propaganda model than Habermas's concept of the public sphere. However, this section also shows that the propaganda model can be utilised just as effectively against a government as it can in its favour, as can be clearly seen in the case of Venezuela. Both cases also show that media proprietors prioritise their own interests, both financial and power-based, before any considerations of media independence or concepts of truth, and ally themselves with whichever power sectors best serve those interests. In both these cases the media has shown considerable autonomy of movement, despite a certain dependence on external powers, and is not, therefore, as helplessly subject to omnipotent authoritarian rulers as is sometimes supposed. The media in Venezuela took an autonomous decision to participate in opposition campaigns against the government, and indeed act as a vanguard in them, and in Peru media owners entered freely into negotiations with Vladimiro Montesinos for their own financial benefit, but also because of the close ideological and personal relations between business and government. In this context the repeated protests of the Venezuelan media over threats to freedom of expression are indeed, as Lichtenberg states, examples of calls for the protection of property and privilege.[113]

Judging by its more recent actions, however, the Chávez government has fought back, using elements of the propaganda model to get its views across. Chief among these has been its use of 'flak', and an emblematic case of this was the Chávez government's refusal to renew the license of Venezuela's oldest television station, RCTV in 2007. This provoked a worldwide outcry and was taken as proof that Chávez was a 'dictator'. RCTV was one of the government's most vociferous critics, yet this criticism went beyond mere commentary as it was deeply involved in the 2002 coup and the 2003 oil stoppage. Furthermore, unlike other broadcasters such as Venevision, owned by billionaire Gustavo Cisneros, it refused to moderate its anti-government output after these attempts at overthrowing the government failed. It was primarily for this reason that the government did not renew its license, a perfectly legal decision that was nonetheless executed with little transparency.

The government also fought back by increasing the number of pro-government broadcasters. Apart from the traditional state channel, VTV, the government also opened the satellite broadcaster TeleSUR (see Chapter 7), as well as other minor television channels. It replaced RCTV with a public broadcaster, TVes, supposedly modelled on the BBC. It also funded a huge explosion in community radio and television, thus democratising media output to a great degree. Whether such initiatives lead to an improvement in the public's right to accurate and reliable information and the quality of democracy is, however, a case for further research beyond the remit of this study.

e) Associational autonomy

In the areas of associational autonomy we also see important differences between the governments of Fujimori and Chávez. Let us first look at the situation in Peru.

Before the arrival of Fujimori, Peru experienced one of the greatest periods of popular mobilisation in its history. The left was in the ascendant after democracy was restored in 1979 and social movements flourished. The years of the Alan García presidency (1985–90) and the grave economic and social crisis which it engendered, however, decimated the left. The arrival of Fujimori, and the implementation of his shock economic programme, deepened this crisis in social movements.[114] Popular organisational energies were diverted from public demands for incorporation to private strategies for survival. Formal employment, especially industrial and mining employment, once the stronghold of the union movement, reduced sharply during the

García and Fujimori presidencies. The April 1992 self-coup, the high legitimacy of the Fujimori government, and the weakness of the opposition added to the pressures which quelled any possible popular unrest. Fujimori and Montesinos developed sophisticated and effective mechanisms to identify and stop opposition developing amongst social movements. Authoritarianism, clientelism, inclusion, recognition and meritocracy were all strategies used by the government to weave local needs together with government aims.[115]

The political parties could not provide an effective response to *fujimorismo* and remained powerless politically. APRA, the most popular and well established party, polled only 8% in the 1995 elections, while the other main parties individually polled less than 5%.[116] The tight control of state resources exercised by Fujimori, ensured that most leaders of community and social organisations remained neutral or aligned themselves with the government.[117] These movements in any case were not loci of ideological resistance but of pragmatic survival and thus did not present a serious autonomous challenge to the Fujimori regime, although they were not uncritical.[118] In sum '[t]he relationship between popular sectors and the state under Fujimori was characterised by a strong pragmatism, arising from the weakness of collective identities, a crisis of the state and of the various support groups, in a context of high levels of violence and a crisis of governability'.[119] Popular sectors became demobilised according to Tanaka, and emphasis was placed on private initiative and public opinion, with the media rather than popular organisations acting as mediator. Low levels of collective collaboration were evident amongst the public.[120]

Venezuela, on the other hand, had not experienced the massive mobilisations of popular sectors seen in Peru during and after the military regime up until the late 1980s. From the *caracazo* of 1989, however, mobilisation became a favoured method of voicing dissent among all sectors of Venezuelan society, especially with the arrival of Chávez.[121] Similarly, social organisations and movements became more prominent after the *caracazo*, particularly as a result of decentralisation policies pursued by the state from the late 1980s.[122] When the Chávez government installed the ANC (National Constituent Assembly) in 1999, the participation of civil society was 'dynamic and successful' due to mutual coincidences in some of their's and the ruling coalition's aims, with some 50% of their proposals being incorporated into the constitution.[123] Social organisations saw the Bolivarian constitution as a satisfactory framework from which to fashion new relations between state and society. They became dissatisfied, however, as they perceived an increasing breach developing between the precepts of the constitution and official discourse on the one hand, and the president's divisive discourse and partisan governmental practice on the other. Polarisation developed and mobilisation increased, with class cleavages becoming more apparent as the middle and upper classes demonstrated against the government and the popular classes in support of it. Chávez responded to increased middle- and upper-class mobilisation with cooptation and direct propagation of popular organisations. Participation for the government, García-Guadilla concludes, means 'winning legitimacy without losing power'.[124]

Associational autonomy is prejudiced too by tendencies of personalisation and weakening of party politics as noted in Peru, and a centralisation of state resources and power, making party lists more dependent on loyalty to party leaders.[125] While the 1999 constitution requires parties to hold elections to decide on candidates, this provision is rarely observed by these more personalist parties or movements, including the governing party, the MVR (although its successor party the PSUV has held extensive internal elections – see below).[126]

Nonetheless, a more grassroots approach, based on autonomous popular participation within a radical democracy paradigm on the one hand, and the more statist approach, dependent on state action from above, on the other, coexist in the formation of public policy in Venezuela.[127] Grassroots activism was central to the survival of the government during the 2002 coup and the 2003 oil stoppage. Government policy deliberately encourages popular organisation as a counterweight to party elite domination. Yet both remain in tension with each other, despite the fact that, as Ellner points out, they have coexisted during the Chávez period. An attempted synthesis of both approaches will lie in the creation of mechanisms allowing genuine grassroots input into debate and leadership selection in the new PSUV, the replacement for the previous MVR aimed at unifying the *chavista* coalition.

Unlike in Fujimori's Peru, where trades unions became largely irrelevant, unions in Venezuela have been one of the centres of ideological and hegemonic struggle. The CTV led a number of strikes against the Chávez government, albeit in concert with the business association FEDECAMARAS. Despite traditionally being dominated by AD, the CTV has successfully avoided being co-opted by the Chávez government while at the same time asserting its autonomy from its erstwhile sponsors. Although its powers of mobilisation have been weakened considerably, it has presented a convincing challenge to the government on a number of occasions.[128] Even labour unions regarded as sympathetic to the government have shown noteworthy discrepancies with government strategies on union policy.[129] The formation of a new labour confederation the National Worker's Union (UNT) has shown wide tactical, strategic and ideological debate, which reflects the different grassroots and statist approaches within the *chavista* movement as a whole rather than a slavish adherence to a dogmatic party line.[130]

Institutional autonomy does not just rest with trades unions, however. The emphasis on popular participation within the Bolivarian revolution ensures that there is popular autonomy from, and therefore popular control over, existing institutions. The successive participatory mechanisms set up, such as the Boivarian Circles, urban land committees, water committees, and neighbourhood health committees have ensured popular input into policy within the *chavista* movement and with the different missions, allowing direct popular controls of the direction of the movement and social service provision structures. While it can be argued that these popular structures feed into a populist relationship between Chávez and the popular classes, Raby notes that they 'have been more sensitive to the real feelings of the people and more democratic in the profound sense, than any conventional party or government mechanism', as they 'give free rein to the popular movement at all levels, without constraint by state and party bureaucracy'.[131]

In sum, there are more differences than similarities in the autonomy of social organisations in Fujmori's Peru and in Venezuela under Chávez. *Fujimorismo* was characterised by a lack of autonomy, both ideological and practical, of social organisations during most of Fujimori's rule. This was achieved through a decline in the left, and a combination of authoritarianism and successful co-optation. Social organisations in Venezuela under Chávez on the other hand have shown a marked autonomy in some cases, or at the very least a qualified cooperation with the government, along with high levels of mobilisation and ideological debate. Although, like in Peru, there have been attempts at co-optation this has met with varying success. The progressive inclinations of the government and its partners and supporters encourages an atmosphere conducive to autonomous popular mobilisation in its support, especially necessary in a context of hegemonic struggle. Political discourse is dominated by left-right ideological identities in Venezuelan party politics, including within the dominant *chavista* movement, thus providing greater programmatic and ideological variety in party discourse, unlike in Peru which has been dominated by a (neo)liberalism installed by Fujimori. Authoritarian practice to assert direct political control over civil society groupings in Venezuela has met with little success, as was the case with the union referendum of 2000, which resulted in defeat for the government and had beneficial though unintended effects for the autonomy of trade unions.[132] In sum, while many social movements remain broadly sympathetic to government aims, which seek increased social and economic participation of the popular classes, this is contingent on the delivery of those aims within a grassroots participatory framework. This gives much greater latitude to the grassroots to influence the general direction of the populist movement and government policy in a collective and organised manner, pointing to the possibility, as Raby states, of it transcending populism towards deeper structural change in the state and its organs.

Comparative analysis

In conclusion therefore, let us summarise findings under each of the policy areas identified in the framework in Table 5.1. To begin with, greater electoral pluralism was found under Chávez than under Fujimori. Authoritarian tendencies and presidential control were found to be weaker in the Chávez presidency than with Fujimori. Human rights have not been violated, nor are they likely to be, as much under Chávez as under Fujimori. While the media was a key actor in Fujimori's Peru in support of the government, it primarily supports the opposition sectors in Venezuela, to the extent that it participated in a number of attempts to overthrow the government. There was a clear lack of associational autonomy under *fujimorismo*, while in Chávez's Venezuela social organisations have a more marked autonomy or at least a qualified cooperation with the government, with higher levels of mobilisation and ideologisation, with the potential to go beyond populism to deeper, more democratic, institutional change.

There are a number of reasons for these differences. First, Venezuelan democracy had much deeper roots than Peruvian democracy, which was only re-established in 1979, as opposed to 1958 in Venezuela. Consequently, in the Peruvian context it was easier for Fujimori to refashion institutions to his own advantage with the aid of many powerful allies.[133] Between them, these groups possessed sufficient knowledge, training and expertise to remodel many of these institutions efficiently, and/or provide the necessary legitimacy to permit those who had previous experience to continue working in them. In Venezuela, on the other hand, the much firmer roots of democratic institutions, under the tutelage of his avowed political enemies, made it more difficult for Chávez to remodel this polity entirely to his own advantage. This ultimately serves as a brake on any supposed 'authoritarian dynamic' of the Chávez administration.

Second, the principal political parties in Venezuela, AD and COPEI, monopolised almost the entire institutional and popular structure of Venezuelan society, dividing it between them according to the rules of the Punto Fijo pact.[134] As these opposed Chávez from the outset, it was more difficult for the government to gain complete control of the state apparatus. Furthermore the Chávez administration lacked the high-powered alliances that the Fujimori regime had, relying on the popular classes in the *barrios*, led by left-wing community activists, a number of small left-wing parties, associated academics, and sections of the armed forces. Although many knowledgeable people are found within these groups, many lacked the expertise of government administration.[135] Extensive resistance on the part of the opposition sectors contributed to a continuous struggle between sectors of the bureaucracy and the government, especially in sensitive areas such as health and education, and an intense vigilance of the behaviour of democratic institutions for signs of bias. Chávez faced a continual series of small and large-scale strikes in the health and education sectors, and education was one of the great battlegrounds during the December 2002 strike/lockout. Fujimori faced little such opposition, as he reduced the bureaucracy numbers, and due to his business and international legitimacy secured the cooperation of trained technocrats. Unions were extremely weak and in general, as we have seen above, the government developed efficient mechanisms to deal with opposition if and when it did arise.

Third, the nature of the alliances upon which both presidents built their power is radically different. While Fujimori relied on a coalition of the very rich and the very poor – business groups and the informal sector – backed by the US and other powerful countries, Chávez's social base rests primarily, as we have seen in Chapter 2, on the popular classes with outright hostility from the middle and upper classes backed by the US and some European countries. The social base of the Chávez coalition, however, unlike Fujimori's, is mobilised in support of what they believe as their project, that is the inclusion of the heretofore excluded marginalised classes into the social, economic and political life of the country. While Chávez is a crucial part and symbol of that project, he is not the sum of it, and he is dependent on their mobilisation, and not just their vote, for the continuation of the Bolivarian project. The repeated and well-attended marches in support of Chávez and his government and more localised grassroots activity not only show the support of the popular classes for the president, but the presence of an organisational infrastructure of militants and activists with convoking power in the *barrios*. This support has remained consistent even when little tangible economic benefit was forthcoming, indicating a strong identificatory link in programmatic and ideological aims. It is doubtful that these groups will allow an authoritarian project solely benefiting the president and his closest associates over the development of the participative and protaganistic model set out in the 1999 constitution. Indeed this was proven when Chávez's constitutional amendments, proposing more centralised power in the executive, were rejected by Venezuelans in a 2007 referendum.

This situation contrasts sharply with Fujimori; under him the popular classes were entirely demoralised and demobilised as a result of the different crises which afflicted Peru in the 1980s and early 1990s and did not participate in an *active* sense in the government nor the governing movement. Fujimori did not have, nor did he want, a grassroots network of militants and party faithful despite, or perhaps because of, having high levels of legitimacy due to the defeat of hyperinflation and terrorism. Mobilisation was therefore dependent almost solely on the media, the armed forces and the SIN and not on ideological or programmatic considerations. Furthermore Fujimori did deliver economically to his poor electoral base, and quite blatantly used that economic power over them for electoral ends.

Fourth, the Venezuelan opposition was, initially at least, much stronger and more active in opposing the Chávez government than its counterpart in Peru ever was. In Peru, congressional opposition was muted and broadly supportive in many respects, despite expressing reservations at the more draconian measures being proposed.[136] The media initially took a critical but broadly supportive stance and latterly became almost entirely subject to the government.[137] Popular movements as we have seen, were gravely weakened, as were the political parties. This is not entirely the case in Venezuela; political opposition may have been weakened electorally, but it still has considerable organisational structure, and alliances and penetration of important social movements. Furthermore, opposition allies such as the Church, the business community and the media, as well as the parties themselves, have considerable power and, like Fujimori, powerful international allies who view Chávez with distrust if not outright distaste.[138] The opposition is equally as mobilised as the Chávez coalition and has, in turn, managed to mobilise the international community to take part in a vigilant observation of the process.

Fujimori, on the other hand, was intimately involved with the international community, which saw him as a stabilising factor in an extremely unstable and precarious country. It was in the interests of the international community to preserve Fujimori in power, a factor which considerably weakened the opposition.[139] The Peruvian opposition had few of the advantages of the Venezuelan opposition listed above, least of all financial, logistical and strategic support from the US. Only near the end of his second term, when unrest became common and electoral fraudulence all too apparent, did the OAS become involved as interlocutor and even then Fujimori continued in power. Fujimori thus had little or no internal or external opposition of weight to inhibit the installation of his authoritarian regime. In the case of Chávez the situation is almost the obverse of the Peruvian situation and augurs against his achieving an authoritarian government like that of Fujimori, if indeed that is his intention.

One of the reasons for this high international support for Fujimori as opposed to Chávez must also rest in Fujimori's firm commitment to an orthodox neoliberal economic model. While in the present study we have found a much higher level of authoritarianism and lack of democracy in the Fujimori presidency, accusations against Fujimori of authoritarianism were relatively rare, especially internationally. Chávez on the other hand has been subject to such accusations incessantly since coming to power in 1998. To give an example, in a 2005 study by FAIR (Fairness and Accuracy in Reporting), nearly a hundred news commentaries on Venezuela in the principal newspapers of the United States were reviewed; of those, 95% expressed clear hostility to Chávez. Most commentaries, rather than commenting on the increased participation brought about by the Chávez government in Venezuela, 'frequently disparaged Chávez as a political "strongman," treating him as if he were the country's sole and all-powerful political actor'. In effect the US media offers a portrait of Chávez which differs little in content from Rumsfeld's summation of him as akin to Hitler. Fujimori rarely suffered such treatment in the US media, and it can only be surmised that this was at least partially because he favoured market-based economics. The radicalism of the Chávez movement, and its firm rejection of 'savage neoliberalism' show it to be a serious obstacle to international capitalism in Venezuela, and possibly South America, and herein may lie the true reason for the countless accusations of authoritarianism against Chávez.[140]

Finally, it is often asserted that both presidents are anti-institutional and anti-party. The Chávez government has shown itself, however, to be much more institutionally minded than Fujimori, as we have seen in our review in this chapter. Furthermore, the Chávez government has been much more dependent on established parties as coalition partners. Chávez went into government as part of a broad alliance of parties, many of them with strong left-wing backgrounds. Whilst in government that alliance was weakened on a number of occasions, such as the Movement Towards Socialism (MAS) party split. Nonetheless the president has been mindful of keeping what remains of these parties within the project, due, amongst other things, to their organisational and technical capacities. Furthermore, the establishment of the PSUV shows a commitment to construct a popular, institutionalised party with strong grassroots input, although this could involve the demise of the coalition parties. Fujimori, on the other hand was entirely free of such alliances and had no such considerations. He could afford to act freely, paying little heed to other parties including his very own movement.

The Fujimori regime was democratic until 1992, when as a result of the *autogolpe* it became autocratic. Yet even then it had high levels of legitimacy and this and its electoral origins prompted many to look on it as a hybrid regime. In 1995, it regained democratic legitimacy when Fujimori was re-elected in what were considered to be questionable but generally speaking legitimate elections. It was not until the late 1990s that the Fujimori regime became primarily authoritarian as Grompone maintains. The picture in Chávez's Venezuela, while similarly betraying signs of hybridism, is, however, much more complex, as Hellinger and Ellner assert.[141] Most certainly there are some indications of authoritarianism, such as a degree of government dominance of institutions; continued impunity in the case of human rights violations; and threats to the freedom of the press and the right to information. These, however, do not constitute authoritarianism as defined by Rueschemeyer et al., though it could be seen as a 'restricted democracy' according to this analyst's terminology.[142]

Nonetheless, as we have seen there are strong countervailing factors which act as important checks against those tendencies. The difficulty for

Venezuelans, however, is that many of those sectors in the opposition which act as guardians against authoritarianism have themselves shown similar authoritarian tendencies. The danger, therefore, is not simply the authoritarian tendencies within the Chávez administration, although these must be guarded against without doubt, nor the authoritarian tendencies of sectors of the opposition, which must be equally guarded against. Rather, the danger lies in a substratum of authoritarianism, a lack of commitment and ambivalence to democracy, which runs through Venezuelan public life in general. This seam of authoritarianism, this autocratic faultline in Venezuelan public life, is barely acknowledged by the principal actors in the Venezuelan drama, who instead mutually accuse each other of sins which they themselves can be guilty of. There is a ready willingness to use the concept of democracy for discursive ends in the government and the opposition, but few programmatic proposals emerge from the opposition as to how to ensure the undoubted participation that the popular sectors enjoy under Chávez. And it is this 'experience of participation', as Germani termed it, which ultimately makes Chávez different from Fujimori, and provides him with much deeper legitimacy. Any alternative to Chávez which denies this experience of participation, and the opportunity to develop and deepen it, will destroy the possibilities of genuine democracy for Venezuela. As Rueschemeyer et al. baldly state, 'democracy means nothing if not a share of political power controlled by the many'.[143] Unfortunately for Venezuela and Venezuelans, few of the alternative political actors to Chávez seem to be offering that opportunity.

To conclude, this chapter draws our attention to a number of observations on populism. The comparison shows us that while both Fujimori and Chávez can be termed populist, the characteristics of their populism are quite distinct. Fujimori's populism was highly authoritarian and neoliberal in its manifestations – neopopulist in essence. Chávez on the other hand bases his support, rhetoric and policies on the marginalised poor and shows some authoritarian tendencies, but the emphasis on the participation and mobilisation of the popular classes, his links with grassroots leftist organisations, and his opposition to 'savage' neoliberalism, amongst other characteristics, clearly differentiates him from Fujimori's neopopulist model and points to a much more radical populism, with the potential to transcend it to a more deliberative democracy in the Heldian sense. Such participation also is central to concepts of democracy as discussed by Rueschemeyer et al. and Dahl, reinforcing the link between participation, populism and democratisation.

Despite this emphasis on participation, most analysts of populism contend that its impact is harmful to democracy and its institutions. Indeed one of the principal claims of the opposition to Chávez is that he harms democracy, or rather the 'institutionality' which democracy depends on. The next chapter will look at these claims in more detail.

Notes

1 Laclau, E., and Mouffe, C., 2001, *Hegemony and Socialist Strategy: Towards a Radical Democratic Politics*, 2nd ed. London and New York: Verso.

2 Rueschemeyer, D., Stephens, E. and Stephens, J. D., 1992, *Capitalist Development and Democracy*. Cambridge: Polity Press; Dahl, R. A., 1989, *Democracy and its Critics*. New Haven and London: Yale University Press.

3 This is an amalgam of the Spanish words *democracia* (democracy) and *dictadura* (dictatorship).

4 López Jiménez, S., 1993, 'Perú, 1992: De la Dictablanda a la Democradura', in *Quehacer* 82: 34–41, p. 37.

5 Mauceri, P., 1997, 'Return of the caudillo: autocratic democracy in Peru', in *Third World Quarterly* 18(5): 899–911, p. 909.

6 Conaghan, C., 1996, *Public Life in the Time of Alberto Fujimori*. Working Paper Series Number 219. Washington DC: Woodrow Wilson International Center for Scholars, p. 3.

7 Cameron, M.A., 2001, 'Venezuela's Hugo Chávez: saviour or threat to democracy?', in *Latin American Research Review* 36(3): 255–266, p. 265.

8 1 represents 'totally free' while 7 'totally unfree'. Freedom House, 2008. 'Map of freedom: country report, Venezuela'. Available from: www.freedomhouse.org. Accessed 17 April 2008.

9 Tanaka, M., 2002, *De la crisis al colapso de los sistemas de partidos y los retos de su reconstrucción: los casos de Perú y Venezuela*. Mimeo, Instituto de Estudios Peruanos, p. 1.

10 Triangulo, El, 2001, 'Fujimori y Chávez: Hay cercanía entre los dos?', Televen 26 July. (Panel members: Luis Cristensen, Consultores 21, polling firm; Mary Mogollon, political analyst; Omar Meza Ramirez, MVR political leader (government); Carlos Raul Hernandez, political writer. Various other personalities interviewed.) Archived in Cinema and Video Centre, National Library, Caracas.

11 Cited in Cotler, J. and Grompone, R., 2000, *El fujimorismo: ascenso y caída de un régimen autoritario*. Lima: Instituto de Estudios Peruanos, p. 80.

12 Cited in Diamond, L., Hartlyn, J., Linz, J. J. and Lipset, S. M. (eds), 1999, *Democracy and Developing Countries: Latin America*, 2nd ed. Boulder, CO and London: Lynne Rienner, p. 311.

13 Naím, M., 2001, 'La Venezuela de Hugo Chávez', in *Politica Exterior* XV(82): 51–73, p. 69; Caballero, M., 2000, *La gestación de Hugo Chávez: 40 años de luces y sombras en la democracia venezolana*. Madrid: Catarata, p. 162.

14 Latinobarómetro, 2007, *Informe Latinobarómetro, 2007: Banco de datos en línea*. Available from: www.latinobarometro.org. Accessed 2 May 2008, p. 88.

15 Rueschemeyer et al., *Capitalist Development*, p. 43.

16 Ibid., p. 44.

17 Ibid., p. 46.

18 Dahl, *Democracy*, p. 222.

19 *Sendero Luminoso* (Shining Path) is a Maoist splinter group of the Communist Party of Peru who took up arms against the Peruvian State in 1980. The *guevarista* Movimiento Revolucionario Tupac Amaru (MRTA) also launched a war against the Peruvian state, but they were not as effective or as active as *Sendero*.

20 Montoya, D., 1995, 'Escenario electoral en las zonas de emergencia', in *Quehacer* 93: 46–50.

21 Ibid., p. 48.

22 Ibid., p. 47.

23 Schady, N. R., 1999, *Seeking Votes: The Political Economy of Expenditures by the Peruvian Social Fund* (FONCODES), 1991–1995. Washington: World Bank Poverty Division/Poverty Reduction and Economic Management Network Policy Research Working Paper 2166. Available from: www.econ.worldbank.org/docs/611.pdf. Accessed 6 August 2003.

24 Montoya, 'Escenario electoral'.

25 Planas, P., 2000, *La democracia volátil: Movimientos, partidos, líderes políticos y conductas electorales en el Perú contemporáneo*. Lima: Friedrich Ebert Stiftung.

26 OAS, Unit for the Promotion of Democracy, 1997, *Executive Summary, Electoral Observation, Peru 1995*. OAS: Washington, p. 29; Conaghan, *Public Life in the Time of Alberto Fujimori*, notes that there was a failure on the part of the press to follow up on this due to newspaper reliance on official sources: 'when the Jurado Nacional de Elecciones and the Attorney General's Office went silent on the matter, news coverage of the matter virtually ceased' (p. 16).

27 Planas, *La democracia volátil*, p. 354.

28 Tanaka, *La Situación de la democracia en Colombia, Perú y Venezuela a inicios de siglo*. Lima: Comisión Andina de Juristas, p. 51.

29 OAS, *Executive Summary*.

30 Ibid., p. 28.

31 Tanaka, *La Situación de la democracia*, p. 51.

32 Kornblith, M., 2001, 'Confiabilidad y transparencia de las elecciones en Venezuela: examen de los comicios del 30 de julio de 2000', in J. V. Carrasquero, T. Maingon and F. Welsch (eds), *Venezuela en transición: elecciones y democracia 1998–2000*, Caracas: Consejo Nacional de Ciencia y Tecnología (CONICIT)/Red Universataria de Estudios Políticos de Venezuela-Redpol/CDB Publicaciones, pp. 133–164, p. 136.

33 PROVEA, 2001, *Situación de los Derechos Humanos en Venezuela: Informe Annual Octubre 2000/Septiembre 2001*. Caracas: PROVEA, p. 17.

34 OAS, 2001, *Electoral Observations in the Americas Series, No.26/Electoral Observation in Peru, 2000*. Available from: http://upd.oas.org/lab/Documents/publications/electoral_observa tion/2000/pbl_26_2000_eng.pdf. Accessed 6 August 2003, pp. 15–16.

35 Julia Buxton, personal communication. See also: Buxton, J. D., 2001, *The Failure of Political Reform in Venezuela*. Aldershot: Ashgate.

36 Ibid., p. 84.

37 Ibid., pp. 51–60.

38 Conaghan, *Public Life in the Time of Alberto Fujimori*, p. 17.

39 Fujimori had been in power for five years as opposed to Chávez being in power less than two. The main opposition leader in Peru, Alan García, was in exile while all the major opposition candidates to Chávez were still in the country, and the parties still maintained substantial support in the National Assembly and in local government.

40 OAS (Organisation of American States), 2002, *General elections Venezuela 2000: electoral obser-vations in the Americas Series No. 30*. Available from: www.upd.oas.org/lab/Documents/publications/electoral_observation/2000/pbl_30_2000_eng.pdf. Accessed 6 August 2003, p. 58.

41 Abstention increased by 40% in Venezuelan presidential elections between 1973 and 2000 (Ryan, J. J., 2001, 'Painful exit: electoral abstention and neoliberal reform in Latin America'. Paper prepared for delivery at 2001 meeting of the Latin American Studies Association, Washington D.C., 6–8 September. Available from: http://136.142.158.105/Lasa2001/RyanJeffrey.pdf. Accessed 6 August 2003, p. 17). Almost 50% abstained in the elections of 1998; 62% in the referendum convoking a Constituent Assembly (April 1999); 54% in Constituent Assembly election (July 1999); 56% in referendum approving the new constitution

(December, 1999); 43% in the 2000 presidential elections; 76.50% in trade union leadership referendum (December 2000). Peréz Baralt identified three reasons for electoral abstention: 'progressive loss of credibility of the obligatory vote, erosion of party loyalties and a negative attitude to the political system' (Peréz Baralt, C., 2001, 'Cambios en la participación electoral', in Carrasquero et al. (eds), *Venezuela en transición*, pp. 123–133, p. 125). Buxton concurs and adds that in relation to the Chávez government, its radical institutional reform was carried out without the expressed support of a majority of Venezuelans (Buxton, J., 2000, 'Hugo Chávez and populist continuity in Venezuela'. Paper for the Political Studies Association – UK 50th Annual Conference 10–13 April, London. Available from: www.psa.ac.uk/cps/2000/Buxton%20Julia.pdf. Accessed: 6 August 2003). Despite this however Coppedge shows that: 'The size of Chávez's base of electoral support ... remains solid in comparative perspective [with previous Venezuelan presidents and other Latin American leaders]' (Coppedge, M., 2002, 'Venezuela: popular sovereignty versus liberal democracy'. Kellogg Institute Working Paper No. 294. Available from: www.nd.edu/~kellogg/WPS/294.pdf. Accessed 6 August 2003, pp. 4–5). Furthermore there have been improvements recently, with the 2006 presidential elections having an abstention rate of approximately 25%, an historic low for Venezuela in recent times.

42   Haussman, R. and Rigobon, R., 2004. *En busca del cisne negro: Análisis de la evidencia estadística sobre fraude electoral en Venezuela*. Available from: www.sumate.org. Accessed 17 April 2008.

43   Weisbrot, M., Rosnick, D., and Tucker, T., 2004, *Briefing Paper: Black Swans, Conspiracy Theories, and the Quixotic Search for Fraud:A Look at Hausmann and Rigobón's Analysis of Venezuela's Referendum Vote*. Available from: www.cepr.net. Accessed 18 August 2008.

44   See for example: McCoy, J., 2004, 'What really happened in Venezuela?' Available from: www.venezuelanalysis.com/articles.php?artno=1271. Accessed 17 April 2008. See also: OAS, 2004, 'Press Release, statement of OAS electoral observation mission of venezuelan presidential referendum, August 18, 2004'. Available from: www.oas.org. Accessed 25 August 2004.

45   European Union Election, 2006, Observation Mission Presidential Elections Venezuela 2006, 'Preliminary Statement, 5th December 2006'. Available from: http://ec.europa.eu/external_relations/human_rights/eu_election_ass_observ/venezuela_2006/prelim.pdf. Accessed 17 April 2008.

46   Grompone, R., 2000, 'Al día siguiente: el fujimorismo como proyecto inconcluso de transformación política y social', in J. Cotler and R. Grompone, 2000, *El fujimorismo: ascenso y caída de un régimen autoritario*. Lima: Instituto de Estudios Peruanos, pp. 77–175, p. 80.

47   Public support for the coup reached more than 80% of the population according to opinion polls. See Tanaka, M., 2001, *Las Fuerzas Armadas en la Region Andina: No deliberantes o actores políticos?* Lima: Comisión Andina de Juristas, p. 48.

48   Ibid., p. 51.

49   Ibid., p. 52.

50   Grompone, 'Al día siguiente', p. 107.

51   Tanaka, *Las Fuerzas Armadas*, p. 52.

52   A number of notable examples are the political analyst Miriam Kornblith, the constitutionalists Richard Combellas and Alan Brewer Carías, the writer Angela Zago, and journalist and former Metropolitan mayor Alfredo Peña, to name but a few who have become powerful critics of the government.

53 García-Guadilla, M. P., 2003, 'Civil society: institutionalisation, fragmentation, autonomy', in Ellner, S. and Hellinger, D. (eds), 2003, *Venezuelan Politics in the Chávez Era: Class, Polarization and Conflict*. Boulder, CO and London: Lynne Rienner, pp. 179–197.

54 Álvarez, A. E., 2003, 'State reform before and after Chávez's election', in Ellner and Hellinger (eds), *Venezuelan Politics in the Chavez Era*, pp. 147–161, p. 155. Indeed political parties are not mentioned in the constitution and are only referred to once as 'associations with political ends'. Furthermore, state funding for parties was abolished; see López Maya, M. and Lander L. E., 1999, 'Triunfos en Tiempos de Transición: Actores de Vocación Popular en las Elecciones Venezolanas de 1998', in *America Latina, Hoy* 21 (Abril): 41–50.

55 Norden, D. L., 2003, 'Democracy in uniform: Chávez and the Venezuelan armed forces', in Ellner and Hellinger (eds), *Venezuelan Politics in the Chavez Era*, pp. 93–113, p. 93.

56 Youngers, C., 2000, *Deconstructing Democracy: Peru under President Alberto Fujimori*. Washington: Washington Office on Latin America, p. 34.

57 PROVEA, 2007, *Informe Anual 2006–2007*. Available from: www.derechos.ve.org. Accessed 10 June 2008, p. 275.

58 Youngers, *Deconstructing Democracy*.

59 Conaghan, *Public Life in the Time of Alberto Fujimori*, pp. 9–11.

60 Álvarez, 'State reform before and after Chávez's election'.

61 Mauceri in Youngers, *Deconstructing Democracy*, p. 46.

62 Manrique, M., 2001, 'La participación política de las Fuerzas Armadas venezolanas en el sistema política (1998–2001)', in Tanaka, *Las Fuerzas Armadas*, pp. 305–337.

63 Wilpert, G. 2007, *Changing Venezuela by Taking Power: The History and Policies of the Chávez Government*. London and New York: Verso, p. 49.

64 Ibid., p. 50.

65 Tanaka, *Las Fuerzas Armadas*, p. 52.

66 Buxton, J., 2003, 'Economic policy and the rise of Hugo Chávez', in Ellner and Hellinger (eds), *Venezuelan Politics in the Chávez Era*, pp. 113–130.

67 Gonzales de Olarte, E., 1998, *El Neoliberalismo a la Peruana: Economía, Políticia del ajuste estructural, 1990–1997*. Lima: Consorico de Investigación Economica/Instituto de Estudios Peruanos, p. 41.

68 The most notorious human rights violations in recent Venezuelan history was the repression of the *caracazo* on 27/28 February 1989 leading to the deaths of anything from 400 to 3,000 people (see below). For information on these events and other cases of human rights violations in Venezuela see the Cofavic website: www.cofavic.org.ve/.

69 It has been estimated that total deaths during the conflict (1980–95) at the hands of both *Sendero Luminoso* and the security forces amounted to 30,000 people, with 4,236 people forcibly 'disappeared' by security forces, 600,000 displaced and around 2,000 innocent people incarcerated, of which 546 have been liberated. See the Peruvian Truth Commission website at www.cverdad.org.pe/. See also Cuya, E., 1999, *La dictadura de Fujimori: marionetismo, corrupción y violaciones de los derechos humanos*. Available from: http://derechos.org/diml/doc/cuya4.html. Accessed 9 July 2003; ANIL (Associación Nacional de Inocentes Liberados), 2002, *Informe Final de la Comisión Especial de Asistencia a los Indultados Inocentes (CEAII) creado mediante Decreto Supremo N° 002-2002-JUS*. Lima: ANIL. For more information on human rights violations under Fujimori see also the Equipo Nizkor website on Peru at http://derechos.org/nizkor/peru/informes.html and the Washington Office on Latin America website at www.wola.org/andes.

70 See reports on Fujimori's court case at www.wola.org/andes. Accessed 12 June 2008.

71 See Coordinadora Nacional de Derechos Humanos, no date, 'Dossier Fujimori: Las leyes que destruyeron el Estado de Derecho'. Available from: www.dhperu.org. Accessed 10 June 2008, p. 10.

72 PROVEA, 2005, *Situación de los Derechos Humanos en Venezuela: Informe Annual Octubre 2004/Septiembre 2005*. Available from: http://derechos.org.ve/. Accessed 6 August 2007, pp. 53 –55, own calculations based on PROVEA statistics

73 PROVEA, 2004, *Situación de los Derechos Humanos en Venezuela: Informe Annual Octubre 2003/Septiembre 2004*. Available from: http://derechos.org.ve/. Accessed 6 August 2007, p. 288.

74 PROVEA, *Informe Anual 2006–2007*, pp. 355–358.

75 Socorro, M., 2003. 'La gran tragedia de la democracia venezolana es la impunidad' . Available from: http://cofavic.org.ve/p-noticias-310303.htm. Accessed 24 July 2003.

76 The *caracazo* massacre carried out by the security forces during the second Pérez presidency in 1989, for example, is commemorated annually by *chavismo* as emblematic of the cruelty of the previous *puntofijista* regime.

77 PROVEA, *Informe Annual Octubre 2004/Septiembre 2005*, p. 53, own calculations based on PROVEA statistics.

78 PROVEA, 2003, *Situación de los Derechos Humanos en Venezuela: Informe Annual Octubre 2002/Septiembre 2003: Las muertes de abril*. Available from: www.derechos.org.ve/. Accessed: 9 January 2004.

79 For an opposition account of the coup and its aftermath see Tablante, C., 2002, *Primer Borrador de la Comisión Política que investiga los sucesos del 11,12,13,y 14 de abril*. Available from: www.logiconline.org.ve/primerborrado1r.htm. Accessed 6 August 2003. For the government perspective see AN (Asamblea Nacional de la Republica Bolivariana de Venezuela), 2002, *Informe de la comisión parlamentaria especial para investigar los sucesos de abril de 2002*. Available from: www.urru.org/11A/Interpelaciones/Informe_Conclusiones_Chavistas10.htm. Accessed 10 December 2002. For a theoretical discussion on the nature of the coup see Rey, J. C., 2002, 'Consideraciones políticas sobre un insólito golpe de Estado'. Available from: www.analitica.com/bitblioteca/juan_carlos_rey/insolito_golpe.asp. Accessed 25 October 2002.

80 Control of the National Guard was unclear at that moment, as some senior officers of that force were involved with or sympathetic to the coup. Armed civilians from both sides were also alleged to have been shooting at demonstrators, and those who died were from both the opposition and the government sides (PROVEA, 2003). Venevision TV repeatedly showed a video clip of government supporters, among them MVR councillor Richard Peñalver, allegedly shooting at demonstrators. However, a documentary by O'Briain and Bartley showed that there were no demonstrators within range of their guns, suggesting rather that they were shooting defensively as the accused claim. O'Briain, D. and Bartley, K., 2002, *The Revolution Will Not Be Televised*. Dublin: Power Pictures. See online: www.chavezthefilm.com. See also Lemoine, M., 2002a, 'Carta abierta al director de 'El Universal'. Available from: www.lainsignia.org/2002/junio/ibe_051.htm. Accessed 17 August 2003. See *El Nacional*, 2002, 'Mal número, '14 fallecidos', 13 April, pp. C/6, C/7, for political affiliation of some of the victims on 11 April.

81 The Carmona government, according to PROVEA, 2003 (no page no.), used 'classical practices of dictatorships: political persecution and torture for political reasons, prisoners of conscience, closing of media outlets and a repression of a number of demonstrations which exceeded the daily average of the last eight years … It is a paradox that a large part of those who organised, facilitated and elaborated the coup,

had formulated legitimate criticisms of the Chávez government, for the same rights and principles that the government of Carmona ended up violating in a most radical manner.'

82 Ibid.

83 See Villegas Poljak, E., 2003, 'When the press sacrifices its credibility to overthrow a government'. Available from: www.vheadline.com/readnews.asp?id=9573. Accessed 16 July 2003.

84 Lichtenberg, J., 2002, 'Foundations and limits of freedom of the press', in D. McQuail (ed.) 2002, *McQuail's Reader in Mass Communication Theory*. London: Sage.

85 Ibid., p. 176.

86 Ibid., p. 181.

87 Ibid.

88 Habermas, J., 2000, *The Structural Transformation of the Public Sphere*. Cambridge, MA: MIT Press.

89 Herman, E. S. and Chomsky, N., 1994, *Manufacturing Consent: The Political Economy of the Mass Media*. London: Vintage, p. 2.

90 Ibid.

91 The Inter American Press Association (IAPA) has been critical of both the Fujimori and Chávez governments with respect to freedom of expression. Concluding a visit to Peru in February, 1999 the IAPA reported that there were 'serious threats to the liberty of the press in Perú' from the Peruvian government (IAPA, 1999, 'La Prensa Bajo Amenaza en Perú', IAPA press release, 24 February. Available at: www.sipiapa.com/pressreleases/srchcountrydetail.cfm?PressRelease ID=81. Accessed 16 July 2003). Daniel Arbilla of the AIPA, concluding a visit to Venezuela, compared Fujimori and Chávez in the way both used 'subtle dubious legalities to intimidate the media and limit freedom of expression' (AFP (Association France Presse and AP (Associated Press), 2002, 'La SIP responsabiliza a Chávez por ataques a los medios', in El *Nacional*, 26 February, p. 4). The IAPA similarly states that there is 'no press freedom [in Venezuela]' and emphasises 'the impunity that protects attacks against journalists and the media' (IAPA, 2003, *2003 Report on Press Freedom in Venezuela*. Available from: www.sipiapa.com/publications/report_venezuela2003.cfm. Accessed 16 July 2003.) For Peru see also HRW (Human Rights Watch), 1999, *World Report*. Available from: www.hrw.org/. Accessed 20 November 2003; and HRW, 2000, *World Report*. Available from: www.hrw.org/. Accessed 20 November 2003. For Venezuela see Vivanco, J. M., 2003, 'Venezuela: limit state control of media/letter to President Chavez'. Available from: http://hrw.org/press/2003/06/venezuela 062303-ltr.htm. Accessed 6 August 2003. See also Bourgeat, R., 2003, 'Venezuela: caught between an authoritarian president and intolerant media'. Available from: www.rsf.fr/IMG/pdf/doc-2047.pdf. Accessed 6 August 2003. For the Peruvian general election see RSF (Reporters Without Borders), 2000, *Peru General Election: 9 April 2000*. Available from: www.rsf.org/rsf/uk/html/ameriques/cplp/cp/230300.html. Accessed 6 August 2003.

92 Wood, D., 2000, 'The Peruvian press under recent authoritarian regimes, with special reference to the autogolpe of President Fujimori', in *Bulletin of Latin American Studies* 19: 17–32.

93 Ibid.

94 Ibid., p. 32.

95 Conaghan, *Public Life in the Time of Alberto Fujimori*.

96 Ibid., p. 3.

97 Such as left of centre tabloid *La Republica* and popular tabloid *El Popular*. 'Quality' newspaper *El Comercio* was also known for its professional ethics and a certain editorial

independence (see Fowks, J., 2000, *Suma y resta de la realidad: medios de comunicación y elecciones generales 2000 en el Perú*. Lima: Friedrich Ebert Stiftung, p. 111).

98 Vladivideos are a library of thousands of video tapes recorded secretly by the president's 'assessor' and de facto head of the SIN, Vladimiro Montesinos, showing prominent politicians, media owners, business people and even entertainers receiving bribes in exchange for favours. When the first of these videos came to light, showing prominent opposition congressman Alex Kouri receiving a bribe to pass to the government benches after the 2000 elections, this led to Fujimori's flight to Japan and subsequent removal from office by Congress.

99 Conaghan *Public Life in the Time of Alberto Fujimori*, pp. 16–17.

100 Herman and Chomsky, *Manufacturing Consent*, pp. 29–31.

101 Lugo, J. and Romero, J., 2003, 'From friends to foes: Venezuela's media goes from consensual space to confrontational actor', in *Sicronia*, Spring. Available from: http://sincronia.cucsh.udg.mx/lugoromero.htm. Accessed 20 August 2003.

102 Klein, N., 2003, 'Venezuela's media coup', in *The Nation* 276(8): 10. The Cisneros Group has important business in beer, bread and telecommunications and is one of the wealthiest companies in Latin America. Klein notes that the Cisneros Group are deeply involved in franchise agreements with important US companies such as AOL, Coca-Cola and Pizza Hut, and is fully committed to free trade and globalisation.

103 See Lugo and Romero, 'From friends to foes', p. 40, notes 56 and 57.

104 Villamediana, C., 2000, 'Crónica massmediática de un triunfo anunciado', in M. Bisbal (ed.), *Antropología de unas elecciones*. Caracas: Universidad Católica Andrés Bello, pp. 69–85.

105 Lugo and Romero, 'From friends to foes'.

106 Ibid., p. 30.

107 A press conference called by the attorney general, Isaias Rodriguez, was hastily taken off the air when he began to denounce the action as a coup (González Plessmann, A. J., 2002, 'Venezuela: oposición y estado de derecho', in *Observatorio Social de América Latina* III(7): 19–23, p. 19). The de facto government of Carmona closed down the state television station VTV, community radio stations such as Radio Catia, and many of their workers were arrested and some tortured. PROVEA reports that apart from the closing of VTV, five community stations were raided, three journalists detained and one of them tortured. (PROVEA, 2002, *Situación de los Derechos Humanos en Venezuela: Informe Annual Octubre 2001/Septiembre 2002*. Available from: www.derechos.org.ve/. Accessed 6 August 2003.) There was a blackout on news of pro-government demonstrations resulting in demonstrations outside some television stations demanding that the truth be shown, and the resignation of some media staff, for example Andrés Izarra, chief of information at RCTV. See González Plessmann ('Venezuela', p. 20). See Bourgeat ('Venezuela', p. 5) and PROVEA (*Informe Annual Octubre 2002/Septiembre 2003*) and O'Briain and Bartley (*The Revolution Will Not Be Televised*). A satellite relayer DirecTV (owned by the Cisneros company) stopped the signal of Colombian satellite station Caracol as it began to broadcast the return of Chávez live from the Presidential palace (PROVEA, *Informe Annual Octubre 2002/Septiembre 2003*). Newspapers, excepting *Ultimas Noticias*, did not publish on Sunday 14 April, after Chávez's return to power, continuing the news blackout (fieldwork observation).

108 González Plessmann, 'Venezuela'.

109 Bourgeat ('Venezuela') reports on the private media operating as a cartel and exchanging footage, providing non-stop reports of opposition protests (pp. 5–7). Simultaneous live transmission was provided every evening of strike leaders and opposition press conferences. Commercial advertising was replaced entirely by pro-opposition spots urging the population to take part in demonstrations and protests,

including non-payment of taxes. According to government estimates the television stations broadcast an average of 700 pro-opposition advertisements every day during the strike (Klein, 'Venezuela's media coup'). Even when some normal programming was resumed, split-second subliminal pro-opposition messages were inserted into films and children's entertainment (Villegas Poljak, 'When the press sacrifices its credibility').

110 Supporters of Chávez are regularly referred to as 'hordes' and the pro-government Bolivarian Circles as 'terror circles' (Reporters Without Borders (RSF), 2003, *Venezuela 2003 Annual Report*. Available from: www.rsf.fr/article.php3?id_article=6230 &Valider=OK. Accessed 6 August 2003, p. 15, quoting government Minister Nora Uribe).

111 For Ibeyise Pacheco's role in coup see Lemoine, M., 2002, 'How hate media incited the coup against the president: Venezuela's press power'. Available from: http://mondediplo.com/2002/08/10venezuela. Accessed 26 July 2003. For Pacheco reporting false information against the government (Ali Rodriguez, head of PdVSA) see O'Donoghue, P., 2003, 'Opposition editor Ibeyise Pacheco eating humble pie for OTT accusations' . Available from: www.vheadline.com/readnews. asp?id=9736. Accessed 24 July 2003. On Patricia Poleo's role in the coup see Poleo, P., 2002, 'La verdadera historia de un gobierno que duró sólo horas por estar susten- tado en los intereses particulares y no en los del colectivo', in *El Nuevo País*, 16 April, pp. 3–4; and on making false paramilitary videos see Villegas, V., 2002, 'Mentiras y videos', in *El Mundo*, 13 June. Available from: www.analitica.com/bitblioteca/ vladimir_villegas/mentiras_y_videos.asp. Accessed 10 December 2002. Marta Colomina broadcast the location of government officials and those linked to the government as she celebrated the coup against Chávez along with fellow broadcaster Cesar Miguel Rondón on Union Radio (fieldwork observation). Colomina also has described the ruling party parliamentarians as 'ridiculous', the government as 'farcical' and its political programme as a 'third rate revolution' (RSF, 2003, p. 16, quoting government minister Nora Uribe).

112 The coup itself is evidence of opposition subterfuge with media cooperation. Large caches of arms were found in the house of prominent businessman and coup supporter Issac Perez Recao (Palacios, M., 2002, 'Incautaron armas de guerra en la casa de Isaac Pérez Recao', in *El Nacional*, 26 April, p. 8). Police investigations have revealed that the shooting of three demonstrators at a pro-opposition rally in support of dissident military officers occupying a public square in Caracas was organised by persons linked to those officers. Bombs outside the Spanish and Colombian embassies and the deaths of three soldiers linked to these officers were also suspected to be the work of this group. All these crimes were prominently blamed on the government by the media and few covered the results of police detective work. See Villegas Poljak ('When the press sacrifices its credibility') and Últimas Noticias, 2003, 'Pesquisas jefes de la Disip y el Cicpc los acusaron de nuevo de ser los reyes del c-4 en Caracas', in *Últimas Noticias*, 24 July, p. 12. Available from: www.ultimasnoti- cias.com.ve. Accessed 24 July 2003.

113 Lichtenberg, 'Foundations and limits of freedom of the press'.

114 Roberts, K., 1998, *Deepening Democracy? The Modern Left and Social Movements in Chile and Peru*. Stanford: Stanford University Press.

115 Degregori, C. I., Coronel, J. and del Pino, P., 1998, 'Government, citizenship and democracy: a regional perspective', in J. Crabtree and J. Thomas (eds), *Fujimori's Peru: The Political Economy*. London: University of London/Institute of Latin American Studies, pp. 243–265, p. 261.

116 Conaghan, *Public Life in the Time of Alberto Fujimori*, p. 19.

117 Over 20% of the national budget was apportioned to the ministry of the presidency in 1995. See Schady, *Seeking Votes*, pp. 3–4.

118 Tanaka points to the near defeat of Fujimori in the referendum of 1993 and defeats in the municipal elections of the same year. See Tanaka, M., 1998, 'From Movmientismo to media politics: the changing boundaries between society and politics in Fujimori's Peru', in Crabtree and Tomas (eds), *Fujimori's Peru*, pp. 229–243.

119 Tanaka, 'From Movmientismo to media politics', p. 235.

120 Conaghan, *Public Life in the Time of Alberto Fujimori*.

121 López-Maya, M., 2002, 'Venezuela after the caracazo: forms of protest in a deinstitutionalized context', in *Bulletin of Latin American Studies* 21(2): 199–219.

122 García-Guadilla, 'Civil society', p. 179.

123 Ibid., p. 186.

124 Ibid., p. 194.

125 Molina J. E., 2001, 'Change and continuity in Venezuelan electoral behaviour in the 1998–2000 elections', in *Bulletin of Latin American Studies* 21(2): 219–248.

126 Ellner, S., 2001, 'The radical potential of Chavismo in Venezuela: the first year and a half in power', in *Latin American Perspectives* 28(5): 5–32, p. 18.

127 Steve Ellner, 2008, *Rethinking Venezuelan Politics: Class, Conflict, and the Chávez Phenomenon*. Boulder, CO and London: Lynne Rienner, pp. 175–195.

128 Ellner, S., 2003. 'Organised labor and the challenge of Chavismo', in Ellner and Hellinger (eds), *Venezuelan Politics in the Chavez Era*, pp. 161–178.

129 Ibid., p. 176.

130 Ellner, *Rethinking Venezuelan Politics*, pp. 152–158.

131 Raby, D. L., 2006, *Democracy and Revolution: Latin America and Socialism Today*, London and Ann Arbor MI: Pluto Press and Toronto: Between the Lines, p. 191.

132 Ellner, 'Organised labor'.

133 Ballón, E., 2002, 'El Toledismo y el movimiento social', in E. Ballón, C. Soria, G. Riofrío, E. Castillo, U. Huamala, G. Carrasco, J. Gamero and R. Ruiz, R., 2002, *Perú Hoy: Toledo: A un año de gobierno*. Lima: DESCO Centro de Estudios y Promoción del Desarrollo, pp. 13–60. According to Ballón these associates and allies consisted of 'the cúpula of the Armed Forces, Fujimori's closest [political] associates, the SIN, the principal business groups (mining companies, chief exporters, and the financial system) and transnational capital, whose presence grew notably as a result of the privatisation process, with the blessing of the IMF and multilateral organisations, sectors of the Catholic Church and the subordination of some of the media' (p. 17).

134 Rey, 'Consideraciones políticas'; Buxton, *The Failure of Political Reform in Venezuela*.

135 González-Plessmann, A. J., 2003. 'Venezuela: torn by polarisation'. Available from: www.wola.org/andes/Venezuela/venezuela_update.pdf. Accessed 6 August 2003, p. 3.

136 See McClintock, C., 1996, 'La voluntad política presidencial y la ruptura constitucional de 1992 en el Perú', in F. Tuesta Soldevilla (ed.), *Los enigmas de poder: Fujimori 1990–1996*, 2nd ed. Lima: Fundación Friedrich Ebert, pp. 303–331, pp. 60–66.

137 See Fowks, *Suma y resta de la realidad*.

138 International reaction to the coup, particularly from the US and Spain was favourable to the rebels and it is accepted by a number of political analysts that the US was involved in the preparations for the coup. See Aharonián, A. R., 2002, 'Venezuela: Un golpe con olor a hamburguesa, jamón y petróleo'. Available from www.analitica.com/va/politica/opinion/1578534.asp#HOLA. Accessed 10 December 2002. See Chapter 7 for a more detailed discussion of US involvement in the destabilisation of the Chávez government.

139 For opinions on US knowledge of Fujimori's activities, see, for example, Fienstein, T. and Youngers, C., 2002, 'Shedding light on the past: declassification of US documents'. Available at: www.wola.org/andes/Peru/peru_declassification_report.htm. Accessed 25 July 2003.

140 Delacour, J., 2005. 'The op-ed assassination of Hugo Chávez', in *Extra!*, November/December. Available from: www.fair.org. Accessed 23 April 2008.

141 Ellner and Hellinger, *Venezuelan Politics in the Chavez Era*.

142 Rueschemeyer, et al., *Capitalist Development and Democracy*.

143 Ibid., p. 44.

6 The consequences and impact of populism: institutionalisation and democractisation in Chávez's Venezuela

Introduction

The previous chapter examined some key political elements in order to assess the relative democratic and authoritarian balance of both presidencies. The chapter underlined the fact that for democracy to develop, it is important to expand popular participation at the political level in order to achieve legitimacy. Expanded political participation alone is insufficient, however, and must be accompanied by participation in the economic and social spheres as well (Chapter 4).

This chapter will expand on these ideas by examining in more detail the political consequences and impact of populism. Examining the literature, two principal consequences of populism emerge: (i) increased popular participation; and (ii) diminished institutionalisation. This analysis, I will argue, however, overlooks the influence of ideology on the extent of popular participation in specific populist experiences, and fails to place Latin American populism, and specific populist governments, within a global and regional context.

In order to deal with these issues, the chapter will cover three main areas. The first section will examine some writings on populism by two well-known US-based political scientists, Kurt Weyland and Kenneth M. Roberts, who emphasise the consequence of diminished institutionalisaton. The second section will identify the failings in this analysis, examining it by reference to the current global and regional context, particularly the expansion of democracy in the age of globalisation. The third section will specifically analyse the Chávez presidency to illustrate these arguments, referring once again to the Fujimori presidency for comparative purposes. The chapter will then end with a number of concluding observations.

The consequences and impact of populism

Introduction

As explained in Chapter 1, the literature identifies two main consequences of populism in Latin America, one positive and one negative. On the positive side there is, according to some analysts, increased popular participation, and greater assertiveness and organisation of the popular and middle classes.[1] As a result, many in those classes experience higher living standards through tighter regulation of working conditions and more access to welfare.[2] Furthermore, this contributes to a greater feeling of national consciousness, often expressed culturally through an interest in national customs, music and art.[3]

On the negative side, however, which is emphasised more in the literature, this participation is not seen as genuine or thorough, but rather as a 'pseudo-participation' which does not lead to real structural change and ultimately perpetuates the inequality and exploitation characteristic of the region. A principal reason for this is that representative institutions are weakened, as the centre, usually the executive, exerts most control over popular participation, discouraging group autonomy and reinforcing the political context which can lead to a re-emergence of new populist movements and regimes.[4] Populism, therefore, damages the chances for democratic development and long-term economic improvement. In essence analysts argue that populism is bad for democracy, that it inhibits democratic development and damages democratic institutions.

There are a number of problems with this analysis, however. First there is a failure to pay sufficient attention to the context and causes of the emergence of populism, not just at a national level, but also at a regional and global level. Second there is an equal failure to note the inherent weaknesses of liberal democracy, not just on a practical level but also on the theoretical and philosophical levels. The conclusion we come to is that populism is a reflection of those weaknesses, not their cause or consequence.

Populism and democracy

Two of the best known US-based writers on populism, Kurt Weyland and Kenneth M. Roberts, illustrate these shortcomings particularly well. Both Weyland and Roberts are well known in political science circles for developing the concept of 'neopopulism' to describe congruence between populism and neoliberalism (see Chapter 1). In this section, however, we will look at some of their more general writings on populism, with a particular focus on explicit or implicit comparisons of populism with democracy, and the negative effects of the former on the institutions of the latter.

The main criticism put forward in this chapter to both Weyland's and Roberts's conception of populism is their identification of populist leaders as amoral beings whose only *raison* for being involved in politics is to seek, gain and maintain power. This type of leadership, they argue, sidelines institutions, weakening them and rendering them inoperative and ineffective. Whereas ideology and class may have a role in the leader's ascendance, these are purely instrumental and incidental to the main aim of securing his or her personal power. Equally, the organisation of populist movements, or the lack of, is also as a result of this wish to secure power. Populism therefore, in this view, is reduced to being simply a means for the populist leader to achieve power for its own sake, regardless of the ideological content, class makeup, or organisational structure of the movement. This conception of populism is then, explicitly or implicitly, compared with democracy, which is equated with institutions and which is, often more implicitly, paired with the market to make up the formula which can achieve true – as opposed to pseudo – participation. In other words, populism is but a pale shadow of true democracy, which we can infer, is that which we enjoy in the 'West'.

In one article written by Weyland in 2001 he makes this position quite clear: 'Populism first and foremost', he asserts,

> shapes patterns of political rule, not the allocation of socio-economic benefits or losses. This political redefinition captures best the basic goal of populist leaders, to win and exercise power, while using economic and social policy as an instrument for this purpose. Thus, this reconcepetualisation is most attuned to the opportunities of populist leaders and their weak commitment to substantive policies, ideas, and ideologies.[5]

Hence populist leaders are empty of ideological or programmatic aims. Their over-riding concern is the gaining and maintenance of power. Any policy, in whichever ideological direction, is solely attributable to this thirst for power and not any over-riding political vision or conviction that this leader might have. Indeed, according to this view, a populist leader simply cannot have such a vision, because their desire for power is their only vision.

A corollary to this view, furthermore, is that the 'masses' which follow this leader, are equally devoid of ideology, class loyalty, or political conviction. As each action on the part of the leader, each policy choice, each organisational move, is simply to perpetuate himself in power by currying favour with the 'voters', so the 'voters' assess these moves in terms of their own personal preferences and accept or reject them on polling day on that basis. Hence not only is the leader power-hungry, he is also highly manipulative in his quest for power – and the 'voters' ripe for manipulation on the one hand, while being highly fickle on the other. The opposition meanwhile simply reacts to these power strategies, and in itself is seemingly devoid of ideology or class loyalty.

Institutions in this scenario equally serve the power designs of the leader. The 'direct, quasi-personal relationship' between leader and masses bypasses or deinstitutionalises established intermediary organisation. Weyland, however, does state that populists can 'routinize their charisma' by introducing elements of party organisation or clientelism. These organisations 'succeed', however, when 'party organisation congeals and constrains the leader's latitude'. Political success thus transforms populism into a different type of rule that rests on non-populist strategies. 'It ... transforms itself.'[6] When a populist leader therefore establishes a 'successful' institution, it is despite not because of his power strategies.

In another, more recent, article Kenneth M. Roberts echoes many of these points, but in a more subtle manner being more to the left than Weyland.[7] In this article, Roberts attempts to prove, by using a comparative study of Presidents Fujimori of Peru and Chávez of Venezuela that the organisational nature of populist movements is not only due to 'structural and institutional contexts, but also [to] the nature and degree of conflict between populist movements and elite, extrapartisan power structures'.[8] What Roberts argues is that the way populist movements are organised, specifically the nature and extent of grassroots organisation and mobilisation within those movements, is directly influenced by the intensity of elite-led resistance to the policies and programmes being proposed or implemented by these movements. The core of his argument mirrors Weyland's instrumentalist notion of populist organisation, in the sense that 'organisation is often an instrument to push through social reforms and to wage conflict in extraelectoral spheres of contestation'.[9]

In essence, Roberts argues that organisational efforts on the part of a populist leader function on the logic of power more than on ideology or class interests. There is a leader-fixated notion of populist organisation and a corresponding down-playing of popular agency and autonomy. There is little consideration of the possibility of popular organisation as being a common project built on a partnership between leader and people. Instead, the people are only the supporting cast to the leader as star and chief protagonist, rather than a symbol and facilitator of change dependent on popular legitimacy and support.

Underpinning these observations is Roberts's use of rational choice theory on the one hand and sociological theory on the other. So for example, from rational choice theory parties are seen as liabilities for populists,[10] whereas from a sociological perspective political organisation is a means of collective empowerment, particularly for working and lower class groups.[11] Mass organisation is needed to balance the 'concentrated economic and political dominance of elite groups'.[12]

Nonetheless the sociological reading is still seen primarily as instrumental in the maintenance of power, and not as an exercise of collective empowerment. There remains an overdetermining emphasis, as in Weyland, on leader and elite agency to the detriment of popular agency and ideological structure. Party organisations, thus, are, '*instruments* of collective empowerment that *serve the strategic needs of populist figures* whose *social reforms or rhetoric have engendered serious political conflict* with elite opponents'.[13] The leader is the 'creator' of these organisations mobilising followers 'for political combat'.[14] There is no sense of popular empowerment for its own sake here, no question of the leader *serving* the people in Roberts's conception, no suggestion indeed that a leader may, for example, *believe* in equality, in the eradication of poverty, in the redistribution of wealth and power, in the increased participation of the popular classes in the economic, social, cultural and political life of the nation, more than maintaining his or her power. The cynicism of power for power's sake, in Roberts's account, decisively overshadows the possibility of politics as redemption, as the locus of passions, as a zone of transformation and a path to 'Utopia'.

Nor is there sufficient recognition of wider global change and populist leaders' involvement in this change. Where Roberts maintains that social and political conflicts are '*unleashed* by populist movements',[15] he is underestimating the influence of the historical fissures along race or class lines, and the increased inequality caused by the implementation of neoliberal structural adjustment policies (SAPs) in Latin America in creating that polarisation. Rather he seems to be suggesting that such deeply engrained polarisation did not predate the election of populist leaders. Nor do we see any evidence of the class and ideological based nature of elite resistance contributing to such polarisation. The depiction of populist leaders as 'power-hungry' masks the fact that populist leaders, like any other political leader, represent and reflect particular groups and sections of society in their policy actions.

In conclusion, both Roberts's and Weyland's analyses overemphasise the 'rational choice' element in political decision-making, a utilitarianism which eclipses ideology and class differences. There is an absence of consideration of wider contextual and historical influences, most particularly class fissures, on the organisational make-up of populist movements and regimes. The role of ideology both in the causation of conflict and polarisation, and in the creation of specific populist movements is underemphasised. Instead, if they do exist they are to serve the interests of power, and are not aimed at changing structures. Moreover, populism is posited as democracy's opposite; both are juxtaposed as distinct types of political organisation. And in this comparative portrayal populism is seen to be inherently wanting in relation to democracy, largely because of the absence or weakness of institutions. Yet the relationship between populism and democracy is much more complex than this, and democracy in both the developed world as well as in the developing world is equally wanting, as we shall see in the next section.

Democracy in peril

The genesis and decline of 'Western' democracy

Nabulsi points out that it is struggle, not institutions, which create democracy:

> It is not only after one possesses democratic institutions that one practices democracy, nor is democracy merely a set of institutions or mechanisms such as elections. Democracy only holds if it emerges by customary practice in the public sphere, and in the case of Europe this custom developed through organised resistance to unrepresentative rule over generations.[16]

Furthermore, Jacques draws attention to the fact that democracy as a universal prescription for the developing world may be unsuitable for the purposes of development as it has usually been authoritarian, rather than democratic, regimes which have achieved economic development for the countries of the West, and the newly industrialised countries (NICs) of East Asia.[17]

Jacques goes on to itemise the different malaise affecting Western democracy which have a familiar ring in the context of democracy's problems in Latin America, as will be discussed below. He reports that Western democracy is suffering due to 'the decline of parties, the fall in turnout, a growing disregard for politicians, the displacement of politics from the centre-stage of society'.[18] The reasons for this are 'the decline of traditional social-democratic parties … [leading to] the erosion of choice … voting has become less meaningful. Politics has moved on to singular ground: that of the market.'[19] Jacques points out that it is the market, money, which now moves party politics, turning democracies, such as that of the US, into plutocracies. The media now determines political choice and electoral results, and is concentrated into the hands of powerful tycoons. Democracy, however, argues Jacques, traditionally acted as a constraint on the market, which evolved, as Nabulsi also points out, through the struggles of working people. Now that the market has superseded it: '[d]emocracy comes under siege.'[20]

Thus we can surmise from this brief discussion the following points. First, democracy is not simply the sum of its institutions, but evolves through practice which is often established through struggle, much of that outside the established laws and institutions of the existing regime. Second, democracy has evolved specifically, according to Jacques, through the organised struggles of the working classes to put checks on the market and so protect their positions. The global decline of democracy is due to that structure of checks on the market ceding to the market's supremacy, and neoliberal policies are the means by which this process is taking place. The rise of the market, therefore, is democracy's nemesis, and not, as is often claimed, its corollary.

As Harvey points out in his *Brief History of Neoliberalism*, neoliberalism has 'all along primarily functioned as a mask for practices that are all about the maintenance, reconstitution and restoration of elite class power'[21] and as such, is 'profoundly anti-democratic'.[22]

Democracy in Latin America under neoliberalism

Some who have analysed Latin American politics have also noted neoliberalism's negative effect on the quality and effectiveness of democracy in the region. Ryan, for example, has argued that neoliberal reform in Latin America is probably one of the principal reasons for the high levels of electoral abstention observed there in the 1990s.[23] Ellner shows quite graphically the role of neoliberalism and globalisation in undermining democratic institutions in Latin America.[24] He points to the use of deceit by politicians, in promising centrist policies then implementing ferocious pro-market programmes (i.e. Fujimori). He also points to the poor record of democratic politicians and institutions in defending the hard-won gains of Latin American working people, such as welfare and favourable labour policies, from the neoliberal onslaught. Institutions such as Congress in particular are perceived as irrelevant as a result of these tendencies, and those who introduce and defend the reforms within institutions are seen as being beholden to foreign interests.

This decline of democracy in Latin America is further illustrated in a 2004 report on democracy published by the UNDP. The report informs us that while democracy is the preferred system of government in Latin America, that support is highly qualified. Latin Americans have little faith in democracy's ability to improve living standards or in the institutions of democracy, particularly political parties.[25] The report emphasises that to achieve full democracy a citizen must be a 'full participant' in society – that is each citizen should have political, civil and social citizenship.[26] Political citizenship is high in the region, it claims, but confidence in political parties is low, as is trust in systems of justice, reflecting low levels of civil citizenship, and with 43.9% of the population living in poverty, social citizenship is equally low.[27] Furthermore, although the report does not highlight this fact, its statistical information shows that neoliberal policies have contributed to this situation, bringing low growth, increased poverty, increased inequality, and increased unemployment and underemployment.[28]

Unsurprisingly, as a result, citizens' perceptions of democracy have become increasingly negative. Most Latin Americans (57% in 2002) express support for democracy, but of those that do, almost half (48.1%) value economic development more highly, and would support an authoritarian government if it solved the country's problems (44.9%).[29] Furthermore, those who show the least faith in democracy are those who live in countries with higher levels of inequality, illustrating graphically the link between lack of confidence in 'actually existing democracy' and inequality.[30]

Furthermore, in a survey carried out amongst 231 leaders in the region, many of them serving presidents or former presidents, those surveyed identified two major problems with democracy in Latin America: 'the role of political parties, and the tension between institutional powers, and what they refer to as de facto power centres.'[31] Parties, survey respondents claim, have 'abandoned their ideologies and programmes'.[32] Instead they act in accordance with 'the interests of individuals, and are under immense pressure from legal and illegal power groups'.[33] While illegal power groups are mostly identified with drug cartels, the legal groups are the business and financial sectors, together with the communications media.[34] Moreover, the United States/US Embassy was seen as slightly more powerful than the armed forces (22.9% against 21.4%), while multilateral agencies were recognised as being more powerful than national legislatures (16.6% against 12.8%).

Thus, current de facto powers in Latin America are perceived by political leaders as business and financial sectors, the media, the USA/US Embassy, and the multilateral agencies, that is, the IMF, the World Bank, and the World Trade Organisation (WTO), as opposed to the traditional de facto powers of army, oligarchy and church. The most powerful institutions in Latin America are therefore mostly unelected, unaccountable to the electorate, and organically linked as operators within, or defenders of market supremacy.

A more recent survey of Latin American attitudes to democracy show little improvement from those in the UNDP report. 54% of Latin Americans surveyed believe that democracy is the most preferable form of government, while 17% believe that an authoritarian government is necessary in certain circumstances and a further 20% are indifferent to a government being democratic or authoritarian. This relatively low support for democracy is directly linked to the level of satisfaction with the provision of public goods such as education, health, transport and pensions amongst others. Hence, the report asserts that 'the development of state services with improving levels of quality is a demand of democracy and its consolidation depends on it'.[36] As the main aim of neoliberal reform in Latin America and throughout the world is to reduce the size and role of the state, this supports Laclau's observation that the main danger to democracy is neoliberalism and not populism.[37]

The limitations of institutional reform

So what's to be done? Kenneth M. Roberts, in a paper presented to a conference in 2000 on 'Populism and Democracy', outlines populism's 'inherently ambiguous relationship with political democracy'.[38] On the one hand populist leaders helped to incorporate the working and lower classes into the political process, expanding the ranks of democratic citizenship and broadening the social base of democratic regimes.[39] They also shepherded the tumultuous transition from oligarchic politics to mass democracy, providing a new sense of dignity and self-respect for subaltern sectors of society, who were encouraged to recognise that they possessed social and political rights.[40]

On the other hand, however, populists often use undemocratic methods to achieve this, showing little respect for the rule of law, political pluralism and democratic checks and balances.[41] As a result, they polarise the political arena in ways that make democratic cohabitation all but impossible.[42] Furthermore, they have conflicts with democratic institutions, especially legislatures, frequently using decree powers or altering institutional rules. And they use plebiscitary tactics to strengthen their power base, rely on the military, and so weaken institutional checks and balances.[43] This erodes the transparency of the public administration, Roberts argues, and undermines the capacity of democratic regimes to monitor and control corrupt or incompetent behaviour.[44] Moreover, populists degrade democratic citizenship by not honouring electoral promises, denying citizens the right to establish policy mandates. Instead, they develop clientelistic relationships to ensure their permanence in power.[45]

To remedy this, Roberts recommends that parties be strengthened and relegitimised, that electoral systems be changed to a mixed proportional representation/plurality system, and that political decentralisation be introduced to strengthen parties at the local level. Debate should be encouraged on varying models of capitalism and parties shouldn't be pressured by international actors to adhere to a '"Washington Consensus" that undermines their programmatic functions by artificially narrowing the range of responsible development alternatives'.[46]

The role of civil society should be strengthened, with greater input into policy-making, and the running of institutions, and the fostering of greater transnational linkages. The civil service, judiciary, and legislature should also be strengthened with greater professionalistion and the development of more transparent procedures.[47] The international community should provide greater safeguards for democratic procedures.[48] Finally, Roberts adds that in terms of policies the 'progress' made in macroeconomic stability should allow attention to shift to policies which reduce social inequalities and integrate society better, thus eradicating the essential causes of populism and strengthening the basis of democracy.[49] The UNDP offers a similar set of reforms but also within the market context.[50]

Weyland, however, has no time for reform, recommending for Venezuela, for example, 'a truly competitive, liberal political regime' with a state run by 'experienced, well-trained experts' as a 'remedy' to Chávez.[51] In a later article he explains that such a regime should be installed alongside 'market-oriented policies', which are the only realistic possibility in any case.[52] All then offer liberal democracy alongside the market, either as it is (Weyland) or after undergoing complex reform (Roberts and UNDP).

There are a number of problems with these recommendations. First, it is paradoxical to recommend that democratic institutions reform themselves in order to strengthen democracy and restore people's faith in it, given the profound and deep-set lack of confidence Latin Americans have in those institutions. It is not explained how these institutions will find the will, the capacity or the resources to enact such complex changes, nor why, given people's lack of faith in them, Latin Americans should trust them to do so.

Second, few recognise that democracy is failing in the region precisely because the neoliberal model is damaging to democracy. While Weyland, Roberts and the UNDP all recognise to some extent that neoliberalism is increasing inequality, none truly questions the viability of the model or its supposed role as a 'companion to democracy'. Gibbs, in her criticism of the UNDP's report, points to its supposition that progress towards democracy and towards clear and legitimate macroeconomic norms are mutually reinforcing.[53] Institutional reform therefore is not aimed at installing a responsive and indigenous model of democracy in the region, but rather, as Gibbs pithily puts it, is 'to make neoliberalism a little friendlier'.

Indeed Gibbs asks: 'How can the agenda of neoliberal reform – macro-economic stability and liberalising markets – be up for discussion when the outcome of that discussion must be that neoliberal reforms are essential?' By emphasising institutional reform accompanied by market policies, all these studies place the emphasis on what Latin Americans need to do 'to get it right' within the current context, underemphasising the need for international actors to examine their part in the increasing instability of Latin American democracy. Given that, as pointed out earlier, the decline in democracy is a worldwide trend linked to the rise of neoliberalism, it is quite reasonable to surmise that these recommendations should be at least more equally balanced.

Moreover, all these analyses underestimate the real difficulties for Latin American countries in contesting the centralising tendencies of the neoliberal model, which lead to reductions in policy-making autonomy for national governments, and the unwillingness of core countries, multilateral agencies and the business and financial sectors – the de facto powers – to modify those tendencies. In other words, they emphasise agency over structure as a 'solution' to the problem. Both Roberts and the UNDP are suggesting, in a nutshell, that Latin American governments implement far-reaching, and no doubt very expensive, institutional reforms, which in tandem with a more 'caring' neoliberal model would suffice to revive democracy and thus prevent authoritarianism or populism from emerging in the region. This proposal seems to be well intentioned, but it is essentially insufficient and most probably unrealistic as it refuses to recognise that at the very least such reforms are needed on a global basis, as much in 'mature' democracies as at the global institutional level.

A third important issue is that the whole thesis rests on the assumption that 'we' have it 'right'. Western nations are not required to implement similar reforms, thus putting in doubt their commitment to supporting them in Latin America. In all likelihood structural reform running counter to neoliberal policies would need to be effected in tandem with such institutional reform, a situation unlikely to be permitted by the *de facto* powers. Indeed governments who attempt such reforms are conversely charged with being 'undemocratic' and 'anti-institutional' by those same *de facto* powers, who then sometimes participate in thoroughly undemocratic measures to remove such governments, as vividly illustrated by the repeated attempts to overthrow the democratically elected government of Venezuela.

Indeed Clement draws our attention to how such 'institutionalist' readings of democracy are deeply interlinked with 'democracy promotion' policies pursued by the United States in the developing world, particularly Latin America.[54] The National Endowment for Democracy (NED), a US government-funded but privately run agency, spent $93 million dollars in 'democracy promotion' in the region between 1985 and 2000.[55] Quite a number of well-known 'institutionalist' scholars have received NED grants, such as Larry Diamond, Laurence Whitehead, or the think tank Inter-American Dialog, all of whom, like Roberts and Weyland, recommend liberal institutions coupled with market reforms as the key to establishing democracy in the developing world. 'Semi-authoritarian' governments in particular were identified for attention, including Venezuela, and the key objectives here 'were strengthening the independent media, civil society, and political parties and building 'effective governing coalitions and business associations, trade unions, and policy institutes that can mediate between the state and the market and effect real economic reform'',[56] quite similar to the recipes cited above by Roberts, the UNDP and Weyland. By 2002, the year of the coup against Chávez, Venezuela was the most heavily NED-funded country in the region, receiving over $1 million, all of it going to opposition groups.[57]

Clement concludes that the underlying preoccupation with such 'democracy promotion' is not the furtherance of democracy but rather US foreign policy objectives. 'The preoccupation with party building and the "semi-authoritarian" tag ... demonstrates a growing awareness that political liberalization does not necessarily result in populations or regimes that readily fall in line with free-market principles or US-defined global security priorities. Experimentation and departures from the authorized model of political liberalization are frequently identified as threats to democratic consolidation.'[58] In effect the real thrust behind these 'democracy-promotion' programmes is not moral and is not really concerned with establishing democracy, but rather uses 'moral rhetoric that casts the intransigent leaders (even elected ones) as dubious political actors with undemocratic intentions' in order to 'accomplish regime change'.[59]

Implications for theory on populism

Returning to Weyland's and Roberts's criticisms of populism in the light of the above discussion we can, therefore, draw the following conclusions. Populists can according to their reading, provide a pseudo-participation for the popular classes, but usually through 'undemocratic' (i.e. non-institutional) means, thus prejudicing democracy. As Nabulsi points out, however, democracy is often advanced by challenging accepted practices through what are often perceived as 'undemocratic' means.[60] It is feasible, therefore, to suggest that the great populist leaders such as Perón, Vargas, and Cárdenas, and their millions of supporters in Latin America, were that region's form of struggle against the unrepresentative rule of the so-called democracies which existed there up until the 1930s. In effect these so-called undemocratic means can be responses to the anti-democratic tendencies of 'really existing democracies', which reinforce inequality and stifle popular participation.

Weyland and Roberts argue that populists are personalist and authoritarian, or at least 'semi-authoritarian'. Yet liberal democratic governments are becoming increasingly authoritarian and insulated from public opinion, as well as contemptuous of the rule of law, as the continuing war on Iraq, launched in 2003 amply demonstrates.[61] Will Hutton shows how the war in Iraq has 'subverted and polluted' the institutions of both the US and Britain. Iraq and the whole doctrine of pre-emption offers 'an open door to lawlessness, arbitrary government, lack of accountability and warlordism ... [giving] enormous powers to the executive branch of government ...'.[62] Institutions are thus under fierce attack in two of the leading democracies in the world and becoming increasingly subject to strong personalist leadership. There are, however, no 'democracy promotion' campaigns being aimed at them, nor are they identified as populist or semi-authoritarian by political scientists concerned with democratic consolidation.

An alternative to the institutionalist view put forward by both Weyland and Roberts is instead to look at the wider ideological context, both nationally and globally. In the present era of neoliberalism, the emphasis is on regulation, instead of democratic accountability. This reduces the ability of democratic institutions to fulfil their historic role of checking the excesses of the market. 'Classic' populists, on the other hand, made some of the greatest contributions to institutionalisation in the region, with some of its most enduring parties, such as APRA in Peru, and the Justicialista party in Argentina, being formed by populist leaders, and trade unions, and other enduring popular organisations being nurtured by populist governments. Latin Americans saw some of their highest standards of living for the greatest numbers of people in their region, much of that agreed through corporatist institutions, advancing a more holistic citizenship and a more complete form of democracy. These governments, however, unlike right-wing, neoliberal populists such as Fujimori, were articulated with social-democratic,

nationalist ideologies, which prioritised nation-building, state-led development and institution-building.

As we have seen, neoliberalism has undone much of this work, and
instead increased inequality and people's sense of disenfranchisement. As
Laclau claims, the nature of a populist government is influenced, not as
Roberts and Weyland maintain, by the power-hunger of the populist leaders,
but by the type of ideology to which that populist movement is wedded,
because all populist leaders are advancing some form of ideological model.[63]
In the following section we will demonstrate this by showing how the
Chávez government has advanced a more participative and inclusive model of
democracy, based on a clear commitment to serious but flawed institutionality. Rather, the Chávez case illustrates that what is judged as being 'undemocratic' is often based more on how widely that populist government has
departed from the prevailing economic and political ideology rather than
concrete 'undemocratic' behaviour, illustrating the connection between the
decline of democracy and neoliberalism.

The impact of populism in Venezuela

Democracy's lack of legitimacy

In Chapter 2 of this study, we argued that the weakness of the *puntofijista* liberal
democratic regime in Venezuela was as a result of its eventual inability to
respond adequately to the demands of its citizens for more equality and
participation. As discussed in that chapter, Habermas shows us that developed
societies achieve legitimacy through a combination of formal democracy and
spreading of economic and social benefits through a class compromise.[64]
Democracies in developing countries, however, are often unable to provide
the second part of the bargain to the majority of their citizens, thus rendering
some of their institutions almost redundant for these groups, and so endan-
gering the legitimacy of the democratic state. It was for this reason that in the
midst of profound crises Venezuela's liberal democratic system collapsed,
clearing the way for Chávez to gain power and profoundly restructure the
state. Furthermore, it is important to note that Venezuela had already
undergone an attempt at reform under COPRE in the late 1980s, which had
singularly failed to provide a state more responsive to the demands of its
citizens.

In short, Venezuelan democratic institutions had already proven
themselves to be thoroughly weak and incapable of satisfying popular
demands for greater equity and participation, failing to heal its profound
cleavages along class/race lines and, as a result, losing its legitimacy and
effectiveness. Another important point to stress is that Chávez was a *product* of
this historical class/race polarisation, not the *cause* of it, as Roberts, Weyland

and many other analysts claim, although he did capitalise on this polarisation in his discourse and policies

Gramsci, and Laclau and Mouffe underline the importance of antagonism in efforts to achieve hegemony.[65] In other words change is difficult to achieve without an antagonistic challenge to the status quo. Chávez successfully challenged the existing delegitimised institutions in an antagonistic fashion, offering a radical alternative. In the previous chapter we already dealt with the autonomy of institutions in Venezuela, finding that the Chávez government has a demonstrated commitment to institutionalisation, despite its imperfections.

Nonetheless much analysis charges that the basis of Venezuela's present institutionality was conceived in an illegitimate manner, so it is worthwhile to revisit this charge in the context of the current chapter. The Canadian political scientist, Maxwell A. Cameron, for example, has no doubt that the Chávez government implemented a 'slow motion constitutional coup'.[66] According to Cameron, Chávez did this by arbitrarily terminating Venezuela's Congress through a referendum of 'dubious legality', convening elections for a Constituent Assembly, and organising the elections for this assembly in such a manner as to ensure his party's domination of it, and thus ensuring the writing of a 'partisan Constitution rather than a statement of broad agreement on Constitutional essentials'.[67] Moreover, Chávez arbitrarily or illegally appointed officials and judges by using an 'executive-dominated and appointed legislature ... to stack the courts, thus degrading constitutional checks and balances',[68] amongst other moves.

Cameron, however, ignores a number of important points in his assessment. Chávez's referendum of 'dubious legality', for example, was allowed by Venezuela's pre-Chávez Supreme Court, whose imprecision in its judgement allowed for legal uncertainties to creep in, but not to the extent that it could be called legally dubious. Furthermore as Wilpert points out, Chávez had a clear mandate for change, transition periods can lead to legal uncertainties, the existing Congress 'caved in all too easily' to the demands of the Constituent Assembly, and all the officials and judges appointed were ratified with a two-thirds majority in the National Assembly.[69] Finally, Wilpert continues, while there is a problem of checks and balances in the Venezuelan government, with most branches having some level of sympathy towards the government, this is 'a problem typical for democracies, which democracies have not resolved particularly well'. Wilpert goes on to cite, for example, the three branches of the US government, which at that time (December 2003) were controlled by sympathisers of the Republican Party. In this situation 'one would have to say, at the very least, that Venezuela is no less democratic than the US, given the parallel'. The transition period and its results were far from perfect, but it is incorrect to claim that it amounted to a 'slow motion coup', whatever that may mean.

While it is true that the Constituent Assembly (ANC) was dominated by the Chávez-led Patriotic Pole (PP), Cameron ignores the fact that the PP at that time was a very broad church indeed. Many of the most prominent members of the ANC, such as the well-known constitutionalist Alan Brewer-Carías, and prominent political scientist Miriam Kornblith, are now equally prominent members of the opposition. Furthermore, Cameron also ignores the high level of public participation in its deliberations, as García Guadilla vividly recounts (see Chapter 4).[70] Far from being a 'partisan constitution' as Cameron claims, Venezuela's constitution is regarded by many Venezuelans as a fair and balanced document that seeks to protect and preserve many fundamental social and political rights for all its citizens. The recent referendum on the constitutional amendments partially failed it could be said as a result of a sense of ownership felt by Venezuelans for the 1999 constitution.

Finally, Cameron almost completely glosses over the frequent assaults on the rule of law perpetrated by the opposition in their repeated attempts to overthrow the constitutional government of Venezuela. López Maya enumerates these as follows:

> The coup of 11 April, 2002, the indefinite general strike with a sabotage-stoppage of the oil industry, petitions for consultative referendums which falsely tried to constitute themselves as recall referendums against the President, *guarimbazos* (violent protests), paramilitary operations, military disobedience, calls to tax disobedience, liberated territories, insurrectional marches, institutional crises seeking to provoke ungovernability.[71]

The opposition's activities therefore have shown little respect for Venezuela's institutionality and have done much to undermine it.

The Chávez government's commitment to institutionality is not perfect by any means, but neither can it be said to be anti-institutional. Separation of powers does exist in Venezuela to the extent that as Wilpert again points out 'no other branch, such as the Executive, can remove another part at will'.[72] This is not greatly different to the situation existing in many other democracies, both in Latin and North America.

These moves on the part of the Chávez government must also be put in the context of the undoubted extension of participation and democracy to previously excluded sectors in Venezuela. In Chapter 4 we saw how the Chávez government has extended greater participation to greater numbers of Venezuelans, extending access to health, education, training, and land and home ownership, involving them in the design and running of these programmes. Other programmes have extended access to identity cards and hence to other benefits, not least the right to vote. Venezuelans are much more deeply involved in politics on a local level, through neigbourhood committees, and on a national level, through referendums and the massive mobilisations which have become commonplace in Venezuela. Minorities, indigenous populations, and women have seen their rights extended under the constitution, and by much of government policy.

Democracy is in the eye of the beholder

It is instructive once again to compare this record with that of the Fujimori government, where we find a greater and graver disregard for the law and institutions, and a much lesser corresponding extension and participation of democracy for Peruvian citizens in comparison with their Venezuelan counterparts. Fujimori, for example, promised a centrist programme on the election trail, to implement one of the most radical neoliberal SAPs seen in Latin America on achieving power, undermining Peruvians' faith in democracy. The Fujimori government was riddled with human rights abuses: numerous massacres, mass jailings of innocents, summary justice procedures, electoral fraud, domination of the media, harassment and intimidation of the opposition. Many of the gravest violations affected specific ethnic groups disproportionately, those who were living in the poorest parts of the country.

Fujimori's economic and social policies saw millions thrown out of work and into poverty, saw the removal of many social rights, the deliberate destruction of worker protections, increased unemployment, underemployment and informality, the domination by the executive of poverty programmes creating direct clientelistic relations between the poor and Fujimori, and the wholesale domination of much of the economic and administrative apparatus of the country by foreigners. Importantly too, much of this took place with the acquiescence, and often the active encouragement, of many of the *de facto* powers; the business and financial sectors, the media, the armed forces, and the IFIs, supported by the international community, most notably the US.

Yet it is the Chávez government which faces the greatest international opprobrium and the most frequent destabilisation attempts. The international media by and large echo uncritically the Venezuelan private media's consistently negative portrayal of the Chávez government, and portray the opposition in an equally consistent positive light. Fujimori, in comparison, was portrayed, at least until the latter stages of his second term, as the 'saviour' of Peru. The inescapable conclusion that must be drawn is that this was not due to either president's perceived commitment to democracy, but rather to the ideology with which each project articulated itself: Fujimori's consistent support for neoliberalism, and Chávez's vehement rejection of that ideology in favour of a more constrained capitalism with greater levels of state interventionism and government control of the economy, which eventually radicalized into his conception of twenty-first century socialism. The opposition and the institutions controlled by them in Peru, as well as the *de facto* powers, failed or refused to limit the excesses of the Fujimori regime for the majority of his two terms. In the case of Venezuela, on the other hand, the opposition and the *de facto* powers used a series of legal and illegal strategies to overthrow Chávez, who instead managed to increase his popular support.

Blame for deinstitutionalisation, therefore, is not as simple as blaming the leader. Democratic institutions, such as political parties, civil society (including trade unions), the media, the business classes, transnational corporations, democratic governments of developed countries (especially the US) and multilateral organisations, amongst others, all participated in these political dramas and processes, in both Venezuela and Peru, more often than not in pursuit of the implantation of neoliberalism. Democracy, democratic institutions, and other factors like human rights, are often used as discursive smoke screens to maintain or challenge power for ideological ends in often undemocratic and sometimes illegal ways.

Radical populism

This typification of the Chávez government, using institutionalist arguments, can be clearly seen in an article by Weyland about Chávez, published in the US international relations magazine *Foreign Affairs* in 2001, a few months before the April 2002 coup in Venezuela.[73] In this article, Chávez is repeatedly referred to with stirring language, such as 'firebrand', and Weyland emphasises throughout the piece how the Chávez government implemented partic-ular policy options only to perpetuate the Venezuelan president in power.

Firstly Weyland emphasises that ideology is simply a power strategy and not a theoretical structure for policy making. Hence, '[t]he oil price boom has allowed [Chávez] to … avoid the conversion to neoliberalism that Menem and Fujimori were forced to make to ensure stability and growth', implying that Chávez's repeatedly strong attacks on neoliberalism were mere rhetorical flourishes which could be abandoned peremptorily to maintain power.[74] Ideology is irrelevant to this greater aim of maintaining power, and Chávez is in essence empty of ideologically driven policy. So for example, 'Chávez is in the process of debilitating, marginalising, or taking over major interest groups that might otherwise oppose him, notably trade unions and business associations',[75] implying that it is only because 'he' is doing that to them that they are resisting, and not because they are class actors who see in govern-ment policy a threat to their interests. Similarly, business feels 'threatened' by Chávez's 'outbursts', and 'belligerent rhetoric'[76] – though we do not learn about specific policies nor their aims – except that they are 'wild', 'spend-thrift' and 'misguided'.[77] Business here is again painted as a passive, relatively neutral actor who is being subject to the abuse of an authoritarian and unpre-dictable *caudillo*.

Indeed, in general, class is elided from the discussion. Hence government supporters are 'masses', or indeed 'lower-status masses', while Venezuelans in general are 'voters' or 'common people'. These 'ordinary citizens', lacking firm organisation, remain 'fickle and dissipated' ready to abandon their leader once the latter fails to deliver on promises.[78] They will remain so, also, as Chávez 'disdains any party institutionalisation that might constrain his personal autonomy'.[79] The Venezuelan people remain undifferentiated; the wide cleavages in Venezuelan society along class and racial lines, the implications of which we explored at length in Chapter 2, are nowhere to be seen in Weyland's reading of contemporary Venezuela. Yet some of the language used by Weyland is redolent of that disqualifying language used by the Venezuelan opposition against Chávez supporters. Hence, Chávez 'depends on strong, widespread backing from the Venezuelan *masses*',[80] but 'many *citizens* are now growing restive',[81] thus Chávez supporters are unthinking 'masses', while 'citizens' we can logically surmise are reflexive, thoughtful beings who logically gravitate towards the opposition.

In effect, Weyland empties the Chávez government and its opponents of ideological content, while instead concentrating on the threat to institutionalism posed by the 'undemocratic' Chávez. Populism and democracy are juxtaposed as opposites, with the former representing a threat to the latter. In essence, however, the relationship between populism and democracy is much more complex, as Francisco Panizza explains.[82]

Populism as a mirror of democracy

For Panizza populism bases much of its discourse on antagonism, as antagonism is central to the construction of political identities in politics and therefore the construction of alternatives to the current status quo. Antagonism therefore is the essence of politics as without it, citing Laclau, 'we have no politics but administration'.[83] The absence of antagonism in modern democracies is the denial of the political and represents the absence of the concept of popular sovereignty.[84] Conversely, however, taken to an extreme populism can also descend into totalitarianism. In the end, Panizza asserts, populism reminds us of the tensions within democracy between the need to assert the will of the people and those who wish to limit that will, democracy's 'democratic and non-democratic logics'.

> In modern global society, populism raises uncomfortable questions about those who want to appropriate the empty site of power, but also about those who would like to subordinate politics to technocratic reason and the dictates of the market. By raising awkward questions about modern forms of democracy, and often representing the ugly face of the people, populism is neither the highest form of democracy nor its enemy, but a mirror in which democracy can contemplate itself, warts and all, and find out what it is about and what it is lacking.[85]

David Held in his *Models of Democracy* enumerates the 'warts' of neoliberal – or, as he terms it, 'legal democracy' – in other words the actually existing democracy of our time.[86] The asymmetries of power between market and consumer remain unrecognised by liberal democrats, putting the citizen at a distinct disadvantage against the distorting nature of economic power within existing democracies. The rolling back of the state implemented by successive waves of neoliberal reform has served to remove the few protections afforded the vulnerable in all areas of the globe. The concept of 'liberty' within liberal democracies is highly limited, as it refers only to questions of individual taste, views, talents and ends. This removes 'distributional' questions from political debate, ignores the wide variety of cleavages along class, gender, racial and other lines, and fails to recognise the need to have the material and cultural resources to pursue different courses of action.[87]

With such 'warts', it is unsurprising that many in Latin America turn away from liberal democracy and seek alternatives. Populism has traditionally been such an alternative in Latin America to the extent that one analyst asks if it is indeed the constitutive form of democracy in the region.[88] Furthermore, populism in its most radical form can have a transformative or even revolutionary potential, as may be the case with the Chávez government.[89] As Raby states, 'populism as a political movement … has a dynamic force of mass mobilisation which easily displaces or overwhelms established political parties and institutions, and this is what gives it a revolutionary potential'.[90]

Weyland in his 2001 article on Chávez dismisses the latter's Bolivarian ideology as 'an odd mix of nationalist, militaristic, autocratic, plebicitarian, and leftist ideas'.[91] Yet it is these 'leftist' ideas that have particularly come to the fore in Venezuelan government policy in recent years. In the area of ownership of strategic industries and services for example, we have seen the progressive 'renationalisation' of the state oil company, PdVSA; the launching of new state-owned services such as in the aviation industry; the nationalisation of strategic services such as electricity generation and telecommunications, and more recently in cement and steel production; and, experimentation in different kinds of ownership and/or management of the means of production, such as cooperatives, worker-management-run industries and so on.

There is a process of ideological clarification taking place, as Ellner points out, with Chávez's declaration of 'twenty-first century socialism' in 2005, the holding of the World Social Forum in Caracas in 2006, and an ideological congress in 2007, with the formation of the PSUV in the same year.[92] Experimentation is also taking place as we have seen in previous chapters in different forms of popular participation in the delivery of services and in the running of neighbourhood councils. Indeed all these policies and measures go far beyond being simply 'leftist ideas', but rather point to a process of practical experimentation, grounded in socialist thought and past experience, as well as on more recent 'anti-globalisation' thought, which aims to seek viable alternatives, in the economic, social and political spheres, which are more responsive to local contexts and conditions than the one-size-fits-all model of market-oriented liberal democracy prevalent today.

With this reading, Chávez can be seen as the element seeking to extend democracy, and the opposition, including the business and trade union elites, seeking to limit it. In essence what institutionalists, the US government and many of the so-called 'advanced' democracies fear in populism is the radical democratising potential behind the combination of politically aroused and mobilised popular classes and a responsive, visionary, and fearless leader united against 'actually existing democracy' and its subservience to the market.

What is worse is that this deadly combination has emerged through an exhaustive democratic process, making it all the more important to discredit its democratic legitimacy. This is the basis of the charges of 'deinstitutionalisation', but this ignores the wish on the part of the Venezuelan people to prioritise change over existing democratic institutions because those institutions had proved themselves incapable of delivering that change. Instead, the Chávez government and its supporters have set themselves on an experimental path to find new sets of institutions and formal mechanisms more suitable to the Venezuelan context and more apt to deliver the changes they want – namely the eradication of the profound inequalities based on class, gender and ethnicity which divide their society. Tackling these inequalities must be the first priority of any government, and the form and nature of institutions which can deliver that change will flow from this. This requires leadership and daring, rather than cautious, expensive and slow institutional reform.

Conclusion

Analysts, as we have noted, have identified two main consequences of populism. On the positive side greater participation and democratisation; on the negative side a disregard for institutions and a consequent lessening of institutionalisation, which ultimately damages democracy. In this chapter, however, the following main arguments have been made. First, democratic institutions in Latin American are inherently weak and have low levels of legitimacy due essentially to the great social cleavages affecting the region. It is a central contention of the present study that regardless of the effects of populism, this situation will be difficult to reverse if these social cleavages are not seen to be attended to.

Second, institutions are not the summation of democracy but a product of democratisation. For the majority of Latin Americans institutions are perceived as perpetuating the very social cleavages which need to be eradicated in order to grow democracy. Institutions, therefore, can be anti-democratic in their effects. It can be necessary, as many populists have done, to step outside and act against the existing institutional arrangements, in order to further social justice and citizenship and so create a new institutionality which is conducive to making the search for equality permanent. Populists, therefore, should be judged not just on their 'rule-breaking', but rather on how much they have contributed to the creation of a fairer, more equitable, and more truly democratic society – in the substantive sense of the word. Analysts should, as Canovan warns, take seriously populist claims to democracy.[93]

The revolutionary potential of populism, as has been emphasised throughout this study, depends very much on the wider contexts in which it seeks change. Internal historical contexts often provide the basis from which populism can emerge, but equally the international context can dictate the form it takes and its chances of survival. In the next and final chapter of this study, therefore, we shall return to the themes introduced in the Introduction, namely the influence and impact of globalisation, neoliberalism and development on the emergence and prospects for survival of Bolivarian Venezuela within the current global context.

Notes

1 Germani, G., 1965, *Politica y Sociedad en una Epoca de Transicion: de la Sociedad Tradicional a la Sociedad de Masas*. Buenos Aires: Editorial Paidos; Lynch, N., 2000, 'Neopopulismo: un concepto vacío', in N. Lynch (ed.), *Política y Antipolítica en el Perú*. Lima: DESCO Centro de Estudios y Promoción del Desarrollo, pp. 153–180; Stein, S., 1980, *Populism in Peru: The Emergence of the Masses and the Politics of Social Control*. Madison and London: Harcourt Brace Jovanovich, p. 14; Torres Ballesteros, S., 1987, 'El Populismo: Un concepto escurridizo', in J. Alvarez Junco (ed.), *Populismo, Caudillaje y Discurso Demagogico*. Madrid: Centro de Investigaciones Sociologicas: Siglo XXI, pp. 159–180, p. 177.

2 Drake, P. W., 1982, 'Conclusion: requiem for populism', in M. L. Conniff, (ed.), *Latin American Populism in Comparative Perspective*. Albequerque: University of New Mexico Press, pp. 217–247, p. 241.

3 Conniff, M. L. 1982, 'Introduction: toward a comparative definition of populism', in Conniff (ed.), *Latin American Populism in Comparative Perspective*, pp. 3–29, p. 20.

4 Ibid., pp. 14–15; Crabtree, J., 2000, 'Populisms old and new: the Peruvian case', in *Bulletin of Latin American Research* 19(2): 163–176, p. 176.

5 Kurt Weyland, 2001, 'Clarifying a contested concept: populism in the study of Latin American politics', in *Comparative Politics* 34(1), October: 1–22, p. 11.

6 Ibid., p. 14.

7 Kenneth M. Roberts, 2006, 'Populism, political conflict, and grass-roots organization in Latin America', in *Comparative Politics* 38(2): 127–147.

8 Ibid., p. 128.

9 Ibid.

10 Ibid., p. 136.

11 Ibid.

12 Ibid.

13 Ibid., p. 137, my italics.

14 Ibid.

15 Ibid, p. 136, my italics.

16 Nabulsi, K., 2004, 'The struggle for sovereignty', in *The Guardian*, 23 June, p. 19.

17 Jacques, M., 2004, 'Democracy isn't working', in *The Guardian*, 22 June, p. 17.

18 Ibid.

19 Ibid.

20 Ibid.

21 Harvey, D., 2005, *A Brief History of Neoliberalism*. Oxford: Oxford University Press, p. 188.

22 Ibid., p. 205.

23 Ryan, J. J., 2001, 'Painful exit: electoral abstention and neoliberal reform in Latin America'. Paper prepared for delivery at 2001 meeting of the Latin American Studies Association, Washington D.C., 6–8 September. Available from: http://136.142.158.105/Lasa2001/RyanJeffrey.pdf. Accessed 6 August 2003.

24 Ellner, S., 2002, 'The tenuous credentials of Latin American democracy in the age of neoliberalism', in *Rethinking Marxism* 14(3): 76–93.

25 UNDP, 2004, *Ideas and Contributions: Democracy in Latin America*. Available from: www.undp.org. Accessed 10 June 2008, pp. 24–25.

26 Ibid., p. 30.

27 Ibid., p. 73.

28 Ibid., Table, Reforms and Realities, p. 50.

29 Ibid., p. 52.

30 Ibid., p. 58.

31 Ibid., p. 62.

32 Ibid.

33 Ibid.

34 Ibid.

35 Latinobarómetro, 2007, *Informe Latinobarómetro 2007: Banco de datos en linea*. Available from: www.latinobarometro.org. Accessed 2 May 2008, p. 79.

36 Ibid., p. 84.

37 Laclau, E., 2006, 'La deriva populista y la centroizquierda latinoamericana', in *Nueva Sociedad* 205, Septiembre/Octubre: 57–61, p. 61.

38 Roberts, K. M., 2000, 'Populism and democracy in Latin America'. Paper delivered to *Threats to Democracy in Latin America Conference*, University of British Columbia, Vancouver, Canada, 3–4 November. Available from: www.iir.ubc.ca/pwiasconferences/threatstodemocracy/. Accessed 25 August 2004, p. 2.

39 Ibid., p. 9.

40 Ibid.

41 Ibid.

42 Ibid., p. 10.

43 Ibid.

44 Ibid., p. 12.

45 Ibid.

46 Ibid., p. 16.

47 Ibid., pp. 18–19.

48 Ibid., p. 19.

49 Ibid., p. 20.

50 UNDP, *Ideas and Contributions*, pp. 67–70.

51 Weyland, K., 2001, 'Will Chávez lose his luster?', in *Foreign Affairs* 80, November-December: 73–87, p. 81.

52 Weyland, K., 2003, 'Neopoplism and neoliberalism in Latin America: how much affinity?', in *Third World Quarterly* 24(6), December: 1095–1115, p. 1110.

53 Gibbs, T., 2004, *Democracy's crisis of legitimacy in Latin America*. Available from: www.nacla.org/art_display.php?art=2447. Accessed 9 September 2004.

54 Clement, C. I., 2005, 'Confronting Hugo Chávez: United States "democracy promotion" in Latin America', in *Latin American Perspectives* 32(3): 60–78.

55 Ibid., p. 64.

56 Ibid., p. 4.

57 Ibid., p. 72; see also Golinger, E., 2006, *The Chávez Code: Cracking US Intervention in Venezuela*. London and New York: Pluto Press.

58 Clement, 'Confronting Hugo Chávez', p. 74.

59 Ibid.

60 Nabulsi, 'The struggle for sovereignty'.

61 See, for example, Global Issues, 2008, *Global Issues on Media, Propaganda, and Iraq*. Available from: www.globalissues.org/HumanRights/Media/Propaganda/Iraq.asp. Last accessed 6 May 2008.

62 Hutton, W., 2008, *The Writing on the Wall: China and the West in the 21st Century*. London: Abacus, p. 319.

63 Laclau, E., 1977, *Politics and Ideology in Marxist Theory: Capitalism-Fascism-Populism*. London: New Left Books.

64 Habermas, J., 1976, *Legitimation Crisis*. Cambridge and Oxford: Polity Press.

65 Gramsci, A., 1971 [1947], *Selections from the Prison Notebooks*. Edited and translated by Q. Hoare and G. Nowell Smith. New York: International Publishers; Laclau, E. and Mouffe, C., 2001, *Hegemony and Socialist Strategy: Towards a Radical Democratic Politics*, 2nd ed. London and New York: Verso.

66 Cameron, M. A., 2003, 'The slow-motion constitutional coup in Venezuela', in *Informed* 6: 1–3. Available from: www.governmentrelations.ubc.ca/informed/. Accessed 9 September 2004.

67 Ibid., p. 2.

68 Ibid.

69 Wilpert, G. and Boyd, A., 2004, *Debate on the Legitimacy and Effectiveness of the Chavez Government*. Available from: www.venezuelanalysis.com. Accessed 27 May 2004, no page no.

70 García-Guadilla, M. P., 2003, 'Civil society: institutionalisation, fragmentation, autonomy', in S. Ellner and D. Hellinger (eds), *Venezuelan Politics in the Chávez Era: Class, Polarization and Conflict*. Boulder, CO and London: Lynne Rienner, pp. 179–197.

71 López Maya, M., 2004, *Exposición con motivo del reconocimiento en la Asamblea Nacional de la ratificación del Presidente: 27 de agosto de 2004*. Available from: www.eluniversal.com/2004/08/29/apo_art_29107Z.shtml. Accessed 9 September 2004, no page no.

72 Wilpert, G., 2004, *Dictatorship or Democracy?* Available from: www.venezuelanalysis.com. Accessed 27 May 2004.

73 Weyland, 'Will Chávez lose his luster?'.

74 Ibid., p. 79.

75 Ibid., p. 74.

76 Ibid., p. 80.

77 Ibid., p. 74.

78 Ibid., p. 76.

79 Ibid., p. 84.

80 Ibid., p. 75.

81 Ibid., p. 78, my italics.

82 Panizza, F., 2005, 'Introduction: populism and the mirror of democracy', in F. Panizza (ed.), *Populism and the Mirror of Democracy*. London: Verso, pp. 1–32.

83 Ibid., p. 28.

84 Mouffe, C., 2005, On the Political. London and New York: Routledge.

85 Panizza, 'Populism and the mirror of democracy', p. 30.

86 Held, D., 2006, Models of Democracy, 3rd ed. Cambridge: Polity Press.

87 Ibid., pp. 205–208.

88 De la Torre, C., 2006, 'Es el populismo la forma constitutiva de la democracia en América Latina?'. in José María Cardenas (ed.), Debate sobre la democracia en América, Caracas: UCV, CEA, pp. 139–151.

89 Raby, D. L., 2006, Democracy and Revolution: Latin America and Socialism Today, London and Ann Arbor MI: Pluto Press and Toronto: Between the Lines; Ellner, S., 2008, Rethinking Venezuelan Politics: Class, Conflict, and the Chávez Phenomenon. Boulder, CO and London: Lynne Rienner.

90 Raby, Democracy and Revolution, p. 243.

91 Weyland, 'Will Chávez lose his luster?', p. 85.

92 Ellner, Rethinking Venezuelan Politics, p. 172.

93 Canovan, M., 1999, 'Trust the people! Populism and the two faces of democracy', in Political Studies XLVII: 2–16.

7 Venezuelan international relations in the age of globalisation

Introduction

In the introduction to this book, it was argued that while the literature on populism can help us understand the Chávez phenomenon, it was necessary to place the latter in a broader context to fully comprehend it in all its complexity. It was imperative in particular to examine *chavismo* within the wider context of globalisation. Populism is essential for explaining *chavismo*, but much of the literature on populism fails to take sufficient note of this wider context, viewing it primarily from narrower institutionalist perspectives.

In the previous chapter populism was examined in the context of democratisation processes, and how democracy's spread throughout Latin America remains incomplete. The present chapter will concentrate specifically on globalisation, looking at it particularly from the perspective of its impact on development theory. To do this the chapter will examine Anthony Payne's ideas on 'the global politics of unequal development', which neatly brings together the concepts of globalisation and development into one overarching theory, in order to place the book's findings on Chávez into this wider context. Venezuelan foreign policy will then be examined in the light of these discussions arguing that it has sought to expand on and safeguard its emerging model by putting greater emphasis on a much more Latin Americanist and internationalist perspective, rather than the traditional pro-US and anti-communist policies of previous governments.

The Global Politics of Unequal Development

Payne, in his book *The Global Politics of Unequal Development*, contends that every state in the world pursues its own national 'development strategy' but that each individual 'development strategy' takes place within a wider context, which has four elements.[1] First, Payne states that in the contemporary context the world is facing the end of US hegemony and the beginning of a new phase in the world order. He explains that in the post-World War Two era up until the 1970s, the US achieved dominance based, in the Gramscian sense, on consent – in other words the US was the undisputed hegemonic power in the Western world.

With the economic crises and turbulence of the 1970s, US 'hegemony' began to give way to US 'dominance'. In order to reassert its hegemony it adopted neoliberalism to resolve these economic crises, most notably during the Reagan administration. Furthermore in the Third World it introduced similar neoliberal adjustment either through force or through the multilateral agencies in which its voice was critical (such as the IMF and the World Bank). This attempt to reconstitute US hegemony only partly succeeded in that it achieved dominance but not through consent – in other words 'hegemony' became 'domination'. Thus the role of the US in the global order remains undeniably preponderant, but the 'US is no longer powerful enough to shape largely on its own the rules of a consensual hegemonic order'.[2]

Second, there is a process of globalisation taking place which manifests itself as ongoing structural change in the world economy. It is, according to Payne, best understood as a 'social process unfolding at the global level and driven forward by a mixture of forces (public and private, political and non-political) within which states, although still likely to be highly significant, are not always necessarily the only or the most important influence'.[3] Payne stresses that globalisation processes are, nonetheless, deliberate policy decisions taken by states, and not as some portray it, an inexorable, unstoppable force. In this sense therefore '[w]hat has been created at present is a particular sort of globalisation, which some have labelled neoliberal globalisation'.[4] Any examination of current populism therefore must be considered within this wider context of a 'globalising liberal political economy'.

Nevertheless, as is apparent from the preceding paragraph, the state still has a central relevance within these globalisation processes, and should be considered as a third contextual element. Within globalisation debates the state was seen to have lost significance as new international and local actors took over many of its functions, such as the IFIs, multinational corporations, financial institutions, as well as local NGOs providing many of the services previously provided by the state. The state was therefore seen by some as being 'irrelevant'.[5] Payne, however, contends that the state rather is being subject to a profound reorganisation and restructuring which is facilitating and implementing globalisation policies and therefore remains as a 'key political actor on the global stage'.[6] As such, despite the many variations between states in terms of size, power, historical background and rationales, all of them must 'come into interaction with each other as they proceed to pursue their perceived interests beyond their boundaries within the international, or inter-state, environment'.[7] These actions and interactions are driven forward, furthermore, by the 'real' or 'constructed' interests of each state.

Finally, Payne contends that development should be seen not simply as a strategy confined to the 'underdeveloped' world but rather as one 'by which all countries seek to orient themselves (that is, their economies, polities and societies) to the new globalizing order'.[8] Development theory has undergone considerable transformations in recent decades, leading to what was generally recognised as an impasse in its identity. Yet as Payne points out, classic development theory has 'been undone not so much by theoretical failures, as by fundamental changes in the world order; namely the ending of the era of US hegemony and the attendant unwinding of the original Bretton Woods system of regulated capital movements and international trade'.[9] In this sense 'neoliberalism has laid effective claim to be the new mainstream development paradigm'.[10] The dominance of neoliberalism in development theory and practice, exercised through the multilateral organisations, most notably the IMF and the World Bank, has changed the agenda of development. Payne cites Hettne in identifying the difficulty for development studies as having become 'trapped somewhere between an obsolete 'nation-state' approach and a premature 'world' approach'.[11] Hettne rather insists that it is necessary 'to analyse development predicaments stemming from the fact that most decision makers operate in a national space but react on problems emerging in a global space over which they have only partial and often marginal control'.[12]

To summarise, therefore, Payne develops four main features of 'a new critical political economy of development'. First, development is seen as a universal process being pursued by all nations and not just those that are seen as in 'need' of development, i.e. the 'developing world'. There are within this conception therefore no rich/poor, North/South dichotomies. Second, development is seen as a strategy pursued by a national economy, society and/or polity through the state. Third, such a strategy 'necessarily involves the interaction, and appropriate meshing, of internal *and* external elements', thus development goals involve states pursuing a position in the global context as much as it involves management of the national context. Finally, development is bounded by time, place and history and is subject to the conjunctural environment dealt by those contexts. Development therefore is seen as a:

> collective building by the constituent social and political actors of a country … of a viable, functioning political economy, grounded in at least a measure of congruence between its core domestic characteristics and attributes and its location within a globalising world order and capable on that basis of advancing the well being of those living within its confines.[13]

Hence according to Payne, all states in the world are bound up in this 'global politics of development' and 'cannot avoid reaching out in pursuit of advantage, interests and position and, in so doing, they come into conflict with the strategies of other countries working to exactly the same dynamic'.[14]

He concludes, however, that these national development strategies take place in a world riven with 'a complex pattern of structural inequalities'. These inequalities manifest themselves first in national indicators of geographical size, gross national income and human development. They also manifest themselves in terms of the structuring of contemporary ideological debate, dominated mostly by the US, supported by the United Kingdom, with neoliberalism at its centre. Few other countries contribute anything to this 'ideational debate about development, political economy and international relations'.[15] Third, global institutions such as the IMF, the World Bank, the UN and the WTO are dominated by the US and its allies, or simply ignored when decisions seen as contrary to its interests are made. Rather global decision-making is now centred on the G7/G8 system, representing the most powerful countries in the world.[16] Other associations of states do exist, such as the G77 of 'Third World' countries, but these rarely have any impact in redressing these profound structural inequalities. Hence, national development strategies must be pursued within the 'global politics of *unequal* development', and that this inequality is a 'very complex inequality'. It is our task, Payne insists to 'get to grips with the detail and [examine] what particular countries, or groupings and alliances of countries, actually do'.[17] This recommendation therefore brings us back to Venezuela in order to examine its efforts to negotiate the 'global politics of unequal development'.

Venezuelan foreign policy in the age of globalisation

Introduction

How then does Venezuela navigate the political waters of unequal global development? Venezuelan foreign policy is currently guided by the latest national plan, the Simón Bolívar Project – the First Socialist Plan.[18] Building on the previous 2001–2007 plan,[19] the foreign policy section in the present plan has three key objectives,[20] as follows:

1   Strengthen national sovereignty by accelerating the conformation of a regional geopolitical bloc and a multipolar world;
2   Diversify political, economic and cultural relations according to the establishment of areas of geostrategic interest;
3   Deepen fraternal dialogue between peoples, the respect for freedom of thought, religion and self-determination.

The main objectives for Venezuelan foreign policy are therefore to move from perceived US domination, the so-called unipolar world, to promote one with a number of power centres based on regional blocs – a multipolar world. In order to do this Venezuela has pursued a policy of developing its own sets of sovereign relations despite US pressures on it to conform to its priorities.

In order to study this in more detail, the chapter will first take a wide-angle view of Venezuelan foreign policy by examining it on the global level. Then it will focus on the regional context, paying particular attention to the Venezuela-Cuba led Bolivarian Alternative for the Americas (ALBA) initiative within the wider context of Latin American, particularly South American integration. Finally it will review Venezuela's relations with its two main trading partners, the US and Colombia. To begin with, however, by way of placing the discussion in context, the chapter will very briefly summarise Venezuela's foreign policy priorities before Chávez.

Venezuelan foreign policy during the Punto Fijo era

Venezuelan political scientist Carlos A. Romero typifies Venezuela's international relations as being a 'mirror-image of the domestic'.[21] According to Romero, Punto Fijo Venezuela saw itself as 'a western country, with a Hispanic colonial history, situated in Latin America and with three strong identities: a democratic, oil-rich country with generous relations with the United States'.[22] Consequently, successive Venezuelan governments of this era pursued foreign policy aims congruent with that self-image, these being to 'maintain stable relations with the United States, keep contained the possibility of authoritarian and other non-democratic governments in Latin America and the Caribbean and preserve the country's frontiers'.[23] While on another level Venezuela at times played a foreign policy which could be considered at various times 'Caribbean, pan-American, Third Worldist and Amazonian', in the essentials it worked hard to maintain its reputation with the US as a stable democratic ally which remained a secure source of oil.[24] Furthermore, Venezuela pursued a vehemently anti-Cuba foreign policy from 1961, when the Caribbean island broke off diplomatic relations with its northern neighbour, until the first Caldera presidency beginning in 1969, which adopted a more conciliatory tone.

Hence, *puntofijista* Venezuela, while being a founding member of OPEC, and disagreeing on some areas of US foreign policy, such as, for example, the latter's support for the UK's war in the Malvinas/Falkland Islands in 1982, 'never questioned the supremacy of the US in the Americas, nor the importance of representative democracy nor the role of private enterprise in national or regional development'.[25] Nonetheless, it is important to note that despite this loyalty to the US, Punto Fijo Venezuela did pursue this Third Worldist vision. The latter would come to the fore with the arrival of Chávez, with Venezuela downgrading the heretofore central relationship with the

United States, and instead privileging the more Third Worldist and Latin Americanist lines of Venezuelan foreign policy, in order to advocate a multi-polar world. Key to this change was the deepening of Venezuela's relationship with Cuba, the bedrock of which was the personal relationship between Chávez and Castro.[26]

From a unipolar to a multipolar world

As Payne notes above, the US attempted to maintain its global hegemony by the imposition of neoliberal globalisation in the developing world through the main IFIs, such as the IMF and the World Bank. Venezuela was eventually a reluctant subject to this strategy, as we have seen in Chapter 2, which was, however, roundly rejected by the Venezuelan people when they chose to first elect Chávez in 1998.

From that point Venezuela instead declared its intention to work towards a multipolar world, rather than one dominated by the US. In its first National Development Plan, for example, foreign policy would be oriented to 'revert the traditional concentration of power in international organisms and to stimulate the concerted action of developing countries, stimulating solidarity and cooperation between different actors in the international system, so that the decisions emerging from it are based on an equitative interaction in global decision making'.[27]

As Romero asserts, Venezuela has always used 'oil as an economic instrument to realise its political objectives'.[28] It is no surprise therefore that in order to achieve its new objectives, one of the first priorities of the Chávez government in its initial stages was the revival of OPEC, of which it was a founding member, in order to newly stimulate the oil market to favour producing countries. During the Punto Fijo era Venezuela acted as a moderate within OPEC and by the late 1990s abandoned OPEC fixed production quotas, adopting a full production policy, with a concomitant lowering of prices. Chávez on achieving office immediately set about reversing that policy. In 2000 he embarked on a tour of all OPEC nations, including, to the annoyance of the US, visiting presidents Saddam Hussein of Iraq and Qaddafi of Libya. That same year the second OPEC summit was held in Caracas and by January 2001, Alí Rodríguez Araqui, an ex-guerrilla and Venezuelan energy minister was installed as secretary general of the organisation.

The main planks of Venezuelan policy were to revive and strengthen OPEC in order to ensure a revived policy of production quotas, initially pegging prices for crude within a $22–28 price band. The policy worked, with even important non-OPEC producers such as Mexico and Russia joining in. Oil prices did not revert to the historic lows of the late 1990s and the price band policy held with revisions to reflect rises in market prices. Prices in recent years have gone well beyond these price bands, however, making the policy somewhat redundant. For the US, as Kozloff points out, it was not so much the price policy which annoyed it, as its oil industry also benefitted, but the 'renewed international profile of OPEC', an OPEC which included such so-called pariah states as Iran, Iraq and Libya.[29]

A second policy thrust of the Chávez government was to diversify Venezuela's foreign relations by establishing firm trading and cooperation links with countries not within its usual US-dominated world view. As part of this policy, Venezuela has been particularly anxious to develop strong relations with the three biggest emerging global economic power houses: China, India and Russia. Venezuela is also pursuing an expanded Third Worldist strategy with groupings of developing countries and with social movements. Let us look at each of these in turn.

China and Venezuela

Sino-Venezuelan relations have developed apace in recent years, with, for example, twnety-five bilateral agreements having been signed between the two countries by 2006. These agreements have advanced cooperation in a whole host of areas, including communications satellites, cellular phones, radar equipment, railways, anti-poverty programmes and agriculture amongst others. The most important, of course, are in energy. One of the latest to be signed, in May 2008, establishes a joint venture company between the Chinese state oil company CNPC and its Venezuelan counterpart, PdVSA, to exploit the Orinoco oil belt in Eastern Venezuela, including the building of a refinery in China to accommodate the oil extracted. The expected investment for this agreement alone should reach $12 billion. Venezuelan oil exports from China have risen from 25,500 barrels per day (bpd) in the first half of 2005 to 350,000 by the end of 2007. The ultimate aim is to see Venezuelan oil exports to China rising to 1 million bpd by 2011 or 2012. This compares to current exports to the US of about 1.5 million bpd.

There are, however, according to some reports, differences between China and Venezuela in their overall geopolitical aims for these moves. Chávez sees China first as an alternative and growing market for its oil and as an alternative source of technology, breaking the hold that mostly US oil companies have in that area. Moreover, Venezuela sees in China an economic model to be pursued in order to break Venezuelan dependence on the 'imperial' power of the US. Hence, at one signing of an agreement with China, Chávez claimed that with such agreements, Venezuela had become 'free' after years of colonialism. In this way, Venezuela, like China, is building a socialism which will 'transform Venezuela into a world power!'[30] Relations with China are therefore seen by the Chávez government as instrumental in breaking the global dominance of the US and redressing the global structural inequalities affecting Venezuela. Furthermore, as costs of transporting oil to China are double those to the US,[31] Venezuela is prepared to accept much lower prices from China than those on the world markets in order to facilitate this.[32]

China, on the other hand, while sharing the Venezuelan desire to usher in a multipolar world, simply 'needs oil' and 'wherever there is oil there are Chinese'.[33] Moreover, the Chinese are not quite as prepared as Venezuela to antagonise the US, which is of much greater significance to it than the Caribbean country.

India, Russia and Venezuela

In similar moves, Venezuela has been pursuing both India and Russia. In April 2007, for example, Venezuela and India signed an agreement worth $400 million to form a joint venture with the Indian state oil company to drill for oil in the Orinoco belt. According to the Indian embassy in Caracas, trade with Venezuela grew from $60 million per year in 2004 to close to $1 billion in 2006, mostly in oil sales.[34]

Russia and Venezuela also have been deepening ties through trade, mostly in the military and energy fields. In July, 2006 a $3 billion agreement was signed for Russia to supply Venezuela with twenty-four fighter planes, and fifty-three attack helicopters. Previous to this Russia agreed to supply Venezuela with 100,000 Kalashnikov rifles. In 2007 discussions were held by Chavez with the then Russian president Vladimir Putin on the construction of oil refineries, a natural gas pipeline, the possible purchase of submarines, and extensions of drilling operations by Russia's state-owned oil company in Venezuela. For Chávez, yet again, Venezuelan-Russian cooperation had clear geopolitical aims when he stated: 'we the people of the world, need Russia, and China, to get stronger and stronger' in order to 'counterbalance 'North American imperialism', or it will 'destroy the world!'.[35] Putin was more sanguine, however, declaring simply to a meeting of his cabinet in October, 2007, that Venezuela 'is one of the countries with the most perspectives from the point of view of joint ventures in the economic sphere'.[36]

'Third Worldism'

In courting China, India and Russia, Venezuela is behaving with little difference to many other countries in the world in their pursuit of trading opportunities with these economic giants. The Chávez government, however, has also sought out relations with what would be considered pariah nations by much of the 'international community', such as Belarus and Iran. Belarus has set up joint ventures with Venezuela in crude oil extraction in the latter country. It has also signed agreements on the manufacturing of trucks, tractors, auto-chassis, televisions and other electronic goods. Venezuela provided Belarus with a $460 million loan and has entered into negotiations on the purchase of a new missile defence systems. In total, twenty-four cooperative agreements were signed between the two countries in the period 2005–2007. Furthermore, the geopolitical implications of such cooperation is shared by both governments, who signed a joint declaration emphasising 'pluralism' and the freedom of the peoples of the world to choose their own model of development and political systems.[37] Indeed, both Chávez and Belarus president Lukashenko are deemed dictators by the West, according to Chávez, because both 'break the neoliberal paradigm of globalisation' and 'resist a unipolar world and … an empire that wants to be the owner of the world'.[38]

From 2005 to 2007 Iran and Venezuela signed an impressive total of approximately 186 agreements in areas such as energy, agriculture, housing, infrastructure, finance, industry, and physical education amongst others. In total, according to President Chávez the investment is worth around $4.6 billion. Furthermore, Chávez, in his fourth meeting with President Ahmadinejad, reiterated Venezuela's support for Iran to 'build nuclear energy for peaceful ends'. Iran and Venezuela are 'two brothers', he said, 'united like a single fist' and 'willing to confront U.S. imperialism in any territory and to defeat it'.[39]

The Venezuelan government has also stepped up its diplomatic activity in the developing world. Venezuela has announced its interest in extending its diplomatic representation in Africa, has shown a greater interest in developing country networks such as the G77 in the UN and the Non-Aligned Movement and hosted the XII G15 Summit in Caracas in 2004. Venezuela also is encouraging the search for grassroots alternatives to capitalism by, for example, hosting the World Social Forum, the alternative grouping for anti-globalisation activists, in Caracas in 2006. The core of this Third Worldist trade and diplomatic activity, however, has been in the Venezuelan government's activities in promoting Latin American integration, as we shall see in the next section.

Bolívar's dream: Venezuela and Latin American integration

In a speech in 1999 at the University of Brasilia, not long after his accession to the presidency of Venezuela, Chávez acknowledged the existence of globalisation and the necessity for Latin America to incorporate itself into globalisation processes, 'but without losing rein of our own processes'. In order to ensure this, it was necessary to return to the thoughts of Simón Bolívar and his attempts to unify Latin America. Only through Latin American unity could the continent survive this 'nefarious globalisation' which tries to impose a unipolar world. 'Either we unite or we are ruined', he declared.[40]

'Nefarious globalisation' already had its own pan-American unity proposal, however, with the Free Trade Area of the Americas (FTAA) initiative, launched by US President Clinton in 1994, at the first summit of the Americas in Miami and discussed at various summits posterior to that event. The main objectives of this proposal, according to its website, include trade and market liberalisation, enhanced competition and market access, the elimination of barriers, restrictions and/or unnecessary distortions to free trade and to the movement of capital and business persons amongst others – in other words a neoliberal 'free trade' system.[41]

This process was largely stopped in its tracks in the Summit of the Americas in Mar de la Plata, Argentina, in 2005, largely due to the opposition from the largest South American nations, amongst them Brazil and Argentina, but also, of course, Venezuela. This opposition was due to a mixture of pressure from social movements and from large national business organisations, especially in Brazil and Argentina. In its place the US pursued a policy of subscribing bilateral Free Trade Agreements with a variety of countries, including Mexico with Canada under the North American Free Trade Agreement (NAFTA, 1994), Chile (2002) the Central American Free Trade Agreement (CAFTA-DR including the Dominican Republic, 2004) and more recently Peru and possibly Colombia (2007). (At the time of writing the US-Colombia FTA remains without approval by the US congress due to human rights concerns, amongst other issues.) These FTAs oblige countries to provide access to markets without discrimination, equal treatment for national and foreign firms, protection of foreign investment and of intellectual property amongst other requirements. There is also a parallel process taking place between the EU and the Central American nations, MERCOSUR, and the Community of Andean Nations (CAN), the EU offering similar agreements to those of the US, but with further 'pillars' of political dialogue and international cooperation alongside the dominant 'free trade' pillar.

In Latin America itself, several regional groupings have also developed. Chief among these is MERCOSUR, created by Brazil, Argentina, Uruguay and Paraguay in 1991, with Venezuela joining in July 2007, though this is undergoing a difficult ratification process in the national parliaments of the member countries, especially in Brazil. Bolivia also has associated status and Ecuador has expressed interest in joining. MERCOSUR has an export-based regional strategy which involves the liberalisation of economic sectors and reciprocity in the opening of markets – in effect a free trade pact. It has no structure for remedying asymmetries between countries; hence Paraguay and Uruguay have on a number of occasions threatened to subscribe to a FTA with the US, forbidden under MERCOSUR rules. Furthermore, although MERCOSUR is a Latin American proposal, it is largely an elite-level process which does not guarantee it will be of interest to the general population.

Another regional grouping is the CAN, beginning in 1969, which as its name suggests joins the Andean nations of Peru, Bolivia, Ecuador and Colombia. Originally the CAN was primarily commercial but has through the years adopted political and social characteristics. Venezuela was a member of the CAN from 1973 until it withdrew in 2006. The main reason cited by Venezuela for its withdrawal was the signing by Peru and Colombia of FTAs with the US, which was seen by Chávez to be incongruent with the needs of the poor, but with little regard for Venezuela's commercial and trade needs. These free trade agreements have also caused problems with Bolivia and Ecuador, although both remain within the CAN.

One of the more recent proposals for South American unification is the proposed Union of South American Nations (UNASUR). UNASUR is an economic and political union proposed by all twelve South American nations at a summit in Cusco, Peru in 2004, and formally constituted in Brasilia, capital of Brazil, on 23 May 2008. One of the principal areas of its work is in energy, and a South American Energy Council has been created to seek a more efficient and unified use of energy within the continent. Another proposal within the UNASUR umbrella is a South American Council for Defence, which according to one analyst, Rosendo Fraga, would be 'a multilateral organism to prevent and resolve conflicts rather than a military alliance'.[42] Its current president is Michelle Bachelet of Chile, who will hold this position until the next summit in Santiago de Chile in 2009. The ultimate aim is to erect a South American union based on the model of the European Union in that it would have political and social, as well as an economic dimension.

Within this context of mostly free trade-based unification proposals, Venezuela placed its own alternative model on the agenda. The Bolivarian Alternative for the Americas (ALBA in its Spanish acronym, which also means 'dawn' in Spanish) was first mooted by Chavez in 2001 but has been developing as a reality since 2004. The ALBA proposal does not have detailed plans for integration but it does have a number of guiding principles. First, ALBA is based not on free trade or competition, but on cooperation, solidarity and complementarity in order to achieve endogenous development. In other words it is seen as a means through which national development can be achieved, through cooperation with other nations, hence providing unity through diversity. It also prioritises the fight against poverty and social exclusion placing human rights, labour rights, women's rights, the protection of environment and the protection of traditional agriculture as central tenets of its philosophy. ALBA looks to eliminate the causes of the blocking of integration, identified as poverty, the inequalities between nations, debt, structural adjustment programmes, media monopolies, and barriers to knowledge transfer, such as intellectual property rights. As a means to overcoming these causes ALBA looks to the strengthening of the state, and the encouragement of popular participation against neoliberal 'reforms'. The emphasis is then on state intervention to reduce the asymmetries between participant countries and the preservation of state sovereignty in regionalisation processes. ALBA has to an extent a double identity in that its core is membership based, with Venezuela, Cuba, Bolivia, Nicaragua, Honduras and the Caribbean island of Dominica being current members. ALBA, however, is also an alternative concept of trade based on the principles above which has informed Venezuelan interaction throughout the Latin America and Caribbean region.

ALBA as a membership-based association began with the first Cuban-Venezuelan ALBA agreement in December 2004, involving the elimination of trade barriers, providing state and mixed enterprises tax-free status and with Cuba providing 30,000 health professionals to run the *Barrio Adentro* health programme. Moreover, 10,000 health scholarships for Venezuelan students in exchange payment for oil and other benefits, alongside social agreements such as joint work in health and literacy programmes in third countries, were also agreed.

Previous to this, however, Cuba and Venezuela had signed a number of important agreements, mostly in the energy field. In 2000, Caracas agreed to provide Cuba with 53,000 barrels per day of oil, as well as opening an office of the Venezuelan state oil company PdVSA and the Industrial Bank of Venezuela. Various agreements have also since been signed between the Cuban state oil company Cuba Petróleo and PdVSA itself, involving Cuba in the refining and distribution of oil within the context of the PetroCaribe initiative (see below), as well as joint exploration operations in Cuban waters. In total, Cuban-Venezuelan trade has expanded from $450 million in 1999 to approximately $3,600 million in 2006. Of this, half consists of oil exports to Cuba from Venezuela, which now reaches 95,000 bpd, plus a further 50,000 to a jointly owned Cuban-Venezuelan oil company, PDV-Cupet.[43] This relationship between Cuba and Venezuela is at the heart of the ALBA project, and its significance is underlined by an ideological affinity between the two countries, based in particular on the special relationship which has developed between President Chávez and Fidel Castro.

ALBA expanded in 2006 when Bolivia, under newly elected President Morales, signed the 'Peoples' Trade Treaty' with Venezuela and Cuba. This treaty reflects the asymmetries between the parties, as Bolivia, the poorest of the three, contributes little. Cuba provides medical centres, personnel and equipment, and scholarships to Bolivia while supporting literacy programmes in that country. Venezuela provides oil and derivatives, cooperation with state companies, and an investment fund of $100m, with $30m donated for social programmes. Bolivia also receives commercial preferences in both countries and lower tariff barriers, whereas it does not have to reciprocate. Furthermore, Venezuela and Cuba buy Bolivian soya, which was left without a market due to loss of trade privileges with the US.

A further expansion took place with Nicaragua joining in 2007, shortly after Daniel Ortega, of the left-wing Sandinistas, won the presidency. This agreement includes the construction by Venezuela of an oil refinery to handle Venezuelan crude and various cooperation projects, such as the development of cooperatives with Venezuelan assistance and the setting up of a development fund with Venezuelan capital. Nicaragua also is part of the Petrocaribe agreement and hence benefits from receiving Venezuelan oil at preference rates. The Caribbean island nation of Dominica joined ALBA in early 2008, as did the Central American nation Honduras later that year and it is also proposed that Ecuador join at a future date.

The concept of ALBA is extended into Venezuela's foreign policy with its Latin American neighbours, presenting alternative proposals to the current neoliberal paradigm in four main areas: development financing; media; social solidarity; and popular participation and energy. In development financing, the most important proposal, first made by President Chávez, was the development of a Bank of the South (Banco del Sur), officially launched on 9 December 2007. Set up by Venezuela, Argentina, Brazil, Bolivia, Colombia, Ecuador, Paraguay and Uruguay with a reputed initial capitalisation from central reserves of up to $7 billion, the bank will be headquartered in Caracas, with branches in Buenos Aires and Bolivia. It will act as an alternative source of development financing for Latin American countries, and perhaps to other developing countries, to the existing US-dominated international financial organisations, such as the World Bank, the IMF, and the Inter American Development Bank.[44]

Unlike these entities, the Bank of the South will insist on few conditions to receive grants and loans. Funds will be provided for infrastructural projects, proposed by individual countries or groups of countries. Funds will also be available for anti-poverty programmes, and for small and medium enterprises. This proposal already had precedents when Venezuela bought Argentinean bonds, valued at $3 billion, allowing it to pay off its IMF debt. Venezuela also provided similar aid to Uruguay and Bolivia. Similarly, in 2008, an ALBA Bank was created between the four member countries, with an initial capital of $1 billion.

The chief plank of ALBA's media strategy was the launching of the satellite news channel TeleSUR, in mid-2005. Based in Caracas, TeleSUR hopes to provide an alternative to CNN, BBC World and other northern-based satellite news providers who provide a 'single discourse which deliberately negate[s] … the right to information'.[45] TeleSUR is primarily financed with Venezuelan capital (46%), followed by Argentina (20%), Cuba (19%), Uruguay (10%), and Bolivia (5%). Ecuador and Nicaragua also participate since 2007.

ALBA also intends to incorporate social movements by including initiatives originating from them. One of the areas in which it incorporates these movements is to recuperate businesses abandoned or bankrupted by previous owners and handing them over to be run by workers. A conference of these worker enterprises was held in Caracas in 2005 leading to the creation of their own network, EMPRESUR. Chavez announced a fund of $5m to help develop its work, promising that 'multinational enterprises will be born but run by workers'.

But of all ALBA's initiatives, the majority and the most important are in energy. Within this area Venezuela has four aims: the diversification of markets and the sidelining of energy multinationals in the region; encouraging and facilitating a process of (re)nationalisation in the region; working against the privatisation and liberalisation policies of the FTAA and securing the energy integration of the peoples of the continent, framed within ALBA, through the medium of a pan-Latin American energy entity, Petroamérica.

The concept of Petroamérica is the summation of three Venezuelan regional energy policies: Petrocaribe, Petrosur, and Petroandina. Petrocaribe was launched with a treaty signed between thirteen Caribbean nations in June, 2005, led by Venezuela. In this agreement Venezuela provides credits of 30% to 50% with up to twenty-three years to repay them at low interest. Included in this is the possibility to pay in goods and services rather than money. It looks also to coordinate energy policy between the nations through technological cooperation, providing energy alternatives and so on. It also provides a social fund. The agreement is strictly between state companies, some of which were created especially to facilitate the agreement. Another important part of the agreement is the construction of refineries in Cuba, Jamaica, and the Dominican Republic.

Petrosur is the summation of agreements or prospective projects between Venezuela and the countries of MERCOSUR. Within this concept there have been agreements on oil prospecting with Argentina and Brazil, and refining with Brazil. Again the concept of reciprocity has been incorporated, hence in exchange for oil from Venezuela, Argentina will provide meat and agricultural machinery. Additionally, Venezuela has ordered four oil tankers from Argentinean shipyards. Deals have been made with Brazil on the production and importation of ethanol and biodiesel. Uruguay has received credit with low interest and long payment terms in exchange for beef. Similarly Petroandina has consisted primarily in agreements with Ecuador, such as the construction of a refinery, and Bolivia, by setting up a joint venture and opening a chain of petrol stations, as well as a proposed gas pipeline across Colombia (see below).

Petroamérica therefore is the summation of these different initiatives which it is hoped will congeal into a South American energy initiative. One of the chief projects within this initiative is the proposed Southern Gas Pipeline, which according to Chávez will be 'the engine of a new process of integration whose objective is the defeat of poverty and exclusion'. This has been agreed in principle by the four state owned oil companies: PdVSA (Venezuela), Petrobras (Brazil), ENARSA (Argentina) and YPFB (Bolivia). The pipeline should be between 8,000 to 10,000 kms, the longest in the world, running from Puerto Ordaz, on the banks of the Orinoco in eastern Venezuela to Buenos Aires in Argentina, with spurs from Bolivia. As a result the pipeline would inevitably pass through fragile ecosystems such as the great plains region of the Gran Sabana in Venezuela and the Amazonia in Brazil. Furthermore there are questions around its commercial viability.

In sum, Venezuelan diplomacy has to a great extent furthered the general move towards South American unity in particular and Latin American and Caribbean unity in general and hence to achieving its objective of a mulit- polar world. At its core is the concept of ALBA, which not only encourages cooperation and reciprocity, but also deliberately excludes large private corporations in favour of state-run companies, and as a result, excludes the United States. Furthermore exchanges of goods between cooperating countries avoid cash deals, facilitating, it is hoped, not only a multipolar world, but also a 'post-dollar' economy for Latin America. Reliance on state companies to carry out the different agreements eliminates intermediaries, freeing up resources for investment in social projects. Increased Venezuelan trade with Latin America and the Caribbean, including the various energy agreements, lessens Venezuelan dependence on the US while simultaneously bolstering the region's economy. It does, however, increase many of the poorer nations' dependence on Venezuela – 76% of Jamaica's energy needs for example are supplied by Venezuela.[46] Most importantly, ALBA represents, despite its flaws, an alternative concept of international trade and cooperation which goes beyond the narrow vision provided by the FTAA. In doing so it therefore challenges directly the hegemonic neoliberal ideology. Not all Latin American countries, however, are sympathetic to ALBA's principles, and the most notable of these is Venezuela's closest neighbour and major trading partner, Colombia, to whom we now turn.

Colombia and Venezuela

Of all the countries in South America, Colombia is the United States' closest ally. Colombia is also notable within the continent for having its oldest and most enduring civil conflict, and one of the few fully fledged neoliberal and right-wing governments. The Colombian state has been fighting the FARC guerrillas in Colombia for over fifty years, none more so than the current president, Alvaro Uribe, with a hard-line policy shunning negotiation in favour of a total war policy, seeking to crush the rebels militarily. Since 1998, the US has worked with Colombia under Plan Colombia, which involves vast transfers of military hardware and funds for drug-eradication administered by the US security contractor, Dyn-Corp. Plan Colombia swallowed up one-third of the $1.6 billion US development aid budget to Latin America in 2007.

Because of these policies few Colombian presidents have been as close an ally of the US as Uribe, and as such Uribe is from Chávez's point of view, the 'only problem we have in South America' in terms of presidential relations.[48] As Romero states, the conflict in Colombia produces destabilising effects on the region, and the decision of Colombia to adhere to US-inspired strategies within Plan Colombia ensures that 'in the Andean countries there is therefore no shared vision of security', creating an even greater possibility for conflict between governments.[49]

Moreover, the shift to the left in Venezuela under Chávez and now in neighbouring Ecuador under Correa has added another dimension to the potential for conflict. Uribe for example supported the US when it invaded Iraq in 2003, agreed to consult with the US if its personnel on Colombian soil were accused of human rights infringements at the International Criminal Court in The Hague, and is an enthusiastic supporter of the FTAA, leading to its signing an FTA with the US in 2007, as noted above. All of these are policy perspectives which diverge greatly from those of Venezuela and Ecuador. Furthermore, Colombia supported the coup against Chávez in 2002, by giving refuge to FEDECAMARA's leader Pedro Carmona, who had been installed briefly as president. This has since been followed by the discovery on a number of occasions of armed Colombian soldiers in Venezuela, accused of being part of a plot to overthrow the Venezuelan government, amongst other incidents.

The incursion in March 2008 by Colombia into Ecuadorian soil to attack a FARC camp, killing twenty people, including Raúl Reyes, the guerrilla organisation's chief international negotiator, has been particularly damaging to relations between all three countries. Venezuela sent troops to the border and broke of diplomatic relations with its closest neighbour. The attack effectively scuppered mediation efforts with the FARC by President Chávéz to gain the release of the hundreds of civilian hostages in the hands of the former, which was beginning to bear fruit, despite Uribe's reneging on original agreements. Worse still, from the Venezuelan point of view, the Colombian government insisted that laptop computers found at the scene proved close links between the Chávez government and the FARC. Colombia had consistently accused Chávez of complicity with the FARC, whereas Venezuela had always insisted in it having a neutral position, while refusing, alongside other Latin American countries such as Brazil, to classify the FARC as terrorists, as Colombia, the US and the EU amongst others had done.

Colombia and Venezuela share a 2,219 kilometre frontier, most of it through very difficult terrain, but which is, despite that, very much 'alive', with smuggling of drugs and other merchandise, refugees, guerrillas, paramilitaries, money laundering, kidnapping and other such illegal or semi-legal activity, presenting an ever-present security challenge to both nations. Much legal activity also passes through the border as Colombia is Venezuela's second largest trading partner after the US. Bilateral trade came to about $4 billion in 2006,[50] and reached $5.2 billion in 2007,[51] with the trade balance favouring Colombia.[52] This further complicates relations as on a bilateral level Colombia and Venezuela have many reasons to cooperate. While tensions due to the internal conflict and larger hemispheric questions may have troubled relations between the two countries, Chávez and Uribe have by and large maintained a cordial and fruitful relationship. For example, both presidents signed a $200 million agreement in 2004 to build a joint pipeline on Colombian soil, thus furthering the concept of an Andean energy network.[53] For this reason, as Romero notes, Venezuela and Colombia have a diplomatic rivalry not so much due to their bilateral relations as due to the deterioration in their hemispheric relations – in other words how each of them relates to the countries in the rest of the hemisphere.[54] Principal among these of course, is each country's respective relations with the United States.

The United States and Venezuela

As we noted above, in the pre-Chávez era, the United States was the central pillar of Venezuelan foreign policy, and although Venezuela showed a certain degree of autonomy in its foreign policy in other areas of the world, this was never allowed to affect the extremely positive bilateral relations between the two countries. The advent of Chávez would change this utterly, and as we have seen in previous sections of this chapter, the Chávez government has directed much of its foreign policy towards reducing the centrality of the US in its trade and diplomatic relations, directing those relations indeed to countries which would be considered by the US as pariah states, most notably Cuba and, more latterly, Iran. Furthermore, this diversification in trade has been accompanied in more recent years with a discourse from the Venezuelan government identifying the US as an imperialist nation bent on world domination. Much of this discourse is justified by perceived interference by the US in Venezuela's internal affairs, including support by the US for a number of opposition attempts to overthrow the democratically elected government of Venezuela, including the April, 2002 coup, the opposition strike/lockout ending in early 2003, and the recall referendum against Chávez in 2004. Despite these profound differences, the US remains Venezuela's most important trading partner and Venezuela remains the US's fourth most important oil supplier.

During the time of the Clinton administration relations between the US and Venezuela were relatively cordial, with a few tense incidents, such as Venezuela's refusal of US military aid during the devastating mudslides in the coastal areas near Caracas in 1999.[55] Relations were also rather fraught between the Chávez government and the new Bush administration before September 2001, due to Venezuela's public rejection of the FTAA and the cancellation by Venezuela of a fifty-year-old military cooperation agreement between the two countries, International Military Education and Training (IMET).[56]

The beginning of the Cold War between the US and Venezuela, however, really dates from Chávez's condemnation of the US-led invasion of Afghanistan in October 2001, shortly after the Al-Qaeda attack on the World

Trade Centre in New York and the Pentagon in Washington on September 11, 2001. It is from this moment, Eva Golinger, a pro-Chávez US-Venezuelan lawyer in her book *The Chávez Code*, relates, when the US realised that '[t]he new Venezuelan government had no plans to be subservient to US interests'.[57] Golinger establishes how from thence on US interference in Venezuela became the US's covert policy. Working through the National Endowment for Democracy (NED), a bi-partisan and state-funded US organisation aimed at 'democracy promotion' and USAID, the US's international development cooperation agency, funding is from thence on consistently channelled to opposition groups in Venezuela from the US. In total Golinger identifies $34 million provided to the Venezuelan opposition between 2000 and 2006, with the bulk of this spent in the 2001–04 period. All the opposition political parties, private media, unions, business and a host of so-called 'civil society' organisations which received funds had one thing in common, Golinger points out: 'a public aversion to President Chávez.'[58]

Golinger provides much evidence to support the case that the US knew of and encouraged the April 2002 coup against Chávez. Numerous meeting between US officials, including Otto Reich, US assistant secretary of state for western hemisphere affairs at the time, and leading opposition figures; a concerted campaign of 'intelligence' briefings and false media reports to discredit Chávez; public support for the coup and its leaders, and a refusal to condemn the coup when it failed. These activities and omissions bring Golinger to declare that 'the highest levels of the US government knew' of the coup.[59]

With the failure of the coup, a newly established USAID Office of Transition Initiatives (OIT), and a shady 'private' consulting firm Development Alternatives Inc. (DAI), with a combined budget of $17 million in 2002, facilitated the formation of a pan anti-Chávez front in the Democratic Coordinator (DC), consisting of all the main NED/USAID funded organisations. The DC spearheaded the two-month lockout and oil stoppage, which when it ended in February 2003 had cost the Venezuelan people approximately $10 billion in economic damage.

DAI also funded training on the use of the media, which contributed to an opposition psych-op campaign during the lockout. The private media, abandoning regular broadcasting, devoted all its airtime to covering the lockout. It also pumped out, free of charge, 700 pro-lockout infomercials daily during the sixty-four-day stoppage.[60] The next attempt at overthrowing the Chávez government was led by the NED-funded organisation Súmate. This organisation was at the forefront of the 2004 recall referendum against Chávez's mandate, whose certified win by NED-funded observers the OAS and the Carter Centre, was as Golinger underlines, a 'huge setback for the United States'.[61]

The situation has not improved in more recent years. First, the war of words continues between the two countries. While on the one hand Chávez regularly accuses the US of imperial ambitions, high-ranking officials from the US often accuse Chávez of being authoritarian and a danger to democracy. Hence, the US secretary of state under George W. Bush identified Chávez as a negative force in the region in January 2005, ex-US defence secretary, Donald Rumsfeld, as we have seen earlier, compared Chávez with Hitler in February 2006, and his successor Robert Gates stated in October 2007 that Chávez was a 'threat to regional stability' and 'to the freedom and economic prosperity of the Venezuelan people'. Equally, Chávez famously announced to the UN General Assembly on 20 September 2006, that 'the Devil was here yesterday ... it still smells of sulphur', referring to President Bush's appearance in that forum the previous day, '[a]s the voice of Imperialism he came to give his recipes on how to maintain the actual scheme of domination, of exploitation and the looting of the peoples of the world'.[62]

Such verbal declarations have been translated into policy arenas. The US stopped Venezuela purchasing arms from Spain and Brazil and attempted to stop Russia selling arms to the Caribbean country. In 2006, Venezuela attempted to fill one of the vacant non-permanent Security Council seats at the UN, which was vehemently opposed by the US, who instead supported Guatemala, alleging that Venezuela would politicise debate and prevent consensus being reached.[63] US annual certification reports on the 'war on drugs' frequently accuse Venezuela of a supposed lack of effort in that area, despite quite a number of high-profile successes carried out by Venezuelan drug enforcement agencies. These reports became particularly critical once Venezuela halted all cooperation with the US Drug Enforcement Agency (DEA), alleging that the agency's activities were more directed at internal interference in Latin America than eradicating drugs.[64]

Even more seriously the US has consistently accused the Venezuelan government of supporting terrorism. US Republican legislators attempted to have Venezuela listed as a state-sponsor of terrorism in 2007, which would require economic sanctions being implemented against it. In the end the annual US State Department report on terrorism of that year stopped short on these demands but insisted that Venezuela was 'not cooperating fully' in the 'war against terrorism'. Venezuelan links with Cuba and Iran were particularly identified as being unhelpful. The production by Colombia of 'evidence' found on laptops confiscated in a FARC camp inside Ecuador in early 2008, supposedly proving that Venezuela supports the FARC (see above) will contribute further to such US accusations being levelled at Venezuela.

In return, Venezuela has continued to pursue its diversified foreign policy efforts which have resulted in it outdoing the US in terms of international aid. According to US magazine, the *New Yorker*, Venezuela outspends the US in development aid to Latin America by a factor of five – that is the US spent $1.6 billion last year compared to Chávez spending $8.8 billion.[65] Chávez regularly delivers his verbal broadsides against the US, including repeated threats to suspend oil exports to that country, which nonetheless have remained merely threats. The Venezuelan government has also attempted to counteract hostile US actions through a variety of what Steve Ellner calls grassroots initiatives.[66] In 2005, for example, PdVSA's US-based subsidiary CITGO launched a home heating scheme for households in poor areas of the US which in 2006–07 served 180,000 households, 250 homeless shelters and 37 Native American tribes, according to the CITGO website (www.citgo.com). Venezuela has made links with progressive elements in the US, including visits from well-known celebrities such as film stars Danny Glover and Sean Penn. Grassroots mobilisation is being encouraged by Venezuelan embassies, not just in the US but in Europe as well, with Venezuelan support committees being formed and networked to counteract negative media portrayals and US government accusations.

Despite all this US-Venezuela trade relations have grown substantially during the Chávez years. In 1999, Chávez's first year in power, the US exported $5,343 billion worth of goods to Venezuela. By 2007 this figure had increased to $10,199 billion, approximately a twofold increase. US imports from Venezuela increased in the same period from $11,334 billion to $39,896 billion, a more than threefold increase, with a trade balance in Venezuela's favour of $8,773 billion.[67] The US is Venezuela's main trading partner, accounting for 41.1% of its total trade in 2006.[68] The majority of Venezuelan exports to the US are oil and related products, amounting to 11% of US oil imports, which in turn amounts to 60% of Venezuela's total oil exports. PdVSA also wholly owns five refineries in the United States and partly owns four refineries, either through partnerships with US companies or through CITGO.[69]

Recent Venezuelan–US relations therefore have been characterised by a profound mutual trade dependence balanced by an equally profound mutual suspicion. Policy statements have sometimes echoed this dichotomy, with most high-profile US officials, including President Bush, secretary of state Condoleezza Rice and John Negroponte, deputy secretary of state, all having issued negative statements against Chávez. Yet Thomas A. Shannon, assistant secretary of state for western hemispheric affairs under President Bush had a more concilitary approach to Venezuela, showing a division in US depart-ments on how to deal with Chávez.[70] Generally speaking for the US, under George W. Bush, Chávez's Venezuela was, as Romero characterises it, 'a semi-democratic government, close to the Cuban regime, capable of exporting its revolution to the hemisphere and with little proof of a willingness to support the pro-democratic, pro-business, anti-terrorist and anti-narcotic policies promoted by Washington on a world, regional and sub-regional levels'.[71]

Meanwhile, the Chávez government viewed the US as an evil Empire seeking to impose its will on a Venezuela which is attempting to free itself from that domination and establish a new more democratic order based on a socialist-inspired economic and social system. Yet trade flourished between the two, despite Chávez's best efforts to diversify it. With such diametrically opposed visions, and such deep contradictions in discourse and action, it seemed that US-Venezuelan relations would remain in a state of turbulence for some time, vacillating between relatively calm periods and episodes of brinkmanship between both nations.

The new US president, Barrack Obama, expressed some similar sentiments towards Latin America on the campaign trail as those held by the Bush administration. For example, in a speech to a group of Miami based Cuban exiles in May 2008, Obama outlined a Latin America policy based on cooperation and increased aid and with a commitment to negotiate with Cuba. He also promised, however, continuing support for present security-based policy in Colombia and reaffirmed Colombia's 'right' to violate neighbouring countries sovereignty in pursuit of 'terrorists'. Moreover, in an apparent threat to Venezuela he strongly condemned 'collaboration' of neighbouring countries with the FARC, which, he said, should be 'exposed to international condemnation, regional isolation and – if need be – strong sanctions'. As Tom Hayden states, there is 'a lingering imperial assumption' beneath the rhetoric which suggests a continuation of many of Bush's failed policies.[72]

Since President Obama's inauguration on 20 January 2009 there has been little sign of change to such sentiments in the new administration's emerging policy on Venezuela. The two countries continue without diplomatic representation since Chávez expelled the US ambassador in September 2008, due to the latter's alleged involvement in a supposed coup plot. President Obama and secretary of state Hillary Clinton have both continued to make negative remarks about Venezuela and Chávez in particular, claiming that Venezuela supports terrorism and that Chávez impedes progress in the region. Chávez had remained relatively restrained in the face of such accusations, but in March 2009, on an edition of his weekly television show, Aló Presidente, Chávez called Obama a 'poor ignorant person', who needed to study Latin America's, and the world's reality more. Nonetheless, Chávez has repeatedly expressed Venezuela's willingness to find mutual areas of cooperation and to re-establish diplomatic relations with the US, providing that country shows respect to Venezuela and to Latin America. Key to this is the dropping by the US of its embargo against Cuba. While the US has made some tentative steps in softening its stance on Cuba – allowing increased visits by Cuban Americans and the sending of more remittances, more frequently to relatives on the island for example – dropping the embargo may still remain quite distant in the future. A crucial test for Obama is his attendance at the 2009 Summit of the Americas in Trinidad and Tobago on 17–18 April, his inaugural engagement with the region and his first encounter with the Venezuelan president. What comes out of that summit and any possible encounter between the two men remains to be seen at the time of writing, but central to Chávez's demands and that of many of his presidential colleagues will be the beginning of the end of Cuba's isolation and a more equal and respectful treatment of the region as a whole.

Venezuelan foreign policy – successes and contradictions

As we have seen throughout this study, the development strategy being set out by the Venezuelan government is profoundly different to the orthodox neoliberal model being put forward by the multilateral agencies led by the United States, and supported in general by western nations. Whereas neoliberalism puts a premium on 'free' markets, a lessening of state influence on the economy, a light regulatory touch, freedom of movement for capital, a reification of private property above the collective, a centralised technocratic state, privatisation of public goods etc., Venezuela has instead insisted on its right to pursue a model reasserting state power within the economy, with increased nationalisation of key industries and services and a rejection of privatisation, with a premium being placed on the right collectively to manage property and enterprise, with workers sometimes having a central role in opposition to corporations, a reassertion of the political over the economic, an emphasis on universal access to public goods etc. It is no surprise then that, as Payne contends, these opposing development strategies should come into conflict with each other, especially given the profound inequalities of power between Venezuela and the United States and other western countries, their heretofore close diplomatic and political relations and the fact that Venezuela is a major oil producer supplying the US with an important proportion of its energy needs.

To what extent then does Venezuela achieve the objectives it has set for itself? If we remember, these objectives, as set out in its latest development plan, were as follows:

1 Strengthen national sovereignty by accelerating the conformation of a regional geopolitical bloc and a multipolar world;
2 Diversify political, economic and cultural relations according to the establishment of areas of geostrategic interest;
3 Deepen fraternal dialogue between peoples, the respect for freedom of thought, religion and self-determination.

As we have seen Venezuela has made a concerted effort to broaden its international relations. It has moved from having the US as the central pillar of its international strategy to forming solid relations with a wide range of countries, including China, Russia and India and other less powerful nations such as Iran and Belarus. Venezuela has worked extremely hard to encourage a regional bloc in South America. It has joined MERCOSUR alongside the largest nations of the continent, Brazil and Argentina, as well as the smaller Uruguay and Paraguay. It has signed a complex series of agreements around energy with the Caribbean nations, MERCOSUR member states and with some of its erstwhile fellow CAN members. It has formed its own trade and solidarity pact in ALBA with Cuba, Bolivia and more lately Nicaragua, Honduras and Dominica. It has put forward successful proposals such as the Bank of the South, which is now a reality as well as being instrumental in putting forward the concept of South American unity, which is now tentatively becoming reality in UNASUR.

In this Venezuela has led the way in a return to the left in Latin America which has provided a beneficial environment for such diplomatic and trade initiatives. While it is true that there are differences between the different left-wing governments in the region – which Jorge Castañeda simplistically characterises as a 'good' left and a 'bad' left, with Chávez of course being the 'leader' of the latter[73] – there are also a core of similarly held values between all these governments despite these differences. These are, according to Ramírez Gallegos:[74]

1   Some degree of return to state development activity;
2   Increased sovereignty in the international context and through regionalism;
3   Some degree of experimentation in economic cooperation between state and society (cooperatives, nationalisations);
4   Democratic innovation – participative, direct or communitarian mechanisms.

In sum there is a new emphasis on the social allied to some form of state intervention, and to political participation within a regionalist context.[75]

In this way it can be said that Venezuela has not rejected globalisation but rather the neoliberal version of globalisation which is seen to be favouring the western nations at the expense of Latin America and other developing countries. Instead, Venezuela has achieved to a great extent its objectives of constructing a multipolar world, which allows for more policy experimentation outside of neoliberal orthodoxy, not just for Venezuela but for other Latin American countries as well. It has contributed to a renaissance of the state in the region and in its dealings outside the region, as most of these agreements have been state-led and with state-owned companies. Venezuela has also contributed to a continuing process of searching for alternatives to neoliberalism both through its own policy experimentation and in its support for groupings of developing nations and alternative groupings of civil society such as the World Social Forum. Chávez in particular has secured a high profile amongst social movements, not just in Latin America but throughout the world. These are all major foreign policy successes for Venezuela, which have a universal impact way beyond its borders. These successes have also mitigated the effects on it of the 'global politics of unequal development', thus providing it with a certain degree of autonomy, an autonomy which, however, is made possible to a large extent by its abundant energy resources.

Nevertheless this has not been achieved without some notable contradictions. First, despite these foreign policy successes, Venezuela still remains highly dependent on the US for trade, and not just the US but that country's chief ally in the region, Colombia – who are also Venezuela's chief ideological adversaries in the hemisphere. As we have seen above, in 2006, 41.1% of all Venezuela's trade was with the United States. Furthermore, 4.3% of its trade was with Colombia, with a trade balance in the latter's favour. If we compare these figures with Venezuela's trade with some of the countries it has been courting in recent years we find that for the same year, total trade with China was 3.9%, with Brazil 2.8%, Argentina 0.7% and Uruguay 0.4% – in other words a mere 3.9% of its total trade is with its future MERCOSUR partners, equal to that of China, but below that with Colombia and well below that with the US.[76] Venezuela therefore has a very long way to go before it has reduced its commercial dependence on the US to a level which leaves it less exposed to the foreign policy demands of the latter country.

It is unsurprising then, although unjustified, that the challenge that Venezuela represents to the US has not gone unpunished. Venezuela's position as a major trading partner, with oil being at the centre of that relationship, its geographical position facing the Caribbean, the 'patio' of the US's Latin American 'backyard', its sharing of a lengthy border with its major ally Colombia, the strong bonds between all three nations and Venezuela's defiant friendship with the US's chief *bête noir* in the region, Cuba, has made it the greatest foreign policy challenge to the US in the western hemisphere since the revolution led by Fidel Castro in that island nation over fifty years ago. It is therefore unlikely that the US will desist in the short term in its attempts to undermine the Venezuelan government, with a view to eventually removing it, unless there is a radical change in attitude from both.

Moreover, the sought-for change to lessen dependence on the US and Colombia would damage those within Venezuela who benefit from this trade. These are found mostly in the middle and upper classes which have shown a willingness to engage in both illegal and legal activities to remove the Chávez government. The Chávez government therefore faces a linked challenge to its authority both from within and from without Venezuela's borders.

Venezuela's foreign policy also shows discrepancies with its own stated objectives and principles for its emerging model. Its energy policy in particular consists of grandiose infrastructural projects, such as the planned

Southern Gas Pipeline, which will run through some of the most ecologically fragile environmental systems in the continent, including its most important, the Amazon. This will have clearly grave consequences not just for these environments, but also for the indigenous peoples which live within them. As US Green Party activist Lorna Salzman states:

> Clearly, radical economic policies declaring independence from the US do not include more deference to the environment. So just what does it mean to declare independence from the old 'imperialist' institutions? Just where are these countries diverging from the economic growth models and agendas of capitalist economies everywhere?[77]

While the Left in Latin America is diverging from IMF/World Bank recipes in general, she claims, 'their hearts remain in the same place, dedicated to untrammelled, unsustainable resource exploitation and economic growth just like their capitalist neighbours to the north but with a few more crumbs allotted to the poor'.

Indeed Salzman's criticism can be extended to Venezuela's trade policies. While on the one hand the Chávez government has rejected the free trade policies incarnate in the FTAA model, it has sought and gained entry to MERCOSUR, which is in essence an equally neoliberal trade-based structure, with no structural recompense for the smaller nations to rectify the glaring asymmetries between them and their much greater neighbours. It remains to be seen if the new UNASUR will go beyond this limited area of action, if indeed it succeeds in achieving any form of unity at all.

Further discrepancies are found between Venezuela's foreign policy and its declared objective of furthering human rights. As we have seen Venezuela has developed close relations with a number of states with questionable human rights records – Belarus, Iran, Syria, China, Zimbabwe and Russia amongst others. As Wilpert states, on the one hand it is understandable that Chávez would have a degree of scepticism about these accusations considering the groundlessness of similar accusations against Venezuela. Nevertheless, he continues, these accusations are serious and Chávez, by supporting these countries 'makes it more difficult for activists in [them] to fight for social justice'.[78]

The Venezuelan government has also placed a great emphasis in its national and international policy on grassroots organising and participation in the formulation and execution of policy. This, however, is largely absent from most of the initiatives reviewed here. Most of the infrastructural projects are being planned with little consultation, including environmental impact studies. Chávez brought Venezuela into MERCOSUR and out of CAN without any popular consultation. Most international agreements subscribed to have been at a statist level with little popular participation. Even ALBA while professing a grassroots approach has seen little actual grassroots participation.

There have been, however, many verbal clashes which have galvanised grass-roots support, as Steve Ellner notes, such as Chávez's dismissal of Mexican president Vincente Fox as a 'lapdog of the empire', or the references to US president George Bush as the 'devil', as well as frequent appearances at mass meetings, such as during the Mar de la Plata Americas summit in 2005.[79] These, however, while important do not constitute an integrated participatory mechanism on the part of Venezuelans in the construction of their country's foreign policy.[80] It is from grassroots movements that the most radical proposals are emerging which point the way to an alternative, more sustainable future, but these by and large have found little impact beyond rhetorical acknowledgement.

Finally Chávez's own role in Venezuelan foreign policy betrays contradictions. On the one hand, Chávez as president has had a preponderant role in the construction of this, in many respects, undeniably successful, and in the current context, radical and alternative foreign policy strategy. He has, moreover, on numerous occasions presented undoubted statesmanship. His frequent public outbursts against fellow leaders, however, while having its uses in terms of galvanizing radical sectors, can be counter-productive in alienating other left-leaning or centrist governments and civil society groupings. Furthermore, it is unknown to what extent this provides fodder for right-wing groups and governments looking to undermine the Chávez government and its many achievements.

To conclude, Venezuela, considering its position as a relatively small nation in a marginalized part of the globe, and even taking into account its status as an important oil producer, has had an impressive impact on the world stage under President Chávez. Its most important contribution has been its furtherance of the idea of the sovereign right of smaller nations to follow their own chosen development path. In this way it has contributed greatly to reorienting the 'global politics of unequal development' in favour of those nations, whilst engaging fully in globalization on its own terms. Venezuela has achieved this, however, not without a price. First, it has paid a price in terms of its own internal stability and its freedom from outside interference. Second, it has paid a price in terms of its contradicting to some extent, through its foreign policy, its stated ethical precepts, such as the promotion of human rights, the right to live in a 'healthy non-contaminated environment' and popular participation.[81] Third, there is a marked incongruence between its searching for a new more ethical model of development and its attraction to countries which practice a modified version of a growth-oriented, resource-exploitative model, such as China, with little regard for the consequences in terms of the environment. These are contradictions, however, which are not just pertinent to Venezuela but are, as Salzman points out, apparent in much thinking on the Left. It is not for this study, however, to attempt to reconcile them.

Notes

1   Payne, A., 2005, *The Global Politics of Unequal Development*. Houndmills, Basingstoke: Palgrave Macmillan.
2   Ibid., p. 27.
3   Ibid., p. 29.
4   Ibid., p. 31.
5   Ibid., p. 32.
6   Ibid., p. 35.
7   Ibid.
8   Ibid., p. 45.
9   Ibid., p. 36.
10 ibid., p. 38.
11 Ibid., p. 39.
12 Ibid., p. 40, citing Hettne, 1995, p. 263.
13 Ibid., p. 234.
14 Ibid., p. 35.
15 Ibid., p. 239.
16 These being the US, Canada, the UK, France, Germany, Italy, Japan (G7) and Russia (G8).
17 Payne, *The Global Politics of Unequal Development*, p. 246.
18 Republica Bolivariana de Venezuela, Presidencia, 2007, *Proyecto Nacional Simón Bolívar – Primer Plan Socialista PPS: Desarrollo Económico y Social de la Nación 2007–2013*. Available from: www.cenit.gob.ve. Accessed 17 May 2008.
19 Republica Bolivariana de Venezuela, 2001, *Líneas Generales del Plan de Desarrollo Económico y Social de la Nación 2001–2007*. Available from: http://portal.gobiernoenlinea.ve/gobierno_al_dia/docs/PlanDesarrolloEconomicoSocial2001-2007.pdf. Accessed 21 May 2008.
20 Republica Bolivariana de Venezuela, Presidencia, *Proyecto Nacional Simón Bolívar*, pp. 43–45.
21 Romero, C. A., 2006, *Jugando con el Globo: La política exterior de Hugo Chávez*. Caracas: Ediciones B.
22 Ibid., p. 98.
23 Ibid.
24 Ibid., p. 99.
25 Ibid., p. 162.
26 Thanks to Julia Buxton for this point.
27 Republica Bolivariana de Venezuela, *Líneas Generales del Plan de Desarrollo Económico*, Section 5, Paragraph 5.1, p. 155.
28 Romero, *Jugando con el Globo*, p. 186.
29 Kozloff, N., 2006, *Hugo Chávez: Oil, Politics and the Challenge to the US*. Houndsmills, Basingstoke: Palgrave Macmillan, p. 26.
30 Carlson, C., 2007, 'Venezuela and China form bilateral development fund – energy, technology and financing, increase supply of oil to China', 7 November. Available from: www.venezuelanalitica.com. Accessed 21 May 2008.
31 Schiller, B., 2006, 'The axis of oil: China and Venezuela', 20 March. Available from: www.opendemocracy.net. Accessed 21 May 2008.
32 Miller Llara, S. and Ford, P., 2008, 'Chávez, China cooperate on oil, but for different reasons', 3 January. Available from: www.csmonitor.com. Accessed 21 May 2008.
33 Ibid.

34 AFP, 2008, 'Venezuela and India sign joint project in Orinoco Oil Belt', 10 April. Available from: www.venezuelanalysis.com. Accessed 21 May 2008.

35 Carlson, C., 2007, 'Venezuela strengthens ties to Russia and Belarus with Chávez visit', 30 June. Available from: www.venezuelanalysis.com. Accessed 21 May 2008.

36 Carlson, C., 2007, 'Russian president praises investment opportunities in Venezuela', 23 October. Available from: www.venezuelanalysis.com. Accessed 21 May 2008.

37 Carlson, 'Venezuela strengthens ties to Russia and Belarus'.

38 Carlson, C., 2007, 'Venezuela and Belarus strengthen strategic alliance', 9 December. Available from: www.venezuelanalysis.com. Accessed 21 May 2008.

39 Carlson, C., 2007, 'Venezuela and Iran strengthen "anti-imperialist" alliance', 20 November. Available from: www.venezuelanalysis.com. Accessed 21 May 2008.

40 Chávez Frías, H., 2006, 'Discurso con motivo del inicio de la Cátedra "Simón Bolívar" en la Universidad Nacional de Brasilia: "O nos unimos o nos hundimos", Brasil, 6 de mayo de 1999', in H. Chávez Frías, *La unidad latinoamericana*, ed. S. Rinaldi. Bogotá: Oceansur, pp. 1–7, p. 5.

41 FTAA (Free Trade of the Americas Agreement), 2003, 'Free Trade Agreement of the Americas, Draft Agreement, Chapter II, General Provisions, November 21, 2003' . Available from: www.ftaa-alca.org. Accessed 22 May 2008.

42 Seitz, M., 2008, 'Una OTAN sudamericana?', 23 May. Available from: www.news. bbc.co.uk. Accessed 23 May 2008.

43 Romero, *Jugando con el Globo*, p. 160.

44 These objectives, however, may be under threat. See Arruda, M., 2008, 'Banco del Sur – riesgo de volverse un proyecto tecnócrata', 23 May. Available from: www.tni.org. Accessed 3 June 2008.

45 www.telesurtv.net.

46 Fritz, T., 2007, *ALBA contra ALCA: La Alternativa Bolivariana para las Américas: una nueva vía para la integración regional en Latinoamérica*, Centro de Investigación y Documentación Chile Latinoamérica (FDCL), Berlin, April. Available from: www.fdcl-berlin.de/index.php?id=1218.

47 Anderson, J. L., 2008, 'Fidel's Heir: the rising influence of Hugo Chávez', in *The New Yorker*, 23 June. Available from: http://www.newyorker.com/reporting/2008/06/23/080623fa_fact_anderson/?currentPage=all. Accessed 23 June 2008.

48 Suggett, J., 2008, 'Venezuela proposes food crisis fund at controversial trans-Atlantic Summit', 20 May 20. Available from: www.venezuelanalysis.com. Accessed 21 May 2008.

49 Romero, *Jugando con el Globo*, p. 139.

50 Marquéz, H., 2007, 'Colombia-Venezuela: possibly the bitterest conflict in a century', 26 November. Available from: www.ipsnews.net. Accessed 24 May 2008.

51 *Wall Street Journal*, 2008, 'War and trade in Colombia', 7 March. Available from: www.blogs.wsj.com Accessed 24 May 2008.

52 Marquéz, 'Colombia-Venezuela'.

53 Kozloff, *Hugo Chávez*, p. 124.

54 Romero, *Jugando con el Globo*, p. 143.

55 Wilpert, G., 2007, *Changing Venezuela by Taking Power: The History and Policies of the Chávez Government*. London and New York: Verso.

56 Ibid., p. 169.

57 Golinger, E., 2006, *The Chávez Code: Cracking US Intervention in Venezuela*. London and New York: Pluto Press.

58 Ibid., p. 51.

59 Ibid., p. 63.

60 Ibid., p. 96.

61 Ibid., p. 123.
62 Chávez, H., 2006, 'Ahora hay que definer el futuro del mundo', in Chávez Frías, *La unidad latinoamericana*, pp. 346–352, pp. 346–347.
63 Ellner, S., 2008, *Rethinking Venezuelan Politics: Class, Conflict, and the Chávez Phenomenon*. Boulder, CO and London: Lynne Rienner.
64 García, G., 2006, 'Venezuela: holding the line against drug trafficking'. Available from: www.coha.org. Accessed 26 May 2008.
65 Anderson, 'Fidel's heir: the rising influence of Hugo Chávez'.
66 Ellner, *Rethinking Venezuelan Politics*, pp. 208–212.
67 US Census Bureau, 2008, 'Trade in goods (imports, exports and trade balance) with Venezuela'. Available from: http://census.gov/foreign-trade/balance/c3070.html#top. Accessed 26 May 2008.
68 European Commission, 2008. 'EU and the world: external trade, Venezuela'. Available from: http://ec.europa.eu/trade/. Accessed 26 May 2008, p. 4.
69 Alvarez, C. J., 2006, 'Venezuela's oil based economy', in *Council on Foreign Relations*. Available from: www.cfr.org. Accessed 26 May 2008.
70 Thanks to Julia Buxton for this point.
71 Romero, *Jugando con el Globo*, p. 167.
72 See Hayden, T., 2008, 'Mixed Blessing', in *The Nation*, 25 May. Available at: www.thenation.com. Accessed 27 May 2008.
73 Castañeda, J. G., 2006 'Latin America's left turn', in *Foreign Affairs* 85(3): 28–43.
74 Ramírez Gallegos, F., 2006, 'Mucho más que dos izquierdas', in *Nueva Sociedad* 205, 'America Latina en los tiempos de Chávez'. Available from: www.nuso.org. Accessed 3 March 2008.
75 For other opinions see: Grandin, G., (2006), 'Latin America's new consensus', in *The Nation*. Available from: www.thenation.com. Accessed 5 May 2006; Solowicz, B., 2004, 'The Latin American left: between governability and change'. Available from: www.tni.org. Accessed 6 July 2005; Weisbrot, M., 2006, 'Latin America: the end of an era'. Available from: www.cepr.net. Accessed 5 June 2006. Also published in: *International Journal of Health Services* 36(4).
76 European Commission, 'EU and the world', p. 4.
77 Salzman, L., 2008, 'The new left in Latin America: what Chomsky didn't tell you', 21 May. Available from: www.countercurrents.org. Accessed 27 May 2008.
78 Wilpert, *Changing Venezuela by Taking Power*, p. 181.
79 Ellner, *Rethinking Venezuelan Politics*, pp. 209–213.
80 For a discusión on this and other ideas in this section see Fritz, *ALBA contra ALCA*.
81 Republica Bolivariana de Venezuela, Presidencia, *Proyecto Nacional Simón Bolívar*, pp. 6–7.

Conclusion: populism and democracy in a globalised age

This book had a number of central questions grouped into four central pillars – what I have called the 'four Cs'- that is context, causes, characteristics and consequences. Hence, the book asked: What were the *contexts* in which Chávez emerged? What were the immediate *causes* of his emergence? What policies have been implemented – in other words what are the *characteristics* of *chavismo*? And finally, what *consequences* is *chavismo* having on Venezuela? These four pillars therefore became the essential guiding structure for the study, giving it both a logical and narrative flow.

The book explored the four pillars through seven chapters. In Chapter 1, populism's theoretical roots and historical trajectory were reviewed to show its ideological and programmatic variety. This chapter found that while the literature can provide us with an essential framework with which to examine *chavismo*, it is necessary to refer to other literatures in order to construct a fuller and more accurate account. The chapter therefore reviewed literature not directly related to populism, such as works by Habermas and Gramsci amongst others. In Chapter 2 the book examined the first two of the four Cs: the overall historic *context* and the immediate *causes* of the Chávez phenomenon. In this chapter, the context of historical cleavages around race and class were found as central to help explain the emergence of Chávez. In Chapter 3 the book focused on the third pillar, the *characteristics* of *chavismo*, examining first *how* Chávez came to power and identifying the political strategies he used to get and maintain power, using the the Gramscian concept of hegemony to help explain this. Following that in Chapter 4 we examined the social and economic policies of the Chávez regime to show to what extent Chávez has departed from established globalisation processes, so gaining legitimacy and establishing hegemony.

In Chapter 5 the book evaluated accusations of authoritarianism against Chávez, assessing the relative levels of democracy and authoritarianism found in the Chávez presidency in five key areas of democracy associated with popular participation: elections, presidential authority and institutional autonomy, human rights, media freedom and the right to information, and associational autonomy. In order to help us assess these claims more fully the neoliberal Fujimori of Peru was introduced as a comparative element. In this way the book better established its central contention that different ideologies can have differing effects on the nature of populist governments. In the penultimate chapter, Chapter 6, the book turned to the question of the impact of the Chávez government on the Venezuelan polity. While much of the literature on populism cites increased democratisation as a consequence of populism, a more common finding is that populism damages democratic institutions and is therefore ultimately bad for democracy. This book questioned many of the assumptions behind the latter argument, arguing that it has a narrow institutional view of democracy and that rather contemporary populism needs to be placed into wider discussions on globalisation and democratisation. In Chapter 7, the book examined Venezuela's foreign policy placing it within Anthony Payne's theory of the 'global politics of unequal development'. Payne argues, as this book does, that national development strategies must be placed within the context of globalisation and the unequal power politics of the international arena. It is argued in this book that in order to advance its heterodox national development strategy, *chavismo* has attempted, through its foreign policy, to advance a multipolar world as opposed to the present unipolar world structure dominated by the United States.

In sum what is argued is that populism is a key explanatory concept for understanding Latin American politics but that it is imperative to place the national context within the wider international structure in order to understand fully the phenomenon. This book has attempted to prove that this is particularly true in the case of the government of Hugo Chávez of Venezuela.

Chávez: a populist president in a globalising world

One of the principal aims of this book was to look at why the concept of populism has emerged back into the mainstream, both in the media and in academia, in recent years, despite having been assigned to the dustbin of history at the end of the Cold War. A further question was to ask why it was that this commentary was by and large so negative. Amongst politicians, Donald Rumsfeld, for example, one time United States secretary for defence under President George W. Bush, in a speech given in March 2006, expressed his concern about Latin Americans turning to 'populist leadership … that clearly are worrisome'. President Alejandro Toledo of Peru expressed the belief that 'cheap empty populism is the danger to democracy'.[1] In the mediaThe Economist, for example, warns that 'populists are leading Latin America down a blind alley'[2] with an article in the British newspaper, *The*

Independent concurring.[3] In the academic world, Argentine analyst Celia Szusterman, for example, in an article published in 2006, warned that what is currently happening in Latin America is a 'populist resurgence which is currently eroding already damaged political institutions'.[4] In Chapter 6 similar academic judgements were examined.

In general it has been argued in this book that these positions fail properly to analyse populism accurately because they do not put it into the wider context of globalisation and neoliberalism. Populism is traditionally associated with state intervention in the economy, with high-tariff barriers, state ownership of strategic industries, and state subvention of much private industry, as well as 'populist' distributivist policies in favour of previously excluded groups.[5] With the advent of globalisation and neoliberalism, populism was recast as 'neopopulism' due to perceived close affinities between it and neoliberalism. 'Classic' populism – that is the traditional populism referred to above - was deemed to be 'dead', never to return.

With the emergence of Chávez, in the late 1990s, however, this was proven not to be the case as he railed against neoliberalism and embarked on a massive spending programme on education and health, with firmer state control of the all-important oil industry in Venezuela, and the renationalisation of strategic areas of the economy such as electricity and telecommunications. This seeming revival of 'classic' populism in the age of globalisation jars with earlier claims of its death and reincarnation as 'neopopulism'. Within this context therefore, populism clearly needed to be reappraised and reassessed, particularly given the apparent affinities in many aspects of Chávez's presidential style with so-called neopopulists such as Fujimori, in spite of stark divergences in terms of policy content. That reappraisal this book argued should focus on three central concepts – ideology, democracy and legitimacy – in the context of globalisation, which were looked at in turn throughout this study.

Damaged democracy, neoliberal style

In this book, globalisation and its impacts were identified as crucial to understanding of the Chávez phenomenon. Globalisation is almost universally recognised as a key explanatory concept for the contemporary world, and globalisation today is primarily identified with two inter-related structures: neoliberalism and liberal democracy. By neoliberalism what is meant is that mix of policy proposals summed up in what was termed the Washington Consensus – financial liberalisation, privatisation of state companies and assets, fiscal discipline, freedom of movement for capital and so on – which have been applied throughout the continent, and the world, over the last thirty years or so. Yet in Latin America a backlash has emerged against neoliberalism in the form of the so-called 'pink tide', with left-wing leaders being elected to power in some of the most important countries in the region, including Brazil (Lula), Argentina (Kirchner and Kirchner Fernandez), and Chile (Bachelet). These leaders, however, by and large have kept within the macroeconomic norms associated with neoliberalism, the Kirchners less so than the others, and the democratic norms set out by liberal democratic theory.

The leader who has attracted most attention, and who receives most charges of populism, is instead President Chávez, and more latterly, Presidents Morales of Bolivia and Correa of Ecuador. These leaders are not attracting this attention because of their populism, it has been argued in this book, but rather because they are carrying through programmes which are opposed to current neoliberal orthodoxy and which challenge liberal democratic norms. Calling them populists rather is, as suggested above, a way of placing them within a long Latin American tradition which has mostly negative connotations, of economic 'irresponsibility' and political 'authoritarianism'. This book examined the populist tradition to find out what it tells us about Chávez in particular, about his electoral successes, about the prospects for offering an enduring alternative to contemporary globalisation in Venezuela.

In contemporary conceptions of globalisation, many consider liberal democracy as its crucial corollary, such as the US-based political scientist, Francis Fukuyama with his famous 'End of History' claim.[6] Latin America has been one of the foremost regions of the world in experiencing democratisation with all Latin American governments except Cuba now being democratic, whereas in the 1970s very few were. Yet, as Chapter 6 shows, economic globalisation processes in Latin America have placed strains on Latin American democracies, leading to popular support for democracy being highly qualified, as a report published by the UNDP in 2004 attests.[7]

The emergence of Chávez, I argue in this book, was strongly influenced by these processes and the effects of neoliberal globalisation. The figure of Chávez emerged due to an economic crisis, much of it caused by neoliberal restructuring. The Venezuelan people rejected these neoliberal reforms, and the political system which implemented them, and Chávez responded to that rejection by running for president on an anti-neoliberal and anti-*puntofijista* ticket (see Chapter 2). Unlike Fujimori, however, who on winning office enthusiastically embraced neoliberalism despite campaigning on a centrist ticket, Chávez kept his word and took an initial cautiously anti-neoliberal approach to Venezuela's engagement with globalisation processes, to later radicalise it in the direction of so-called 'twenty-first century socialism'.

The contrast between the legitimacy of Chávez and that of other presidents deemed 'democratic' is tremendous. Chávez's astounding win in the December 2006 presidential elections, with around 62% of the vote from a turnout of 75%, leaves that legitimacy unquestioned. The Venezuelan vote for

Chávez must be contrasted with pro-neoliberal candidates, such as Felipe Calderón in Mexico who won that country's 2006 presidential elections with a highly questioned 35.88%, only 0.6% ahead of left-wing rival Manuel López Obrador. Of right-wing presidents in Latin America, only Alvaro Uribe of Colombia matches Chávez's popularity, and that due primarily to security rather than economic considerations. As seen previously poll evaluations by Venezuelans of their democracy remains high.

Reasons for this disparity are deeply intertwined with positions towards neoliberalism held by Latin American leaders. In Mexico, for example, neoliberalism is not seen to be working in favour of the poorest members of society, whereas in Venezuela, Chávez's anti-neoliberal polices are considered by the poor to be favourable to their interests. Furthermore, innovations in Venezuelan democracy, making it more participative, have allowed the poorest members of Venezuelan society a greater say in the decisions affecting their everyday lives. Clearly then ideology is a key factor in both cases, with neoliberalism found to be wanting. This then has a knock on effect on attitudes to, and conceptions of, democracy. It is imperative then that, while populism is a key concept to help us understand Chávez it must be placed within wider theoretical and conceptual frameworks, as this book has attempted to do.

The book has centred its argument on placing populist leaders within the broader global context of globalisation, in order to understand their true significance. The main aim of the book therefore, using the government of Hugo Chávez as an example, has been to show that the concept of populism is an essential tool to a deeper understanding of current politics in Latin America as that region grapples with deepening globalisation processes. *Chavismo*, the book argues, is the result of Venezuela's interaction with the broader ideological and structural changes brought about by globalisation.

The main argument put forward therefore, has been that while the Venezuelan leader is undeniably populist, the type of populism practised is deeply rooted in a radical, eclectic, socialist and Latin Americanist ideology. This ideological orientation of the Chávez government necessitates and encourages a high degree of popular mobilisation and participation in order to further its implantation as the hegemonic ideological vision of a new Venezuela. In contrast, it was argued, a similar process was found in the case of Fujimori in Peru, but this resulted in a highly authoritarian and deeply clientelistic regime with extremely low levels of popular mobilisation and participation due to its fiercely neoliberal ideological nature. It is its anti-neoliberal ideology and participative concept of democracy which marks *chavismo* out as a challenge to the orthodox neoliberal version of globalisation – a challenge now joined by other governments in the region, such as those of Morales in Bolivia and Correa in Ecuador.

Nonetheless, using populism as the analytical basis of the book also helped address the weaknesses and limitations of *chavismo*. These were identified variously as being problems of pluralism within the Chávez movement, dominance of the party leadership, particularly that of Chávez himself, corruption within government bureaucracy, weaknesses in and lack of control of the quality of public services and in the *misiones*, political and class/race polarisation amongst others. It now remains to be seen if the Chávez government can surmount these diffculties and truly establish a durable alternative to the current hegemonic neoliberal model.

Notes

1 For Rumsfeld see Rumsfeld, D., 2007, 'Remarks by Secretary Rumsfeld to the 35th Annual Washington Conference of the Council Of Americas', in US Department of Defense, Defense Link. Available from: www.defenselink.mil/transcripts/2005/tr20050503-secdef2681.html. Accessed 3 May 2005. For Toledo see SustainabilityTank, 2008, 'LATIN AMERICA: growth perspective in a shifting poltical landscape'. Available from: www.sustainabilititank.info. Accessed 14 June 2008.

2 See for example *The Economist*, 2006, 'The return of populism', in *The Economist*. Available from: http://www.economist.com/opinion/displaystory.cfm?story_id=6802448. Accessed 17 May 2006.

3 Usborne, D., 2006, 'The big question: should we be worried by the rise of the populist left in South America?', in *The Independent*, 4 May. Available from: http://news.independent.co.uk/world/americas/article361780.ece Accessed 17 May 2006.

4 Szusterman, C., 2006, 'Latin America's eroding democracy: the view from Argentina'. Available from: www.opendemocracy.net/democracy-protest/argentina_erosion_3607.jsp. Accessed 7 June 2006.

5 See Dornbusch, R. and Edwards S. (eds), 1991, *The Macroeconomics of Populism in Latin America*. Chicago: University of Chicago Press.

6 Fukuyama, F., 1993, *The End of History and the Last Man*. London: Penguin.

7 UNDP/United Nations Development Programme, 2004, *Ideas and Contributions: Democracy in Latin America*. Available from: www.undp.org. Accessed 2 May 2004.

Bibliography

Acuerdo Social, 2004, 'Sector Privado – Indicadores Sabía usted que ...' . Available from: www.acuerdosocial.com/index.asp?spg_id=33. Accessed 8 July 2004.

AFP (Association France Presse) and AP (Associated Press), 2002, 'La SIP responsabiliza a Chávez por ataques a los medios', in *El Nacional*, 26 February, p. 4.

AFP, 2008, 'Venezuela and India sign joint project in Orinoco Oil Belt', 10 April. Available from: www.venezuelanalysis.com. Accessed 21 May 2008.

Aharonián, A. R., 2002, 'Venezuela: Un golpe con olor a hamburguesa, jamón y petróleo'. Available from:www.analitica.com/va/politica/opinion/1578534.asp#HOLA. Accessed 10 December 2002.

Álvarez, A. E., 2003, 'State reform before and after Chávez's election', in S. Ellner and D. Hellinger (eds), (2003), *Venezuelan Politics in the Chávez Era: Class, Polarization and Conflict*. Boulder, CO and London: Lynne Rienner, pp. 147–161.

Álvarez, A. E., 2007, 'Venezuela 2007: Los Motores de la Revolución se alimentan con Petróleo', in *Revista de Ciencia Política: Edición Especial 2007*. Available from: www.scielo.cl/pdf/revcipol/v27nEsp/art16.pdf. Accessed 10 June 2007, pp. 265–289.

Alvarez, C. J., 2006, 'Venezuela's oil based economy', in *Council on Foreign Relations*. Available from: www.cfr.org. Accessed 26 May 2008.

Anderson, J. L., 2008, 'Fidel's heir: the rising influence of Hugo Chávez,' in *The New Yorker*, 23 June. Available from: http://www.newyorker.com/reporting/2008/06/23/080623fa_fact_anderson/?currentPage=all. Accessed 23 June 2008.

Anderson, P., 1976, *Considerations on Western Marxism*. London: New Left Books.

AN (Asamblea Nacional de la Republica Bolivariana de Venezuela), 2002, *Informe de la comisión parlamentaria especial para investigar los sucesos de abril de 2002*. Available from: www.urru.org/11A/Interpelaciones/Informe_Conclusiones_Chavistas10.htm. Accessed 10 December 2002.

AN (Asamblea Nacional la Republica Bolivariana de Venezuela)/OAEF (Oficina de Asesoría Económica y Financiera), 2003, 'Impacto de la Huelga General sobre las perspectivas Económicas y Fiscales para 2003 en Venezuela'. Available from: www.oaef.gov.ve/publicaciones2/Informes/Analisis/2003/Finanzas/ia%200303-054%20impacto%20del%20paro%20civico.pdf. Accessed 3 August 2004.

ANIL (Associación Nacional de Inocentes Liberados), 2002, *Informe Final de la Comisión Especial de Asistencia a los Indultados Inocentes (CEAII) creado mediante Decreto Supremo N° 002-2002-JUS*. Lima: ANIL.

Arditi, B., 2004, 'Populism as a spectre of democracy: a response to Canovan', in *Political Studies* 52(1), March: 135–143.

Arruda, M., 2008, 'Banco del Sur – riesgo de volverse un proyecto tecnócrata', 23 May. Available from: www.tni.org. Accessed 3 June 2008.

Ballón, E., 2002. 'El Toledismo y el movimiento social', in E. Ballón, C. Soria, G. Riofrío, E. Castillo, U. Huamala, G. Carrasco, J. Gamero, R. Ruiz, 2002, *Perú Hoy: Toledo: A un año de gobierno*. Lima: DESCO Centro de Estudios y Promoción del Desarrollo, pp. 13–60.

BCV (Banco Central de Venezuela), 2004, *Información Estadística*. Available from: www.bcv.org.ve/c2/indicadores.asp. Accessed 27 July 2004.

BCV, 2008, *Información Estadistica: Reservas Internacionales y Servicio de la Deuda Pública*. Available from: http://www.bcv.org.ve/cuadros/2/231.asp?id=32. Accessed 10 June 2008.

Betancourt, R., 2001 [1956], *Venezuela, Política y Petróleo*. Caracas: Monte Ávila Editores.

Bisbal, M. (ed.), 2000, *Antropología de unas elecciones*. Caracas: Universidad Católica Andrés Bello.

Blanco Muñoz, A., 1998, *Venezuela del 04F-92 al 06D-98: Habla el Comandante Hugo Chávez Frias*. Caracas: Catedra 'Pio Tamayo' CEHA/IIES/FACES/Universidad Central de Venezuela (UCV).

Bourgeat, R., 2003, 'Venezuela: caught between an authoritarian president and intolerant media'. Available from: www.rsf.fr/IMG/pdf/doc-2047.pdf. Accessed 6 August 2003.

Buci-Glucksmann, C., 1982, 'Hegemony and consent: a political strategy', in A. Sasoon (ed.), *Approaches to Gramsci*. London: Writers and Readers, pp. 116–126.

Buxton, J., 2000, 'Hugo Chávez and populist continuity in Venezuela Paper for the Political Studies Association – UK 50th Annual Conference 10–13 April, London, 2000'. Available from: www.psa.ac.uk/cps/2000/Buxton%20Julia.pdf. Accessed 6 August 2003.

Buxton, J., 2003, 'Economic policy and the rise of Hugo Chávez', in S. Ellner and D. Hellinger (eds), *Venezuelan Politics in the Chávez Era: Class, Polarization, and Conflict*. Boulder, CO and London: Lynne Rienner, pp. 113–130.

Buxton, J. D., 2001, *The Failure of Political Reform in Venezuela*. Aldershot: Ashgate.

Buxton, J. D., 2008, 'The Bolivarian Revolution as Venezuela's post-crisis alternative'. Paper presented at the 2nd Global International Studies Conference, Ljubljana, Slovenia 2008. Draft version.

Caballero, M., 2000, *La gestación de Hugo Chávez: 40 años de luces y sombras en la democracia venezolana*. Madrid: Catarata.

Calvert, P., 2002, *Comparative Politics: An Introduction*. Harlow: Longman.

Cameron, M. A., 2001, 'Venezuela's Hugo Chávez: saviour or threat to democracy?', in *Latin American Research Review* 36(3): 255–266.

Cameron, M. A., 2003, 'The slow-motion constitutional coup in Venezuela', in *Informed* 6: 1–3. Available from: www.governmentrelations.ubc.ca/informed/. Accessed 9 September 2004.

Cammack, P., 2000, 'The resurgence of populism in Latin America', in *Bulletin of Latin American Research* 19(2): 149–161.

Canache, D., 2004. 'Urban poor and political order', in J. L. McCoy and D. J. Myers (eds), *The Unravelling of Representative Democracy in Venezuela*. Baltimore and London: John Hopkins University Press, pp. 33–50.

Canovan, M., 1981, *Populism*. New York and London: Harcourt Brace Jovanovich.

Canovan, M., 1999, 'Trust the people! Populism and the two faces of democracy', in *Political Studies* XLVII: 2–16.

Cardenas, J. M. (ed.), 2006, *Debate sobre la democracia en América*. Caracas: UCV, CEA.

Cardoso, F. H. and Faletto, E., 1979, *Dependency and Development in Latin America*. Berkeley: University of California Press.

Carlson, C., 2007, 'Russian president praises investment opportunities in Venezuela', 23 October. Available from: www.venezuelanalysis.com. Accessed 21 May 2008.

Carlson, C., 2007, 'Venezuela and Belarus strengthen strategic alliance', 9 December. Available from: www.venezuelanalysis.com. Accessed 21 May 2008.

Carlson, C., 2007, 'Venezuela and China form bilateral development fund – energy, technology and financing, increase supply of oil to China', 7 November. Available from: www.venezuelanalitica.com. Accessed 21 May 2008.

Carlson, C., 2007, 'Venezuela and Iran strengthen "anti-imperialist" alliance', 20 November. Available from: www.venezuelanalysis.com. Accessed 21 May 2008.

Carlson, C., 2007, 'Venezuela announces increased social spending for 2008'. Available from: www.venezuelanalysis.com. Accessed 5 March 2008.

Carlson, C., 2007, 'Venezuela enters fifth consecutive year of growth'. Available from: www.venezuelanalysis.com. Accessed 8 March 2008.

Carlson, C., 2007, 'Venezuela strengthens ties to Russia and Belarus with Chávez visit', 30 June. Available from: www.venezuelanalysis.com. Accessed 21 May 2008.

Carmona Estanga, P., 2002, 'Decreto del Gobierno Provisional de Pedro Carmona Estanga', in *Observatorio Social de América Latina* III(7): 27–28.

Carrasquero, J. V., Maingon, T. and Welsch, F. (eds), 2001, *Venezuela en transición: elecciones y democracia 1998–2000*. Caracas: Consejo Nacional de Ciencia y Tecnología (CONICIT)/Red Universataria de Estudios Políticos de Venezuela-Redpol/CDB Publicaciones.

Carrasquero, J. V. and Welsch, F., 2001, 'Revolución en democracia o retorno al caudillismo', in J. V. Carrasquero, T. Maingon and F. Welsch (eds), *Venezuela en transición: elecciones y democracia 1998–2000*. Caracas: Consejo Nacional de Ciencia y Tecnología (CONICIT)/Red Universataria de Estudios Políticos de Venezuela-Redpol/CDB Publicaciones.

Carrera Damas, G., 1980, *Una nación llamada Venezuela*. Caracas: Monte Ávila Editores.

Cartaya, V., Magallanes, R. and Dominguez, C., 1997, *Venezuela: Exclusion and Integration – A synthesis in the building?* International Labour Organisation. Available from: www.ilo.org/public/english/bureau/inst/papers/1997/dp90/index.htm. Accessed 22 August 2003.

Carvallo, G. and López-Maya, M., 1989, 'Crisis en el Sistema Político Venezolano', in *Cuadernos de CENDES* 10: 47–53.

Castañeda, J. G., 1993, *Utopia Unarmed: The Latin American Left After the Cold War*. New York: Alfred A. Knopf.

Castañeda, J. G., 2006, 'Latin America's left turn', in *Foreign Affairs* 85(3): 28–43.

CEPAL, 2006, *Anuario Estadistica de America Latina y el Caribe, 2006: Etadisticas Economicas*. Available from: www.eclac.cl/publicaciones/xınl/3/28063/LCG2332B_2.pdf. Accessed 10 March 2008.

CEPAL, 2007, *Economic Survey of Latin America and the Caribbean: Statistical Apendix*. Available from: www.eclac.cl. Accessed 11 June 2008.

CEPAL, 2007, *Preliminary Overview of the Economies of Latin America and the Caribbean: Statistical Annex*. Available from: www.eclac.cl/publicaciones/xml/4/31994/Statistical_Annex.pdf. Accessed 11 June 2008.

CEPAL, 2007, *Social Panorama of Latin America 2007: Briefing Paper*. Santiago: ECLAC. Available from: www.eclac.cl/. Accessed 10 March 2008.

CEPAL/ECLAC, 2003, *Anuario Estadistico de America Latina y el Caribe 2002*. Available from: www.eclac.cl. Accessed 14 November 2003.

Chávez Frías, H., 1993, *El Comandante Hugo Chávez a la Nación: Mensaje Bolivariano*. Yare: No publisher.

Chávez Frías, H., 1994, *A Dos Años del 4 de febrero*. Yare: No publisher.

Chávez Frías, H., 2000, *Seis discursos del Presidente Constitucional de Venezuela, Hugo Chávez Frías*. Caracas: Ediciones de la Presidencia de la República.

Chávez Frías, H., 2006, 'Ahora hay que definer el futuro del mundo', in H. Chávez Frías, *La unidad latinoamericana*, ed. S. Rinaldi. Bogotá: Oceansur, pp. 346–352.

Chávez Frías, H., 2006, 'Discurso con motivo del inicio de la Cátedra "Simón Bolívar" en la Universidad Nacional de Brasilia: "O nos unimos o nos hundimos", Brasil, 6 de mayo de 1999', in H. Chávez Frías, *La unidad latinoamericana*, ed. S. Rinaldi. Bogotá: Oceansur, pp. 1–7.

Civit, J. and España, L. P., 1989, 'Análisis socio-político a partir del estallido del 27 de febrero', in *Cuadernos de CENDES* 10: 35–46.

Clement, C. I., 2005, 'Confronting Hugo Chávez: United States "democracy promotion" in Latin America', in *Latin American Perspectives* 32(3): 60–78.

CNE (Consejo Nacional Electoral), 2003, 'Resultados electorales referendo sindical' . Available from: www.cne.gov.ve/estadisticas/e014.pdf. Accessed 6 August 2003.

CNE, 2004, *Estadisticas Electorales*. Available from: www.cne.gov.ve/estadisticas.asp. Accessed 20 January 2004.

Conaghan, C., 1996, *Public Life in the Time of Alberto Fujimori*. Working Paper Series Number 219. Washington DC: Woodrow Wilson International Center for Scholars

Conniff, M. L. 1982, 'Introduction: toward a comparative definition of populism', in M. L. Conniff (ed.), *Latin American Populism in Comparative Perspective*. Albequerque: University of New Mexico Press, pp. 3–29.

Conniff, M. L., (ed.), *Latin American Populism in Comparative Perspective*. Albequerque: University of New Mexico Press

Constitución de la Republica Bolivariana de Venezuela, 1999. Available from: www.constitucion.ve. Accessed June, 10, 2008.

Coordinadora Nacional de Derechos Humanos, no date, 'Dossier Fujimori: Las leyes que destruyeron el Estado de Derecho'. Available from: www.dhperu.org. Accessed 10 June 2008.

Coppedge, M., 2002, 'Venezuela: popular sovereignty versus liberal democracy'. Kellogg Institute Working Paper No. 294. Available from: www.nd.edu/~kellogg/WPS/294.pdf. Accessed 6 August 2003.

Coronil, Fernando, 1997, *The Magical State: Nature, Money, and Modernity in Venezuela*. Chicago and London: The University of Chicago Press.

Coronil, F. and Skurski, J., 1991, 'Dismembering and remembering the nation: the semantics of political violence in Venezuela', in *Comparative Studies in Society and History* 33(2): 288–337.

Cotler, J. and Grompone, R., 2000, *El fujimorismo: ascenso y caída de un régimen autoritario*. Lima: Instituto de Estudios Peruanos.

Crabtree, J. and Tomas, J. (eds), 1998, *Fujimori's Peru: The Political Economy*. London: University of London Institute of Latin American Studies.

Crabtree, J., 2000, 'Populisms old and new: the Peruvian case', in *Bulletin of Latin American Research* 19(2): 163–176.

Croes, C., 1997, 'El 4 de febrero no ha terminado', in *Quinto Día* 7–14 November: 10–16.

Croes, C., 1999, 'A mí no me van a cerrar la boca', in *Quinto Día* 21–28 May: 14–21.

Cuya, E., 1999, 'La dictadura de Fujimori: marionetismo, corrupción y violaciones de los derechos humanos'. Available from: www.derechos.org/diml/doc/cuya4.html. Accessed 9 July 2003.

Dahl, R. A., 1989, *Democracy and its Critics*. New Haven and London: Yale University Press.

Datanalisis, 2001, *Escenarios Julio*. Año IV, número 3.

De la Torre, C., 2006, 'Es el populismo la forma constitutiva de la democracia en América Latina?', in José María Cardenas (ed.), *Debate sobre la democracia en América*. Caracas: UCV, CEA, pp. 139–151.

Degregori, C. I., Coronel, J. and del Pino, P., 1998, 'Government, citizenship and democracy: a regional perspective', in J. Crabtree and J. Thomas (eds), *Fujimori's Peru: The Political Economy*. London: University of London/Institute of Latin American Studies, pp. 243–265.

Delacour, J., 2005., 'The op-ed assassination of Hugo Chávez', in *Extra!*, November/December. Available from: www.fair.org. Accessed 23 April 2008

Di Tella, T., 1965, 'Populism and reform in Latin America', in C. Veliz (ed.), *Obstacles to Change in Latin America*. London: Oxford University Press, pp. 47–73.

Diamond, L., Hartlyn, J., Linz, J. J. and Lipset, S. M. (eds), 1999, *Democracy and Developing Countries: Latin America*, 2nd ed. Boulder, CO and London: Lynne Rienner.

Dietrich, Heinz, 2007, 'Derrota estratégica en Venezuela; peligro mortal para Bolivia y Cuba', 3 December. Available from: www.aporrea.org. Accessed 10 March 2008.

Dissent Voice News Service, 2002, 'The US and the coup in Venezuela'. Available from: www.thirdworldtraveler.com/South_America/US_Coup_Venezuela.html. Accessed 20 January 2004.

Dix, R. H., 1985, 'Populism: authoritarian and democratic', in *Latin American Research Review* 20(2): 29–52.

Dornbusch, R. and Edwards S. (eds), 1991, *The Macroeconomics of Populism in Latin America*. Chicago: University of Chicago Press.

Drake, P. W., 1982, 'Conclusion: requiem for populism', in M. L. Conniff, (ed.), *Latin American Populism in Comparative Perspective*. Albequerque: University of New Mexico Press.

ECLAC (Economic Commission for Latin America and the Caribbean), 2003, *Anuario Estadistico de America Latina y el Caribe 2002*. Available at: www.eclac.cl. Accessed 14 November 2003

ECLAC, 2008, *Estudios Economico de America Latina y el Caribe, 2007–2008*. Available from: www.eclac.cl. Accessed 25 August 2008.

EIU (Economist Intelligence Unit), 1998, *Venezuela: Country Profile*. London: EIU.

El Nacional, 2002, 'Mal número, 14 fallecidos' pp.s. C/6 and C/7, 13 April.

El Universal, 2004, 'Datanálisis asegura que 38,7% de los venezolanos no objeta ni apoya a Chávez'. El Universal Sección Avances, 9 January. Available from: www.eluniversal.com/2004/01/09/09A1432526.shtml. Accessed 9 January 2004.

El Universal, 2006, 'Rosales's candidacy formally announced', 8 August. Available from: http://english.eluniversal.com/2006/08/09/en_pol_art_09A762409.shtml. Accessed 22 February 2008.

Ellner, S., 2001, 'The radical potential of Chavismo in Venezuela: the first year and a half in power', in *Latin American Perspectives* 28(5): 5–32.

Ellner, S., 2002, 'The tenuous credentials of Latin American democracy in the age of neoliberalism', in *Rethinking Marxism* 14(3): 76–93.

Ellner, S., 2003, 'Hugo Chávez y Alberto Fujimori: análisis comparativo de dos variantes de populismo', in *Revista Venezolana de Economía y Ciencias Sociales* 10(1): 13–37.

Ellner, S., 2003, 'Organised labor and the challenge of Chavismo', in S. Ellner and D. Hellinger (eds), *Venezuelan Politics in the Chávez Era: Class, Polarization and Conflict*. Boulder, CO and London: Lynne Rienner; pp. 161–178.

Ellner, S., 2008, *Rethinking Venezuelan Politics: Class, Conflict, and the Chávez Phenomenon*. Boulder, CO and London: Lynne Rienner.

Ellner, S. and Hellinger, D. (eds), 2003, *Venezuelan Politics in the Chávez Era: Class, Polarization and Conflict*. Boulder, CO and London: Lynne Rienner.

European Commission, 2008, 'EU and the world: external trade, Venezuela'. Available from: http://ec.europa.eu/trade/. Accessed 26 May 2008.

European Union Election, 2006, 'Observation Mission Presidential Elections Venezuela 2006, Preliminary Statement, 5th December 2006'. Available from: http://ec.europa.eu/external_relations/human_rights/eu_election_ass_observ/venezuela_2006/prelim.pdf. Accessed 17 April 2008.

Evans/McDonough Co. Inc./Consultores 30.11, 2007. 'Clima Política Votantes Venezolanos: Presentación de resultados'. Available from: www.rethinkvenezuela.com/downloads/PRESENTACION_ENCUESTA_NACIONAL_NOVIEMBRE_2007.pdf. Accessed 15 January 2008.

Ewell, J., 1984, *Venezuela: A Century of Change*. Stanford: Stanford University Press.

Fienstein, T. and Youngers, C., 2002, 'Shedding light on the past: declassification of US documents'. Available at: www.wola.org/andes/Peru/peru_declassification_report.htm. Accessed 25 July 2003.

Fowks, J., 2000, *Suma y resta de la realidad: medios de comunicación y elecciones generales 2000 en el Perú*. Lima: Friedrich Ebert Stiftung.

Francia, N., 2000, *Antichavismo y Estupidez Ilustrada*. Caracas: Rayuela Taller de Ediciones.

Fukuyama, F., 1993, *The End of History and the Last Man*. London: Penguin

Freedom House, 2008, 'Map of freedom: country report, Venezuela'. Available from: www.freedomhouse.org. Accessed 17 April 2008.

Fritz, T., 2007, *ALBA contra ALCA: La Alternativa Bolivariana para las Américas: una nueva vía para la integración regional en Latinoamérica*, Centro de Investigación y Documentación Chile Latinoamérica (FDCL), Berlin, April. Available from: www.fdcl-berlin.de/index.php?id=1218. Accessed 10 June 2008.

FTAA (Free Trade of the Americas Agreement), 2003, 'Free Trade Agreement of the Americas, Draft Agreement, Chapter II, General Provisions, November 21, 2003' . Available from: www.ftaa-alca.org. Accessed 22 May 2008.

Fuentes, F., 2008, 'The struggle for a mass revolutionary party in Venezuela', 28 January.. Available from: www.venezuelanalysis.com. Accessed 30 January 2008.

Gable, D., 2004, 'Civil society, social movements, and participation in Venezuela's Fifth Republic'. Available from: www.venezuelanalysis.com/articles.php?artno=1103. Accessed 9 February 2004.

García, G., 2006, 'Venezuela: holding the line against drug trafficking'. Available from: www.coha.org. Accessed 26 May 2008.

García-Guadilla, M. P., 2003, 'Civil society: institutionalisation, fragmentation, autonomy', in S. Ellner and D. Hellinger (eds), *Venezuelan Politics in the Chávez Era: Class, Polarization and Conflict*. Boulder, CO and London: Lynne Rienner, pp. 179–197.

Gamble, A. and Payne, A., 2003, 'The world order approach', in Fredrik Soderbaum and Timothy M. Shaw (eds), *Theories of New Regionalism*. New York: Palgrave Macmillan, pp. 43–63.

Germani, G., 1965, *Politica y Sociedad en una Epoca de Transicion: de la Sociedad Tradicional a la Sociedad de Masas*. Buenos Aires: Editorial Paidos.

Germani, G., di Tella, T. and Ianni, O., 1976, *Populismo y contradicciones de clase en Lainoamérica*. Mexico DF: Serie Popular Era.

Gibbs, T., 2004, *Democracy's crisis of legitimacy in Latin America*. Available from: www.nacla.org/art_display.php?art=2447. Accessed 9 September 2004.

Giordano, A., 2008, 'The McCain doctrine: back to the Cold War in Latin America', 22 May. Available from: www.narconews.com. Accessed 28 May 2008.

Global Issues, 2008, *Global Issues on Media, Propaganda, and Iraq*. Available from: www.globalissues.org/HumanRights/Media/Propaganda/Iraq.asp. Accessed 6 May 2008.

Gobierno Bolivariano de Venezuela, Ministerio de Poder Popular para las Finanzas, Oficina Estadisticas de las Finanzas Publicas, 2008, 'Gobierno Central Presupestario'. Available from: www.mf.gov.ve. Accessed 5 June 2008.

Golinger, E., 2006, The Chávez Code: Cracking US Intervention in Venezuela. London and New York: Pluto Press.

Gomez, E., 2002, 'Sólo la presión social puede liberar conciencias', in El Universal, Wednesday 13 February.

Gonzales de Olarte, E., 1998, El Neoliberalismo a la Peruana: Economía, Política del ajuste estructural, 1990–1997. Lima: Consorico de Investigación Economica/Instituto de Estudios Peruanos.

González Plessmann, A. J., 2002, 'Venezuela: oposición y estado de derecho', in Observatorio Social de América Latina III(7): 19–23.

González-Plessmann, A. J., 2003, 'Venezuela: torn by polarisation'. Available from: www.wola.org/andes/Venezuela/venezuela_update.pdf. Accessed 6 August 2003.

Gott, R., 2001, In the Shadow of the Liberator: Hugo Chávez and the Transformation of Venezuela. London and New York: Verso

Gott, R., 2006, 'Venezuela's Murdoch', in New Left Review 39, May–June. Available from: http://newleftreview.org/A2622. Accessed 27 August 2008.

Gott, R., 2007, 'The 2006 SLAS Lecture: Latin America as a white settler society', Institute for the Study of the Americas, London, Bulletin of Latin American Research, April, 26(2): 269–289.

Gramsci, A., 1971 [1947], Selections from the Prison Notebooks, ed. and trans. by Q. Hoare and G. Nowell Smith. New York: International Publishers.

Grandin, G., 2006, 'Latin America's new consensus'. Available from: www.thenation.com. Accessed 5 May 2006.

Greenberg, Quinlan and Rosner, 2004, 'Venezuela, Resultados Estudio de Opinión Pública Nacional: Junio 23, 2004'. Available from: www.rnv.gov.ve/noticias/uploads/encuesta-greenberg-junio-2004.ppt. Accessed 15 January 2008.

Grompone, R., 2000, 'Al día siguiente: el fujimorismo como proyecto inconcluso de transformación política y social', in J. Cotler and R. Grompone (eds), El fujimorismo: ascenso y caída de un régimen autoritario. Lima: Instituto de Estudios Peruanos, pp. 77–175.

Gwynne, R. N. and Kay, C. (eds), 1999, Latin America Transformed: Globalisation and Modernity. London: Arnold.

Habermas, J., 1976, Legitimation Crisis. Cambridge and Oxford: Polity Press.

Habermas, J., 2000, The Structural Transformation of the Public Sphere. Cambridge, MA: MIT Press.

Halebsky, S. and Harris, R. L. (eds), 1995, Capital, Power and Inequality in Latin America. Boulder, CO: Westview Press.

Hall, S., Lumley, B. and Mc Lennan, G., 1977, 'Politics and ideology: Gramsci', in On Ideology. London: Hutchinson, pp. 45–76.

Hall, S.,1992, 'The West and the rest: discourse and power', in Stuart Hall and Bram Gieben (eds), The Formations of Modernity. Cambridge: Polity Press.

Harvey, D., 2005, A Brief History of Neoliberalism. Oxford: Oxford University Press.

Haussman, R. and Rigobon, R., 2004, 'En busca del cisne negro: Análisis de la evidencia estadística sobre fraude electoral en Venezuela'. Available from: www.sumate.org. Accessed 17 April 2008.

Hayden,T., 2008, 'Mixed Blessing', The Nation, 25 May. Available from: www.thenation.com. Accessed 27 May 2008.

Held, D., 2006, Models of Democracy, 3rd ed. Cambridge: Polity.

Herman, E. S. and Chomsky, N., 1994, Manufacturing Consent: The Political Economy of the Mass Media. London: Vintage.

Herrera Salas, J. M., 2005, 'Ethnicity and revolution: the political economy of racism in Venezuela', in Latin American Perspectives 32: 72–91.

HRW (Human Rights Watch), 1999, World Report. Available from: www.hrw.org/. Accessed 20 November 2003.

HRW, 2000, World Report. Available from: www.hrw.org/. Accessed 20 November 2003.

Hutton, W., 2008, The Writing on the Wall: China and the West in the 21st Century. London: Abacus

Ianni, O., 1976, 'Populismo y relaciones de clase', in G. Germani, T. di Tella and O. Ianni, (eds), Populismo y contradicciones de clase en Lainoamérica. Mexico DF: Serie Popular Era

IAPA (Inter American Press Association), 2003, 2003 Report on Press Freedom in Venezuela. Available from: www.sipiapa.com/publications/report_venezuela2003.cfm. Accessed 16 July 2003.

IAPA, 1999, 'La Prensa Bajo Amenaza en Perú', IAPA Press Release, 24 February. Available from: www.sipiapa.com/pressreleases/srchcountrydetail.cfm?PressReleaseID=81. Accessed 16 July 2003.

Ishibashi, J., 2003, 'Hacia una apertura del debate sobre el racismo en Venezuela: exclusión y inclusión esteriotipada de personas negras en los medios de comunicación'. Available from: www.globalcult.org.ve/pub/Rocky/Libro1/Ishibashi.pdf. Accessed 10 June 2008.

Jacques, M., 2004, 'Democracy isn't working', in The Guardian, 22 June.

Janicke, Kiraz, 2007, 'The Battle for the United Socialist Party of Venezuela', 1 December. Available from: www.venezuelanalysis.com. Accessed 30 January 2008.

Kaplan, M., 2001, Neocesarismo y Constitucionalismo: El Caso Chávez y Venezuela. México D.F.: Universidad Nacional Autónoma de México/Corte de Constitucionalidad de Guatemala.

Kay, B. H., 1996, ''Fujipopulism' and the liberal state in Peru, 1990–1995', in Journal of Interamerican Studies and World Affairs 38(4): 35–55.

Kelly, J., 2000, 'Thoughts on the constitution: realignment of ideas about the economy and changes in the political system in Venezuela', prepared for delivery at the 2000 meeting of the Latin American Studies Association, Hyatt Regency, Miami, 16–18 March. Available from: www-personal.umich.edu/~mmarteen/svs/lecturas/lasa2000/kelly2.htm.Accessed 3 August 2004.

Kirby, P., 2003, Introduction to Latin America: Twenty-First Century Challenges. London: Sage.

Klein, N., 2003, 'Venezuela's media coup', in The Nation 276(8): 10.

Koeneke R. H., 2000, 'Cosmovisión e ideólogos del chavismo', in Veneconomia 18(1). Available from: www.veneconomia.com/mensual/mes44.htm. Accessed 16 August 2001.

Kornblith, M., 1994, 'La Crisis del Sistema Politico Venezolano', in Nueva Sociedad 134: 142–157.

Kornblith, M., 2001, 'Confiabilidad y transparencia de las elecciones en Venezuela: examen de los comicios del 30 de julio de 2000', in J. V. Carrasquero, T. Maingon and F. Welsch (eds), Venezuela en transición: elecciones y democracia 1998–2000. Caracas: Consejo Nacional de Ciencia y Tecnología (CONICIT)/Red Universataria de Estudios Políticos de Venezuela-Redpol/CDB Publicaciones, pp. 133–164.

Kozloff, N., 2005, 'A real radical democracy: Hugo Chávez and the politics of race'. Available from: www.venezuelanalysis.com/articles.php?artno=1577. Accessed 20 February 2007.

Kozloff, N., 2006, Hugo Chávez: Oil, Politics and the Challenge to the US. Basingstoke: Palgrave Macmillan.

Laclau, E., 1977, Politics and Ideology in Marxist Theory: Capitalism-Fascism-Populism. London: New Left Books.

Laclau, E., 2005, On Populist Reason. London: Verso.

Laclau, E., 2006, 'La deriva populista y la centroizquierda latinoamericana', in *Nueva Sociedad* 205, Septiembre/Octubre: 57–61.

Laclau, E., and Mouffe, C., 2001, *Hegemony and Socialist Strategy: Towards a Radical Democratic Politics*, 2nd ed, London and New York: Verso.

Lander, E., 1996, 'The impact of neoliberal adjustment in Venezuela, 1989–1993', in *Latin American Perspectives* 23(3): 50–73

Lander, E., 2007, 'El referendum sobre la reforma constitucional', 24 December. Available from: www.tni.org. Accessed 18 February 2008.

Lander, E., 2007, 'Party disciplinarians: the threat to dissidence and democracy in the United Socialist Party of Venezuela'. Available from: www.tni.org. Accessed 21 February 2008.

Lander, E. and Navarette, P., 2007, *The Economic Policy of the Latin American Left in Government: Venezuela*, Briefing Paper 2007:02. Amsterdam: TransNational Institute. Available from: www.tni.org. Accessed 5 June 2008.

Lander, L. E. and Lopez Maya, M., 2000, 'Venezuela: La hegemonia amenazada', in *Nueva Sociedad* 167: 15–25.

Latinobarómetro, 2007, *Informe Latinobarómetro 2007: Banco de datos en linea*. Available from: www.latinobarometro.org. Accessed 2 May 2008.

Lemoine, M., 2002, 'Carta abierta al director de "El Universal"'. Available from: www.lainsignia.org/2002/junio/ibe_051.htm. Accessed 17 August 2003.

Lemoine, M., 2002, 'How hate media incited the coup against the president: Venezuela's press power'. Available from: http://mondediplo.com/2002/08/10venezuela. Accessed 26 July 2003.

Lichtenberg, J., 2002, 'Foundations and limits of freedom of the press', in D. McQuail (ed.), *McQuail's Reader in Mass Communication Theory*. London: Sage.

Lingenthal, M., 1999, 'Elecciones en Venezuela', in *Contribuciones* XVI(1): 219–235.

Lombardi, J.V., 1977, 'The patterns of Venezuela's past', in J. D. Martz and D. J. Myers (eds), *Venezuela: The Democratic Experience*. New York: Praeger, pp. 3–26.

López Jiménez, S., 1993, 'Perú, 1992: De la Dictablanda a la Democradura', in *Quehacer* 82: 34–41.

López Maya, M., 1996, 'Neuvas Representaciones populares en Venezuela', in *Nueva Sociedad* 144: 138–151.

López Maya, M., 2002, 'Venezuela after the caracazo: forms of protest in a deinstitutionalized context', in *Bulletin of Latin American Studies* 21(2): 199–219.

López Maya, M., 2003, 'Hugo Chávez Frías: his movement and his presidency', in S. Ellner and D. Hellinger (eds), *Venezuelan Politics in the Chávez Era: Class, Polarization and Conflict*. Boulder, CO and London: Lynne Rienner.

López Maya, M., 2004, 'Exposición con motivo del reconocimiento en la Asamblea Nacional de la ratificación del Presidente: 27 de agosto de 2004'. Available from: www.eluniversal.com/2004/08/29/apo_art_29107Z.shtml. Accessed 9 September 2004.

Lopez Maya, M., 2005, *Del Viernes Negro al Referendo Revocatorio*. Caracas: Alfadil.

López Maya, M. and Lander L. E., 1999. 'Triunfos en Tiempos de Transición: Actores de Vocación Popular en las Elecciones Venezolanas de 1998', in *America Latina, Hoy* 21, Abril: 41–50.

Lugo, J. and Romero, J., 2003, 'From friends to foes: Venezuela's media goes from consensual space to confrontational actor', in *Sicronia*, Spring. Available from: http://sincronia.cucsh.udg.mx/lugoromero.htm. Accessed 20 August 2003.

Lynch, N., 2000, 'Neopopulismo: un concepto vacío', in N. Lynch (ed.), *Política y Antipolítica en el Perú*. Lima: DESCO Centro de Estudios y Promoción del Desarrollo, pp. 153–180.

McCoy, J. L. and Myers, D. J. (eds), 2004, *The Unravelling of Representative Democracy in Venezuela*. Baltimore and London: John Hopkins University Press.

Malavé Mata, H., 1996, *Las contingencias de bolívar: El discurso de la política de ajuste en Venezuela* (1989–1993). Caracas: Fondo Editorial FINTEC.

Manrique, M., 2001, 'La participación política de las Fuerzas Armadas venezolanas en el sistema política (1998–2001)', in M. Tanaka (ed.) *Las Fuerzas Armadas en la Region Andina: No deliberantes o actores políticos?* Lima: Comisión Andina de Juristas, pp. 305–337.

Marquéz, H., 2007, 'Colombia-Venezuela: possibly the bitterest conflict in a century', 26 November. Available from: www.ipsnews.net. Accessed 24 May 2008.

Márquez, P., 2004, 'Vacas flacas y odios gordos: la polarización en Venezuela', in P. Márquez and R. Piñango (eds), *Realidades y Nuevos Caminos en esta Venezuela*. Caracas: Instituto de Estudios Superiores de Administración, pp. 31–46.

Márquez, P. and Piñango, R. (eds), 2004, *Realidades y Nuevos Caminos en esta Venezuela*. Caracas: Instituto de Estudios Superiores de Administración

Mauceri, P., 1997, 'Return of the caudillo: autocratic democracy in Peru', in *Third World Quarterly* 18(5): 899–911.

MBR-200, no date (1995?), *La Importancia de la Asemblea Nacional Constituyente para el MBR-200*. Mimeo in CENDES Centro del Estudio del Desarrollo.

MBR-200, 1992, *¿Porqué Insurgimos?* Mimeo in CENDES Centro del Estudio del Desarrollo.

MBR-200, 1996, *Agenda Alternativa Bolivariana: Una Propuesta Patriótica para salir del Laberinto/Presentación de Hugo Chávez Frías*. Caracas: MBR-200.

MBR-200 and Pirela Romero, Lt. Col. A., 1994, *MBR-200: El Arbol de las Tres Raíces*. Valencia, Venezuela: No publishing details.

McClintock, C., 1996. 'La voluntad política presidencial y la ruptura constitucional de 1992 en el Perú', in F. Tuesta Soldevilla (ed.), *Los enigmas de poder: Fujimori 1990–1996*, 2nd ed. Lima: Fundación Friedrich Ebert, pp. 303–331.

McCoy, J., 2004, *What Really Happened in Venezuela?*. Available from: www.venezuelanalysis.com/articles.php?artno=1271. Accessed 17 April 2008.

McCoy, J. L. and Smith, W. C., 1995, 'Democratic disequilibrium in Venezuela', in *Journal of Interamerican Studies and World Affairs* 37(2): 113–179.

MEF, 2006, 'Gobierno Central Presupuestario 2006'. Available from: www.mf.gov.ve/archivos/2000020201/Presentaci%F3n%20GCP%20A%D1O%202 006.pdf. Accessed 5 June 2008.

Miles, R., and Brown, M., 2003. *Racism*, 2nd ed. London and New York: Routledge.

Miller Llara, S., and Ford, P., 2008, 'Chávez, China cooperate on oil, but for different reasons', 3 January. Available from: www.csmonitor.com. Accessed 21 May, 2008.

MINCI (Ministerio de Communicación y Información de Venezuela), 2004, 'Gestión del Gobierno'. Available from: www.minci.gov.ve/logros.asp?t=1. Accessed 24 July 2004.

MINCI/Ministerio del Poder Popular para la Comunicación y la Información, 2007, *Misiones Bolivarianas*. Caracas: Coleción Temas de Hoy. Available from: www.minci.gov.ve. Accessed 21 November 2007.

MINCI/Ministerio del Poder Popular para la Comunicación y la Información, 2008, 'Nueve años de revolución: estadisticas de los aspectos sociales' – Presentación. Available from: www.minci.gob.ve/especiales/22/40274/. Accessed 11 June 2008.

MINCI/Ministerio del Poder Popular para la Comunicación y la Información, 2008, 'Nueve años de revolución: Logros Sociales' – Presentación. Available from: www.minci.gob.ve/especiales/22/40274/. Accessed 11 June 2008.

Molina J. E., 2001, 'Change and continuity in Venezuelan electoral behaviour in the 1998–2000 elections', in *Bulletin of Latin American Studies* 21(2): 219–248.

Montoya, D., 1995, 'Escenario electoral en las zonas de emergencia', in *Quehacer* 93: 46–50.

Mouffe, C., 2005, *On the Political*. London and New York: Routledge

Mouzelis, N., 1978, 'Ideology and class politics: a critique of Ernesto Laclau', in *New Left Review* 107: 45–61.

Mouzelis, N. P., 1986, *Politics in the Semi-Periphery: Early Parliamentarism and Late Industrialisation in the Balkans and Latin America*. New York: St. Martin's Press.

Myers, D. J., 1996, 'Venezuela: the stressing of distributive justice', in H. Wiarda and H. Kline (eds), *Latin American Politics and Development*. Boulder: Westview Press, pp. 227–267.

Nabulsi, K., 2004, 'The struggle for sovereignty', in *The Guardian*, 23 June.

Naím, M., 2001, 'La Venezuela de Hugo Chávez', in *Política Exterior* XV(82): 51–73.

Nef, J., 1995, 'Demilitarization and democratic transition in Latin America', in S. Halebsky and R. L. Harris (eds), *Capital, Power and Inequality in Latin America*. Boulder: Westview Press, pp. 81–107.

Norden, D. L., 2003, 'Democracy in uniform: Chávez and the Venezuelan armed forces', in S. Ellner and D. Hellinger (eds), *Venezuelan Politics in the Chávez Era: Class, Polarization and Conflict*. Boulder, CO and London: Lynne Rienner, pp. 93–113.

OAS (Organisation of American States), 2001, *Electoral Observations in the Americas Series, No.26/Electoral Observation in Peru, 2000*. Available from: www.upd.oas.org/lab/Documents/publications/electoral_observation/2000/pbl_26_2000_eng.pdf. Accessed 6 August 2003.

OAS, 2001, *Inter-American Democratic Charter*. Available from: www.oas.org/OASpage/eng/Documents/Democractic_Charter.htm. Accessed 14 June, 2008.

OAS, 2002, *General elections Venezuela 2000: electoral observations in the Americas Series No. 30*. Available from: www.upd.oas.org/lab/Documents/publications/electoral_observation/2000/pbl_30_2000_eng.pdf. Accessed 6 August 2003.

OAS, 2004, 'Press Release, Statement of OAS electoral observation mission on Venezuelan presidential referendum August 18, 2004'. Available from: www.oas.org. Accessed 25 August 2004.

OAS, Unit for the Promotion of Democracy, 1997, *Executive Summary, Electoral Observation, Peru 1995*. OAS: Washington.

O'Briain, D. and Bartley K., 2002, *The Revolution Will Not Be Televised* [documentary film]. Dublin: Power Pictures. See: www.chavezthefilm.com.

Observatorio Comunitario por el derecho a la Salud, 2007, *Derecho a la Salud en Venezuela 2007: Situación del Derecho a la Atención Sanitaria*. Available: /www.derechos.org.ve/Informe_derecho_Salud_2007_.pdf. Accessed 28 April 2008.

OCEI (Oficina Central de Estadistica e Informatica)/ PNUD (Programa Naciones Unidas para el Desarrollo), 2001, *Informe sobre Desarrollo Humano en Venezuela, 2000: Caminos para superar la probreza*. Caracas: CDB Publicaciones,

O'Donnell, G., 1979, *Modernization and Bureaucratic Authoritarianism*, 2nd ed. Berkeley: Institute of International Studies, University of California.

O'Donoghue, P., 2003, 'Opposition editor Ibeyise Pacheco eating humble pie for OTT accusations'. Available from: www.vheadline.com/readnews.asp?id=9736. Accessed 24 July 2003.

O'Donoghue, P. J., 2004, 'Flagship government non status banking system losing bad debt battle'. Available from: www.Vheadline.com/readnews.asp?id=9736. Accessed 14 July 2004.

Organización de Panamerican de Salud, 2006, *Barrio Adentro: Derecho a la salud e inclusión social en Venezuela*. Caracas: OPS. Available from: www.paho.org. Accessed 2 September 2008

PAHO (Pan American Health Organisation), 2006, *Barrio Adentro: Derecho a la Salud y a la Inclusión Social en Venezuela*. Caracas: Organización Panamericana de Salud Available from: www.ops-oms.org.ve. Accessed 10 March 2008.

Palacios, M., 2002, 'Incautaron armas de guerra en la casa de Isaac Pérez Recao', in *El Nacional*, 26 April.

Panizza, F., 2005, 'Introduction: populism and the mirror of democracy', in F. Panizza (ed.), *Populism and the Mirror of Democracy*. London: Verso, pp. 1–32.

Panizza, F. (ed.), 2005, *Populism and the Mirror of Democracy*. London: Verso

París Pombo, M. D., 1990, *Crisis de identidades colectivas en America Latina*. Mexico D.F.: Plaza y Valdes.

Parker, D., 2002, 'Debilidades en la conducción política del proceso también facilitaron el golpe', in *Observatorio Social de América Latina* III(7): 5–10.

Payne, A., 2005, *The Global Politics of Unequal Development*. Basingstoke: Palgrave Macmillan.

Peréz Baralt, C., 2001, 'Cambios en la participación electoral', in J. V. Carrasquero, T. Maingon and F. Welsch (eds), *Venezuela en transición: elecciones y democracia 1998–2000*. Caracas: Consejo Nacional de Ciencia y Tecnología (CONICIT)/Red Universataria de Estudios Políticos de Venezuela-Redpol/CDB Publicaciones, pp. 123–133.

Philip, G., 1998, 'New populism in Spanish America', in *Government and Opposition* 33(1): 81–87.

Planas, P., 2000, *La democracia volátil: Movimientos, partidos, líderes políticos y conductas electorales en el Perú contemporáneo*. Lima: Friedrich Ebert Stiftung.

Plummer, R., 2008, 'Chávez in pre-election cash spree', 26 May. Available from: www.news.bbc.co.uk. Accessed 3 June 2008.

Poleo, P., 2002, 'La verdadera historia de un gobierno que duró sólo horas por estar sustentado en los intereses particulares y no en los del colectivo', in *El Nuevo País* 16 April: 3–4.

PROVEA (Programa Venezolana de Educación Acción en Derechos Humanos), 2001, *Situación de los Derechos Humanos en Venezuela: Informe Annual Octubre 2000/Septiembre 2001*. Caracas: PROVEA.

PROVEA, 2002, *Situación de los Derechos Humanos en Venezuela: Informe Anual Octubre 2001/Septiembre 2002*. Available from: www.derechos.org.ve/. Accessed 6 August 2003.

PROVEA, 2003, *Situación de los Derechos Humanos en Venezuela: Informe Annual Octubre 2002/Septiembre 2003: Las muertes de abril*. Available from: www.derechos.org.ve/. Accessed 9 January 2004.

PROVEA, 2004, *Situación de los Derechos Humanos en Venezuela: Informe Annual Octubre 2003/Septiembre 2004*. Available from: www.derechos.org.ve/. Accessed 6 August 2007.

PROVEA, 2005, *Situación de los Derechos Humanos en Venezuela: Informe Annual Octubre 2004/Septiembre 2005*. Available from: www.derechos.org.ve/. Accessed 6 August 2007.

PROVEA, 2007, *Informe Anual 2006–2007*. Available from: www.derechos.ve.org. Accessed 10 June 2008.

Raby, D. L., 2006, *Democracy and Revolution: Latin America and Socialism Today*, London and Ann Arbor MI: Pluto Press and Toronto: Between the Lines.

Ramírez Gallegos, F., 2006, 'Mucho más que dos izquierdas', in *Nueva Sociedad* 205, 'America Latina en los tiempos de Chávez'. Available from: www.nuso.org. Accessed 3 March 2008.

Ransome, P., 1992, *Antonio Gramsci: A New Introduction*. New York: Harvester Wheatsheaf.

Republica Bolivariana de Venezuela, 2001, *Líneas Generales del Plan de Desarrollo Económico y Social de la Nación 2001–2007*. Available from: www.cenit.gob.ve. Accessed 17 May 2008.

Republica Bolivariana de Venezuela, Presidencia, 2007, *Proyecto Nacional Simón Bolívar – Primer Plan Socialista PPS: Desarrollo Económico y Social de la Nación 2007–2013*. Available from: www.cenit.gob.ve. Accessed 17 May 2008.

Reuters, Panorama, RNV, 2003, 'Venezuela's economy expected to grow by 6.7% in 2004 according to analysts'. Available from: www.venezuelanalysis.com/news.php?newsno=1143. Accessed 26 January 2004.

Rey, J. C., 2002, 'Consideraciones políticas sobre un insólito golpe de Estado'. Available from: www.analitica.com/bitblioteca/juan_carlos_rey/insolito_golpe.asp. Accessed 25 October 2002.

Rivas, E., 2004, 'A Venezuelan miracle?'. Available from: www.venezuelanalysis.com/articles.php?artno=1098. Accessed 3 February 2004.

Roberts, K. M., 1995, 'Neoliberalism and the transformation of populism in Latin America: the Peruvian case', in World Politics 48(1): 82–116.

Roberts, K. M, 1998, Deepening Democracy? The Modern Left and Social Movements in Chile and Peru. Stanford: Stanford University Press.

Roberts, K. M, 2000, 'Populism and democracy in Latin America'. Paper delivered to Threats to Democracy in Latin America Conference, University of British Columbia, Vancouver, Canada, 3–4 November. Available from: www.iir.ubc.ca/pwias conferences/threatstodemocracy/. Accessed 25 August 2004.

Roberts, K. M, 2003, 'Social polarisation and the populist resurgence', in S. Ellner and D. Hellinger (eds), Venezuelan Politics in the Chávez Era: Class, Polarization and Conflict. Boulder, CO and London: Lynne Rienner, pp. 55–73.

Roberts, K. M., 2006, 'Populism, political conflict, and grass-roots organization in Latin America', in Comparative Politics 38(2): 127–147.

Rodriguez, A., 2001, Golpes de Estado en Venezuela, 1945–1992. Caracas: El Nacional.

Rodríguez, F., 2003, 'Las consecuencias económicas de la revolución bolivariana', in Revista Nueva Econômia, 19 abril: 85–142.

Rodríguez, F., 2008, 'An empty revolution: the unfulfilled promises of Hugo Chávez', in Foreign Affairs 87(2), March–April. Available from: www.foreignaffairs.org/20080301 faessay87205/francisco-rodriguez/an-empty-revolution.html. Accessed 10 June 2008.

Rodriguez, F., and Ortega, D., 2006, 'Freed from illiteracy? A closer look at Venezuela's Robinson Literacy Campaign'. Available from: http://frrodriguez.web.wesleyan. edu/. Accessed 10 March 2008.

Rojas, A., 2004, 'Entrevista: Chávez indica a opposición que violencia pudiera ser su final físico: Seguiremos gobernando con o sin reconciliación', in El Universal Sección Política, 12 January. Available from: http://politica.eluniversal.com/2004/entre-vista_chavez.shtml. Accessed 12 January 2004.

Romero, C. A., 2006, Jugando con el Globo: La política exterior de Hugo Chávez. Caracas: Ediciones B.

RSF (Reporters Without Borders), 2000. Peru General election: 9 April 2000. Available from: www.rsf.org/rsf/uk/html/ameriques/cplp/cp/230300.html. Accessed 6 August 2003.

Reporters Without Borders (RSF), 2003, Venezuela 2003 Annual Report. Available from: www.rsf.fr/article.php3?id_article=6230&Valider=OK. Accessed 6 August 2003.

Rueschemeyer, D., Stephens, E. and Stephens, J. D., 1992, Capitalist Development and Democracy. Cambridge: Polity Press.

Rumsfeld, D., 2007, 'Remarks by Secretary Rumsfeld to the 35th Annual Washington Conference of the Council Of Americas' in US Department of Defense, Defense Link. Available from: www.defenselink.mil/transcripts/2005/tr20050503-secdef2681. html. Accessed 3 May 2008.

Ryan, J. J., 2001, 'Painful exit: Electoral abstention and neoliberal reform in Latin America'. Paper prepared for delivery at 2001 meeting of the Latin American Studies Association, Washington D.C., 6–8 September. Available from: http://136.142.158.105/Lasa2001/RyanJeffrey.pdf. Accessed 6 August 2003.

Sachs, J. Y., 1990, Social Conflict and Populist Politics in Latin America. San Francisco: ICS Press.

Salzman, L., 2008, 'The new left in Latin America: what Chomsky didn't tell you', 21 May. Available from: www.countercurrents.org. Accessed 27 May 2008.

Schady, N. R., 1999, *Seeking Votes: The Political Economy of Expenditures by the Peruvian Social Fund* (FONCODES), 1991–1995. Washington: World Bank Poverty Division/Poverty Reduction and Economic Management Network Policy Research Working Paper 2166. Available from: www.econ.worldbank.org/docs/611.pdf. Accessed 6 August 2003.

Schiller, P., 2006, 'The axis of oil: China and Venezuela', 20 March. Available from: www.opendemocracy.net. Accessed 21 May 2008.

Seitz, M., 2008, 'Una OTAN sudamericana?', 23 May. Available from: www.news.bbc.co.uk. Accessed 23 May 2008.

SENIAT (Servicio Nacional Integrado de Administración Aduanera y Tributaria), 2004, *Bolétin Mensual No. 39*. Available from: www.seniat.gov.ve. Accessed19 July 2004

SENIAT, 2007, *Informe de Recaudación Gerencia de Estudios Economicos Tributarios Diciembre 2007*. Available from: www.seniat.gov.ve. Accessed 27 February 2008.

SISOV (Sistema Integrado de Indicadores Sociales de Venezuela), 2008, 'Indicadores; Precios; Tasa de Inflación'. Available from: www.sisov.mpd.gob.ve/indicadores/. Accessed 10 June 2008.

SISOV, 2008, 'Indicadores: Producción, Empleo y Precios'. Available from: www.sisov.mpd.gob.ve/indicadores/EM0301800000000/. Accessed 10 June 2008.

SISOV, 2008, 'Necesidades y Demandas de Trabajo: Ocupados en el Sector Informal'. Available from: www.sisov.mpd.gob.ve/indicadores/EM0200900000000/. Accessed 10 June 2008.

SISOV, 2008, 'Indicadores; Salario Minimo'. Available from: www.sisov.mpd.gob.ve/indicadores/EM0400300000000/. Accessed 11 June 2008.

SISOV, 2008, 'Indicadores; Gasto público en vivienda como porcentaje del gasto social'. Available from: www.sisov.mpd.gob.ve/indicadores/VI0301600000000/. Accessed 11 June 2008.

Socorro, M., 2003, 'La gran tragedia de la democracia venezolana es la impunidad'. Available from: www.cofavic.org.ve/p-noticias-310303.htm. Accessed 24 July 2003.

Solowicz, B., 2004, 'The Latin American left: between governability and change'. Available from: www.tni.org. Accessed 6 July 2005

Sreeharsha, V., 2006, 'Is there a black vote in Venezuela?'. Available from: www.slate.com/id/2154688/. Accessed 3 February 2007.

Stein, S., 1980, *Populism in Peru: The Emergence of the Masses and the Politics of Social Control*. Madison and London: Harcourt Brace Jovanovich.

Stiglitz, J., 2003, 'Populists are sometimes right'. Available from: www.project-syndicate.org. Accessed 5 October 2006.

Strange, S., 1994, *States and Markets*, 2nd ed. London and Washington: Pinter.

Subero, C., 2000, 'Clases sociales tienen distinto candidato', in *El Universal* Sección Nacional y Política, 6 April. Available from: www.eluniversal.com/2000/04/06/06102AA.shtml. Accessed 20 June 2003.

Suggett, J., 2008, 'Venezuela proposes food crisis fund at controversial trans-Atlantic Summit', 20 May. Available from: www.venezuelanalysis.com. Accessed 21 May 2008.

SustainabilityTank, 2008, 'LATIN AMERICA: growth perspectives in a shifting political landscape'. Available from: www.sustainabilitank.info. Accessed 14 June 2008.

Szusterman, C., 2006, 'Latin America's eroding democracy: the view from Argentina'. Available from: www.opendemocracy.net/democracy-protest/argentina_erosion_607.jsp. Accessed 7 June, 2006.

Tablante, C., 2002, *Primer Borrador de la Comisión Política que investiga los sucesos del 11,12,13,y 14 de abril*. Available from: www.logiconline.org.ve/primerborrado1r.htm. Accessed 6 August 2003.

Tanaka, M., 1998, 'From Movmientismo to media politics: the changing boundaries between society and politics in Fujimori's Peru', in J. Crabtree and J. Tomas (eds), *Fujimori's Peru: The Political Economy*. London: University of London Institute of Latin American Studies, pp. 229–243.

Tanaka, M., 2001, *Las Fuerzas Armadas en la Region Andina: No deliberantes o actores políticos?* Lima: Comisión Andina de Juristas.

Tanaka, M., 2002, *De la crisis al colapso de los sitemas de partidos y los retos de su reconstrucción: los casos de Perú y Venezuela*. Mimeo, Instituto de Estudios Peruanos

Tanaka, M., 2002, *La Situación de la democracia en Colombia, Perú y Venezuela a inicios de siglo*. Lima: Comisión Andina de Juristas.

TeleSUR, 2008, 'Hugo Chávez anuncia la creación del partido único bolivariano en 2007', 16 December. Available from: www.telesurtv.net/secciones/noticias/nota/index.php?ckl=4496. Accessed 21 February, 2008.

The Economist, 2006, 'The return of populism'. Available from: www.economist.com/opinion/displaystory.cfm?story_id=6802448. Accessed 17 May 2006.

Torres Ballesteros, S., 1987, 'El Populismo: Un concepto escurridizo', in J. Alvarez Junco (ed.), *Populismo, Caudillaje y Discurso Demagogico*. Madrid: Centro de Investigaciones Sociologicas: Siglo XXI, pp. 159–180.

Triangulo, El, 2001, *Fujimori y Chávez: Hay cercanía entre los dos?* Televen 26 July. (Panel members: Luis Cristensen, Consultores 21, polling firm; Mary Mogollon, political analyst; Omar Meza Ramirez, MVR political leader (government); Carlos Raul Hernandez, political writer. Various other personalities interviewed). Archived in Cinema and Video Centre, National Library, Caracas.

Tuesta Soldevilla, F. (ed.), *Los enigmas de poder: Fujimori 1990–1996: Segunda edición*. Lima: Fundación Friedrich Ebert,

Últimas Noticias, 2003, 'Pesquisas jefes de la Disip y el Cicpc los acusaron de nuevo de ser los reyes del c-4 en Caracas', in *Últimas Noticias*, 24 July: 12. Available from: www.ultimasnoticias.com.ve. Accessed 24 July 2003.

UNCTAD (United Nations Conference on Trade and Development), 2007, *Trade and Development Report 2007*. Available from: www.unctad.org. Accessed 12 March 2008.

UNDP (United Nations Development Programme), 2000, *Human Development Report, 2000*. Available from: www.undp.org. Accessed 11 June 2008.

UNDP, 2004, *Ideas and Contributions: Democracy in Latin America*. Available from: www.undp.org. Accessed 10 June 2008.

UNDP, 2006, *Human Development Report, 2006, Beyond Scarcity: Power, Poverty and the Global Water Crisis*. Available from: www.undp.org. Accessed 10 May 2008.

UNDP, 2007, *Human Development Report 2007*. Available from: www.undp.org. Accessed 11 June 2008.

Union Radio, 2002, 'FMI ofrece colaboración a nuevo gobierno venezolano', 12 April. Available from: www.unionradio.com.ve. Accessed 10 June 2008.

US Census Bureau, 2008, 'Trade in Goods (Imports, Exports and Trade Balance) with Venezuela'. Available from: http://www.census.gov/foreign-trade/balance/c3070.html#top. Accessed 26 May 2008.

Usborne, D., 2006, 'The big question: should we be worried by the rise of the populist left in South America?', in *The Independent*, 4 May. Available from: http://news.independent.co.uk/world/americas/article361780.ece. Accessed 17 May 2006.

Vallenilla Lanz, L., 1984 [1930], *Disgregación y Integración*. Caracas: Centro de Investigación Históricas, Universidad Santa María.

Veliz, Claudio (ed.), 1965, *Obstacles to Change in Latin America*. London: Oxford University Press

Veltmeyer, H., Petras, J. and Vieux, S., 1997, *Neoliberalism and Class Conflict in Latin America: A Comparative Perspective on the Political Economy of Structural Adjustment*. Basingstoke: Macmillan

Venezuelanalysis.com, 2004, 'Rebel Venezuelan ex-military officers ask for a U.S. military invasion of Venezuela'. Available from: www.venezuelanalysis.com/news.php?newsno=1169. Accessed 15 January 2004.

Viciano Pastor, R. and Martínez Dalmau, R., 2001, *Cambio Político y Proceso Constituyente en Venezuela* (1998–2000). Caracas: Vadell Hermanos.

Villamediana, C., 2000, 'Crónica massmediática de un triunfo anunciado', in M. Bisbal (ed.), 2000, *Antropología de unas elecciones*. Caracas: Universidad Católica Andrés Bello, pp. 69–85.

Villegas Poljak, E., 2003, 'When the press sacrifices its credibility to overthrow a government'. Available from: www.vheadline.com/readnews.asp?id=9573. Accessed 16 July 2003.

Villegas, V., 2002, 'Mentiras y videos', in *El Mundo*, 13 June 2002. Available from: www.analitica.com/bitblioteca/vladimir_villegas/mentiras_y_videos.asp. Accessed 10 December 2002.

Vivanco, J. M., 2003, 'Venezuela: limit state control of media/letter to President Chavez'. Available from: http://hrw.org/press/2003/06/venezuela062303-ltr.htm. Accessed 6 August 2003.

Wall Street Journal, 2008, 'War and trade in Colombia', 7 March. Available from: www.blogs.wsj.com. Accessed 24 May 2008.

Weisbrot, M., Rosnick, D., and Tucker, T., 2004, *Briefing Paper: Black Swans, Conspiracy Theories, and the Quixotic Search for Fraud: A Look at Hausmann and Rigobón's Analysis of Venezuela's Referendum Vote*. Available from: www.cepr.net. Accessed 18 August, 2008.

Weisbrot, M., 2006, 'Latin America: the end of an era'. Available from: www.cepr.net. Accessed 21 June, 2006.

Weisbrot, M. and Sandoval, L., 2007, *The Venezuelan Economy in the Chávez Years*. Available from: www.cepr.net. Accessed 10 June 2008.

Weyland, K., 1996, 'Neopopulism and neoliberalism in Latin America: unexpected affinities', in *Studies in Comparative International Development* 31(3): 3–31.

Weyland, K., 2001, 'Clarifying a contested concept: populism in the study of Latin American politics', in *Comparative Politics* 34(1), October: 1–22.

Weyland, K., 2001, 'Will Chávez lose his luster?', in *Foreign Affairs* 80, November–December: 73–87.

Weyland, K., 2003, 'Neopopulism and neoliberalism in Latin America: how much affinity?', in *Third World Quarterly* 24(6), December: 1095–1115.

Wiles, P., 1969, 'A syndrome not a doctrine', in G. Ionescu and E. Gellner (eds), *Populism: Its Meaning and National Characteristics*. London: Weidenfeld and Nicolson.

Williamson, J., 1990, 'What Washington means by policy reform', chapter 2 from *Latin American Adjustment: How Much Has Happened?* Available from: www.iie.com/publications/papers/williamson1102-2.htm. Accessed 8 March 2004.

Wilpert, G., 2003, 'Mission impossible? Venezuela's mission to fight poverty'. Available from: www.venezuelanalysis.com/articles.php?artno=1051. Accessed 11 November 2003.

Wilpert, G., 2004, 'Dictatorship or democracy?'. Available from: www.venezuelanalysis.com. Accessed 27 May 2004.

Wilpert, G., 2004, 'IMF says Venezuela's economy will grow 8.8% in 2004'. Available from: www.venezuelanalysis.com/news.php?newsno=1257. Accessed 27 April 2004.

Wilpert, G., 2007, *Changing Venezuela by Taking Power: The History and Policies of the Chávez Government*. London and New York: Verso.

Wilpert, G., 2007, 'Venezuela's constitutional reform: an article by article summary', 23 November. Available from: www.venezuelanalysis.com. Accessed 17 February 2008.

Wilpert, G. and Boyd, A., 2004, 'Debate on the legitimacy and effectiveness of the Chavez government'. Available from: www.venezuelanalysis.com. Accessed 27 May 2004.

Wood, D., 2000, 'The Peruvian press under recent authoritarian regimes, with special reference to the autogolpe of President Fujimori', in Bulletin of Latin American Studies 19: 17–32.

World Bank, 2001, World Development Report 2000–2001. Oxford: Oxford University Press:. Available from: www.worldbank.org/poverty/wdrpoverty/report/index.htm. Accessed 14 November, 2003.

World Values Survey, 2008, 'Online data analysis, Venezuela – 1996, 2000, sociodemographics – ethnic description'. Available from: www.jdsurvey.net/bdasepjds/wvsevs/home.jsp?OWNER=WVS. Accessed 15 January, 2008.

Wright, W. R., 1990, Café con Leche: Race, Class and National Image in Venezuela. Austin: University of Texas Press

Youngers, C., 2000, Deconstructing Democracy: Peru under President Alberto Fujimori. Washington: Washington Office on Latin America.

Index